WalkiNG L.a.

walking
L.a.

36 walking tours exploring
stairways, streets, and buildings
you never knew existed

Erin Mahoney

WILDERNESS PRESS · BERKELEY, CA

Walking L.A.: 36 walking tours exploring stairways, streets, and buildings you never knew existed

1st EDITION October 2005

Copyright © 2005 by Erin Mahoney

Cover photos copyright © 2005 by Erin Mahoney
Interior photos: Erin Mahoney
Maps: Bart Wright/Fineline Maps
Book and cover design: Larry B. Van Dyke
Book editor: Jessica Benner

ISBN 0-89997-363-9
UPC 7-19609-97363-8

Manufactured in the United States of America

Published by: **Wilderness Press**
1200 5th Street
Berkeley, CA 94710
(800) 443-7227; FAX (510) 558-1696
info@wildernesspress.com
www.wildernesspress.com

Visit our website for a complete listing of our books and for ordering information.

Cover photos:	*Front, clockwise from bottom center:* Chinatown; Beachwood Canyon stairway (and Tuffy); Exposition Park Rose Garden; Walt Disney Concert Hall; Emmy statue; Argyle Hotel; Venice canal. *Back, clockwise from bottom left:* Gregory Ain house; Helms Bakeries sign; Civic Center fountain.
Frontispiece:	Echo Park Lake.

acknowledgments

It's been a busy couple of years since I first embarked on this project, and my husband Tony Harris has been wonderfully supportive throughout with his welcome sense of humor and profound faith in my abilities. The fact that my mother Ann Mahoney is an English teacher sometimes felt like the bane of my existence when I was a student, but I now realize how fortunate I was to have a writing tutor with such a heavy personal investment in my future. I may never have had the guts to try to publish a book without the encouragement of Gloria Lintermans, a dear friend and trusted mentor. Finally, I'd like to thank Adah Bakalinsky and Larry Gordon for the original inspiration to get out and explore Los Angeles on foot.

author's note

The face of Los Angeles is constantly changing, particularly when it comes to residential and commercial architecture, so you may find on your journeys that certain landmarks and features described in this book have changed since it was written. I encourage you to use my directions as a general guide, but to explore each neighborhood at a leisurely pace and make your own discoveries. That said, I also implore you to use common-sense caution on your walks to ensure your safety and comfort: bring a buddy if you're exploring a new neighborhood that you don't feel entirely at ease about visiting; take your walks during the day rather than at night; wear appropriate shoes to prevent blisters; and, finally, if you bring your dog along, keep him/her on a leash at all times, as these are primarily urban routes in close proximity to street traffic.

The boundaries mentioned at the beginning of each walk are meant to give you an idea of the major streets that surround the route in order to make it easier to find. These streets do not always appear on the accompanying maps, so please refer to the Thomas Guide coordinates provided or refer to a separate map if you have trouble locating the start of a walk.

Happy trekking!

Numbers on this locator map correspond to Walk numbers

TaBLe OF CONTENTS

Author's Note v

Locator Map vi

Introduction 1

1 **Castellammare** 3

2 **Northwest Santa Monica** 9

3 **Southeast Santa Monica** 15

4 **Venice Beach** 21

5 **Mar Vista** 27

6 **Playa Vista and the Ballona Wetlands** 31

7 **UCLA Campus** 35

8 **North Culver City** 41

9 **Downtown Culver City** 47

10 **Leimert Park Village** 53

11 **NoHo Arts District** 59

12 **Studio City's Woodbridge Park** 65

13 **Laurel Canyon** 71

14 **Sunset Strip** 75

15 **West Hollywood** 81

16 **Miracle Mile** 87

17 **Carthay Circle and South Carthay** 95

18 **High Tower and the Hollywood Bowl** 101

19 Whitley Heights and Hollywood Boulevard 107

20 Lower Beachwood Canyon 115

21 Upper Beachwood Canyon 121

22 Melrose Hill 127

23 Larchmont Village and Windsor Square 131

24 Koreatown/Wilshire Center 137

25 Los Feliz 143

26 Franklin Hills 151

27 West Silver Lake 155

28 East Silver Lake 161

29 Echo Park and Angelino Heights 169

30 Elysian Heights 175

31 El Pueblo de Los Angeles and Chinatown 179

32 Little Tokyo 187

33 Downtown Civic Center 193

34 Downtown Financial District 201

35 USC and Exposition Park 209

36 Mt. Washington 217

APPENDIX 1: Walks by Theme 222

APPENDIX 2: Points of Interest 224

APPENDIX 3: Calories Burned per Walk 232

Index 236

About the Author 240

INTRODUCTION

Los Angeles has gotten a bad rap.

Sure, it's sprawling, traffic-choked, and smoggy. Its public transportation system leaves a lot to be desired, and the old adage that it takes 20 minutes to drive anywhere in the city is woefully misleading.

But it is a great place to walk. Really, it is—don't be deterred by the maze of freeways and pervasive car culture. Sure, you won't be able to traverse the greater metro area in a day, or even in a weekend, but take it in smaller doses and you'll be rewarded with a deeper understanding of this city's unique blend of culture, architecture, and topography.

Encompassing a total area of 400 square miles, the greater Los Angeles area encapsulates idyllic hills and canyons, sunny coastline, peaceful residential neighborhoods, and gritty urban zones, all within fairly close proximity to each other. Property values, while universally inflated, fluctuate wildly according to geographic location, and you'll find striking juxtapositions between ethnic cultures and economic classes throughout the region.

The purpose of this book is to prove that walking in LA can be an immensely rewarding experience, opening your eyes to hidden pockets of the city that you never knew existed. These walks reflect the many faces of Los Angeles, and I hope that the discoveries you'll make as you explore the vibrant neighborhoods dotting the hills, valleys, and flatlands of this fascinating city will encourage you to dust off your sneakers and leave the car in the garage at every opportunity.

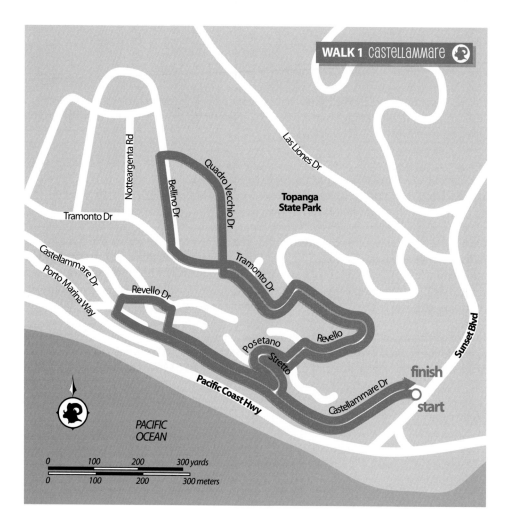

Notteargenta Rd

Belino Dr

Quadro Vecchio Dr

Las Liones Dr

Topanga State Park

Tramonto Dr

Tramonto Dr

Castellammare Dr

Porto Marina Way

Revello Dr

Posetano

Revello

Stretto

Sunset Blvd

finish

start

Castellammare Dr

Pacific Coast Hwy

PACIFIC OCEAN

0   100   200   300 yards

0   100   200   300 meters

1 Castellammare:
Pacific Palisades' "Castle on the Sea"

BOUNDARIES: **Pacific Coast Highway, Sunset Blvd., Topanga State Park. Surfview Dr.**
THOMAS GUIDE COORDINATES: **Map 630; G6**
DISTANCE: **Approx. 1½ miles**
DIFFICULTY: **Strenuous**
PARKING: **Free street parking is available on Castellammare Dr.**

This whimsically named neighborhood in the Pacific Palisades lies just east of the Pacific Coast Highway, and just south of Sunset Blvd.—talk about exclusive real estate! Castellammare's lucky residents enjoy the soothing breezes and sweeping panoramas of the Pacific Ocean from their vantage point high in the hills. Of all the architecturally diverse regions in the greater Los Angeles area, this may represent the best example of the structural incongruity that so annoyed Woody Allen's character in *Annie Hall*. After all, when money is no object, people tend to go nuts building their dream homes. As you might expect on streets with names like Posetano and Tremonto, many of the homes are Mediterranean, but you'll also find a surprising preponderance of traditional, ranch-style, and modern houses in this quietly exclusive coastal enclave.

● **Begin on Castellammare Dr., just southwest of Sunset Blvd. Head uphill on Castellammare, following the road as it curves to the right, affording an expansive (and expensive) view of the ocean below.**

Continue past Stretto Way, admiring the gorgeous Spanish-style home—pale yellow with pretty blue trim and lots of colorful tile work—on the corner at 17501. This stunner is purportedly the former abode of John Barrymore and was recently listed for over five million dollars. Right next door is another Mediterranean-style home with elegantly carved wooden trim; one can imagine the breathtaking sunset views afforded by the row of windows on the second floor.

- When you reach the dead end, press ahead on the dirt path that begins to the left of the wooden barrier, passing between low trees, ice plant, and yucca. Continue straight ahead on Castellammare where the paved street begins once again. You'll pass a stairway on your right before coming to "Nana's Garden," which is delightfully cluttered with numerous funky art pieces including a ceramic face mounted on one of the trees, a colorfully painted bench, and a windmill. As you approach Porto Marina Way, notice the scarecrow standing guard over the garden plot on your left.

- Ascend the stairs at Breve Way on your right; the sound of the surf gets louder as an even more impressive view of the ocean opens up behind you.

- At the top of the steps, turn right on Revello Dr. As you approach Posetano, you'll notice a dead-end staircase leading halfway up the hill on your left. Continue straight ahead on Revello, passing a striking Spanish mission-style house with arched entry-ways and stained glass windows at 17638 on your right. The as-yet undeveloped hillside on your left is covered with cactus and agave plants.

- When you come to the end of Revello, you'll see the remnants of another washed-out staircase on the left. Descend the still-intact stairway on your right, but keep an eye out because a few of the steps are starting to shift with time here, as well. Someone has terraced a portion of the hill on your left and built a freestanding wooden patio overlooking the sea.

- Cross Posetano Rd. and continue down the next flight of stairs.

- Turn left at the bottom of the steps and retrace your steps on Castellammare Dr., across the washout footpath and all the way back to the breathtaking Spanish home at the corner of Stretto Way.

- Turn left on Stretto Way, following the road as it curves sharply to the left. When you reach Posetano Rd., check out the three-story Italian villa climbing the hill at 17531 Posetano. Screen siren Thelma Todd died here of carbon monoxide poisoning in 1935, either by her own hand or that of someone else…the mystery has never been solved. A sign above the garage declares CASTILLO DEL MAR, and this mansion indeed looks like it belongs in a neighborhood known as Castellammare.

- Turn right on Posetano Rd. Ahead you'll notice a striking modern home constructed of stucco, steel, glass, and wood at 17437 Posetano Rd. This is an excellent example of California-born architect Pierre Koenig's work, which uses exposed steel and glass to dramatic effect.

- Look for the stairs on your left just before 17445 and ascend. This stairway is clean and well maintained, vibrantly bordered on the right with bougainvillea, which is abundant throughout this walk.

- At the top of the steps, turn right on Revello Dr., passing by a series of sleek modern homes, including the rear of Koenig's masterpiece, (the address on this side is 17446) which has an entire wall of frosted glass. Follow the road as it curves to the left. At 17426 Revello, a somewhat wacky house catches the eye—its skewed angles and multi-colored façade give it the look of a contemporary art piece. Fragrant plumeria, a relatively rare find outside of the tropics, graces the front yard of the home at 17408.

- Bear left at the intersection to follow Tramonto Dr., pausing to admire the hills of Topanga State Park on your right. As you continue along Tramonto, you'll notice an abundance of traditional-style houses, which provide a stark contrast to the sleekly modern homes on Revello. An awesome panoramic view of the Pacific opens up on your left; stop here to watch the sailboats cruising through Santa Monica Bay.

- Turn right on Quadro Vecchio Dr. This blissfully domestic street is lined with ranch-style homes that couldn't look less Italian. Follow Quadro Vecchio as it curves to the left.

Pierre Koenig house

- Turn left on Bellino Dr., which takes you back to Tramonto Dr.

- Turn left on Tramonto and then retrace your steps back to the intersection with Revello Dr.

- Bear right at the intersection to head back along Revello Dr. Straight ahead is a great view of the Santa Monica beaches. After following the curve in the road, descend the staircase you climbed earlier.

- Turn right on Posetano Rd. at the bottom of the stairs, then bear left at the intersection to curve back around onto Revello.

- Turn left on Castellammare, following the road back to your starting point near the intersection with Sunset Blvd. If you're feeling famished at this point, grab a table overlooking the surf at Gladstone's 4 Fish, located just across PCH at the intersection with Sunset Blvd.

POINTS OF INTEREST

Gladstone's 4 Fish 17300 Pacific Coast Hwy, Pacific Palisades, CA 90272, 310-454-3474

route summary

1. Begin on Castellammare Dr., just southwest of Sunset Blvd. and head uphill on Castellammare.

2. Continue straight ahead on the dirt path to the left of the dead end, and then continue straight on Castellammare when the paved road begins again.

3. Ascend the stairs at Breve Way on your right.

4. At the top of the steps, turn right on Revello Dr.

5. When you come to the end of Revello, descend the stairway on your right.

6. Cross Posetano Rd. and continue down the next flight of stairs.

7. Turn left at the bottom of the steps and retrace your steps on Castellammare Dr., across the dirt path.

8. Turn left on Stretto Way, following the road as it curves sharply to the left.

9. Turn right on Posetano Rd.

10. Acend the staircase on your left just before 17445 Posetano.

11. Turn right on Revello Dr. at the top of the steps.

12. Bear left at the intersection to follow Tramonto Dr.

13. Turn right on Quadro Vecchio Dr.

14. Turn left on Bellino Dr.

15. Turn left on Tramonto and then retrace your steps back to the intersection with Revello Dr.

16. Bear right at the intersection to head back along Revello Dr., and then descend the staircase you climbed earlier.

17. Turn right on Posetano Rd. at the bottom of the stairs, then bear left at the intersection to curve back around onto Revello.

18. Turn left on Castellammare, following the road back to your starting point.

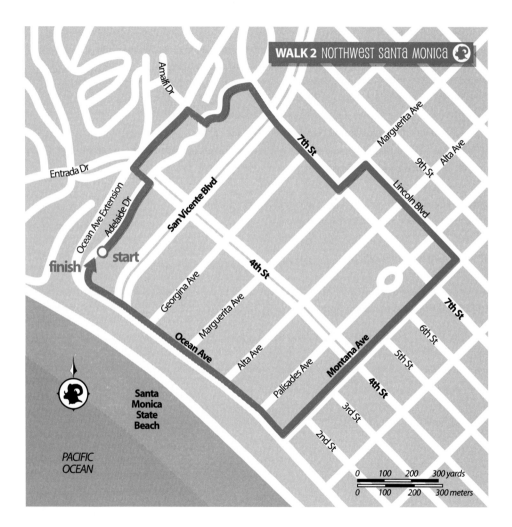

Amalfi Dr

Entrada Dr

Ocean Ave Extension

Adelaide Dr

San Vicente Blvd

Marguerita Ave

9th St

Alta Ave

7th St

Lincoln Blvd

start

finish

Georgina Ave

4th St

Marguerita Ave

7th St

6th St

Ocean Ave

Alta Ave

Palisades Ave

Montana Ave

5th St

4th St

Santa
Monica
State
Beach

3rd St

2nd St

PACIFIC
OCEAN

| 0 | 100 | 200 | 300 yards |
| 0 | 100 | 200 | 300 meters |

2 Northwest Santa Monica: rarefied air North of Montana Ave.

BOUNDARIES: **Ocean Ave., Entrada Dr., Lincoln Blvd., Montana Ave.**
THOMAS GUIDE COORDINATES: **Map 671; C1**
DISTANCE: **Approx. 2 miles**
DIFFICULTY: **Moderate**
PARKING: **Free street parking is available on Adelaide Ave.**

The northernmost reaches of Santa Monica are where you'll find some of the most outrageously priced homes in all of Los Angeles County. And it's no surprise, as this area has it all: the beach, nearby hiking trails, a good school district, and proximity to excellent places to eat and shop. This walk will head up and down Santa Monica's notoriously steep pair of Adelaide staircases before heading over to Montana Ave., Santa Monica's premier shopping and dining district, and then drop down for a quick detour to the beach before returning to the starting point.

Finding the beginning of this walk can be a little tricky, as Adelaide isn't clearly marked with a street sign. As you approach the end of Ocean Ave., you'll see two streets branching off to the right. Turn on the first street, the one that heads uphill, and you're on Adelaide. Park on the right side of the street, paying attention to posted parking enforcement signs.

● Begin by walking east on Adelaide, away from the ocean. Adelaide serves as the northeast border between Santa Monica and the city of Los Angeles—the neighborhood appropriately named Rustic Canyon lies on the other side. On your right are gorgeous multimillion-dollar homes—stately traditional houses of dark-stained wood alongside Spanish mansions. The sprawling shingled Craftsman at 236 Adelaide is particularly envy-inducing.

● At the intersection of 4th St. and Adelaide, descend the long, steep stairway on your left all the way down to Entrada Dr. The secret's out about this stairway and the one you're about to climb, so you may have to yield to the remarkably fit locals doggedly trotting up and down, up and down…

● Turn right at the bottom of the steps, passing by a school on your left before you reach the next set of stairs opposite the intersection with Amalfi Dr. Ascend the long wooden staircase, again watching out for exercise addicts on their quest for buns of steel.

● Turn left at the top of the stairs, continuing along Adelaide. As you approach the intersection with 7th St., notice the unique, pueblo-style home up ahead on your right.

● Turn right on 7th St., passing a sign indicating that you've officially entered Santa Monica city limits or, as some locals wryly call it, "the people's republic of Santa Monica." After one block, you'll cross San Vicente Blvd., which is divided by a wide meridian planted with coral trees. This is a popular path for joggers. It seems that everyone in Santa Monica is into some form of physical activity, be it jogging, biking or stair-climbing. Continue to head southwest on 7th, passing an interesting architectural mix of homes—contemporary, traditional, Spanish, Tudor.

● Turn left on Marguerita Ave. and follow it for one block to Lincoln Blvd. An impressive shingled Cape Cod-style house sits on the southwest corner of Marguerita and Lincoln.

● Turn right on Lincoln Blvd. At the intersection with Alta, notice the interesting modern yellow stucco home with an abundance of small windows on the southwest corner. Continue on Lincoln past the elementary school on your left.

● Turn right on Montana Ave. This street is a popular destination for the well-to-do residents of north Santa Monica, featuring a collection of upscale boutiques, fine restaurants and chic spas and salons in the stretch between 7th and 17th Streets. You may want to explore this street for a few blocks to the east before heading west back toward the ocean. Just east of the intersection with Lincoln is Pioneer Boulangerie, a large bakery that now shares its space with a Panda Express. This is unfortunate, as the scent of fresh baked bread is now stifled by the aroma of Chinese fast food.

● Continue to head west on Montana, passing The Massage Place at 625 Montana Ave. This is a discount massage therapy center ($44 for one hour—not bad at all!) that also offers every type of beauty treatment imaginable at reasonable prices. You'll continue to follow Montana Ave. for about half a mile toward the ocean through a mostly residential area.

● Once you reach Ocean Ave., cross the street and turn right to head northeast for another half mile along the greenway known as Palisades Park—or, more informally, as "the bluffs"—passing a collection of high-rise condos on your right. This exclusive real estate provides an interesting juxtaposition with the many homeless who make Palisades Park their home due to the temperate climate and Santa Monica's relative tolerance for the indigent.

● As you approach the intersection with Adelaide, you'll notice a striking white structure overlooking the ocean at 101 Ocean Ave. Once you reach Adelaide, turn right and walk back up the hill to your starting point.

The Bluffs

POINTS OF INTEREST

Pioneer Boulangerie 804 Montana Ave., Santa Monica, CA 90403, 310-451-4998

Diedrich Coffee 732 Montana Ave., Santa Monica, CA 90403, 310-656-7838

Spumoni Italian Restaurant 713 Montana Ave., Santa Monica, CA 90403, 310-393-2944

Marmalade Café and Catering 710 Montana Ave., Santa Monica, CA 90403, 310-395-9196

The Massage Place and Petit Spa 625 Montana Ave, Santa Monica, CA 90403, 310-393-7007

route summary

1. Begin by walking east on Adelaide, away from Ocean Ave.

2. At the intersection o 4th St. and Adelaide, descend the stairway on your left to Entrada Dr.

3. Turn right at the bottom of the steps, and then climb the stairs on your right opposite the intersection with Amalfi Dr.

4. Turn left at the top of the stairs, continuing along Adelaide.

5. Turn right on 7th St.

6. Turn left on Marguerita Ave.

7. Turn right on Lincoln Blvd.

8. Turn right on Montana Ave.

9. Continue to head west on Montana for about half a mile.

10. Cross Ocean Ave. and turn right.

11. Turn right on Adelaide to return to your starting point.

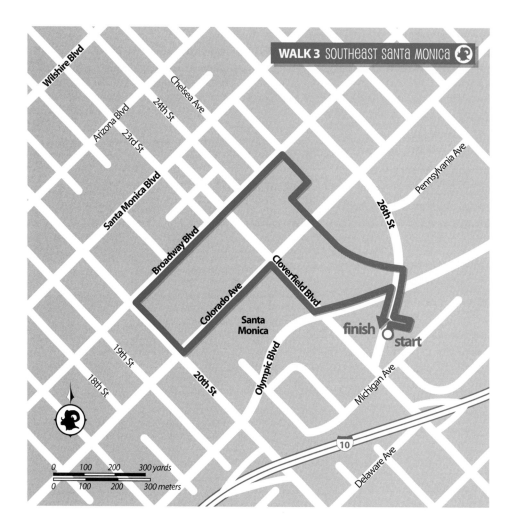

3 SOUTHEAST SANTA MONICA: MIXING BUSINESS WITH PLEASURE

BOUNDARIES: **26th St., Broadway Blvd., 20th St., 10 Freeway**
THOMAS GUIDE COORDINATES: **Map 631; H7**
DISTANCE: **Approx. 1¼ miles**
DIFFICULTY: **Easy**
PARKING: **Metered street parking is available on 26th St.**

When most people think of Santa Monica, they have visions of sun-kissed locals jogging along the waterfront, tourists in wide-brimmed hats and flip flops strolling along the pier, and other images of a beachy nature. But a couple of miles inland, you'll find that Santa Monica is also home to several colossal office parks, teeming with high-powered executives in button-down shirts and ties. This walk will explore the beachside city's recent multimillion-dollar development The Water Garden, as well as Bergamot Station, a sprawling collection of art galleries occupying a former train depot hidden between the 10 Freeway and Olympic Blvd.

● **Begin on 26th St. between Cloverfield Blvd. and Olympic Blvd.**

● **On your right-hand side immediately before Olympic is the rear entrance to Bergamot Station. You should allow yourself some time to wander through this maze of brick and corrugated-metal buildings, most of which house art galleries, museums, and studios. The Santa Monica Museum of Art resides at Bergamot Station, along with notable galleries such as the Shoshana Wayne, Track 16, and the Gallery of Functional Art. You can also grab a bite at the Gallery Café, if you're so inclined…it won't be the only opportunity you have to nosh on this walk, however.**

● **Exit Bergamot Station the same way you came in and continue along 26th St. to the corner of Olympic Blvd.**

● **Cross Olympic and then cross 26th St. so that you are on the same side of the street as The Water Garden office complex—you'll notice a lovely circular fountain on the corner. Follow the perimeter of the fountain around to the point where it spills into a** rivulet, and then follow the water trail into the heart of the Water Garden, where it opens up into the vast collection of pools for which the complex is named.

● Continue through the courtyard, roughly following the same path as the watercourse, which is criss-crossed with bridges and punctuated with fountains and planters brimming with vibrant flowers. The Water Garden is a great place to stop and have a sandwich or a cool drink; there are tables and chairs with umbrellas all over the plaza, and the elaborately constructed pools and fountains are really quite lovely. The peaceful atmosphere is corrupted somewhat by the imposing tinted-glass and concrete office buildings rising on all sides, however.

● When you come to the end of the last pool, you'll notice Café Bizou, an enormously popular French restaurant, on your left, and Colorado Ave. ahead. Cross the street to the entrance of Colorado Center, another office complex that was formerly known as MGM Plaza. Ascend the steps and follow the path into the courtyard.

● You'll notice an elevated seating area marked with a sculpture of a giant water urn to your right. Cross through this area and continue straight along the path through a cute little park planted with palms and ice plant. Just before you reach the reflecting pool that lies ahead to the left of your path, turn left and follow this path out of the park onto Broadway Blvd.

● Turn left on Broadway Blvd. You'll notice the LA Art Exchange across the street on the corner of 25th St.

● Cross Cloverfield Blvd., noticing the colorful graffiti-art covered building on the southwest corner. You'll continue to head west on Broadway Blvd. for about a quarter of a mile. An unprepossessing gray stucco building at 2112 Broadway turns out to be the home to Playboy Studio West. The Lowe Gallery resides at 2034 Broadway, although you may be art-galleried-out at this point in your walk. At 2024, you'll come to Back on Broadway, a pleasant, casual eatery offering tasty sandwiches, salads, and bakery items. This is a good place to stop in for some sustenance if you haven't already picnicked at The Water Garden.

- Turn left on 20th St. The Santa Monica Dog and Cat Hospital sits on the southeast corner.

- Walk for one block to Colorado Ave. and turn left. On the south side of the street is the enormous, rose-colored sandstone Universal/Sony Music complex. Next door to Universal/Sony is the Plaza at the Arboretum, one of those newfangled multi-use commercial/residential developments complete with a selection of casual dining establishments, a dentist and, naturally, a Starbucks. This multicolored monstrosity of a structure manages to be bold, garish, generic, and completely forgettable all at once, a remarkable feat.

- At the intersection of Colorado and Cloverfield, notice the giant Universal globe teetering on its pedestal on the southwest corner. Turn right on Cloverfield and continue for one block to Olympic Blvd., passing a Ralph's grocery store on your right.

- Turn left on Olympic, crossing Cloverfield. (Be warned: this is an exasperatingly long signal.) Don't cross Olympic, as there is no sidewalk on the south side of the street. Continue along Olympic for one block; you'll see The Water Garden on your left.

- Turn right on 26th St., returning to the start of you walk.

The Water Garden

POINTS OF INTEREST:

Bergamot Station 2525 Michigan Ave., Santa Monica, CA 90404, 310-829-5854
Café Bizou 2450 Colorado Ave., Santa Monica, CA 90404, 310-582-8203
LA Art Exchange 2451 Broadway Blvd., Santa Monica, CA 90404, 310-828-6866
The Lowe Gallery 2034 Broadway Blvd., Santa Monica, CA 90404, 310-449-0184
Back on Broadway 2024 Broadway Blvd., Santa Monica, CA 90404, 310-453-8919

route summary:

1. Begin on 26th St. between Cloverfield Blvd. and Olympic Blvd. and head northeast on 26th St. toward Olympic Blvd.

2. Enter Bergamot Station on the right hand side of the street.

3. Exit Bergamot Station the same way you went in.

4. Cross Olympic Blvd. and then cross 26th St. so that you are on the same corner as the Water Garden office complex.

5. Cross through the Water Garden courtyard, roughly following the same path as the waterway.

6. Cross Colorado Ave. and enter the Colorado Center office complex on the other side of the street.

7. Cross through the Colorado Center courtyard toward Broadway Blvd.

8. Turn left on Broadway Blvd.

9. Cross Cloverfield Blvd. and continue to head west on Broadway.

10. Turn left on 20th St.

11. Turn left on Colorado Ave.

12. Turn right on Cloverfield Blvd.

13. Turn left on Olympic Blvd.

14. Turn right on 26th St.

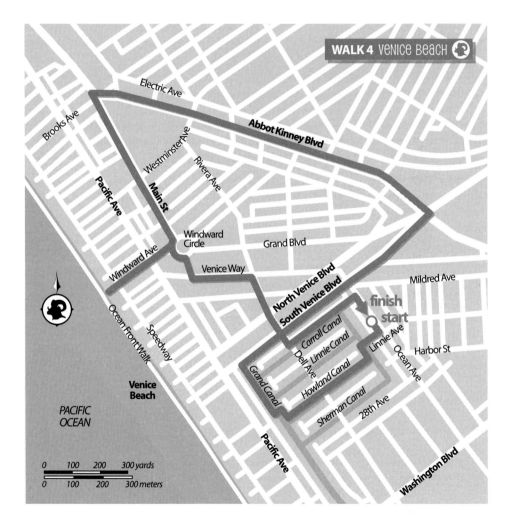

Electric Ave

Brooks Ave

Abbot Kinney Blvd

Westminster Ave

Riviera Ave

Pacific Ave

Main St

Windward Circle

Grand Blvd

Venice Way

Windward Ave

North Venice Blvd

South Venice Blvd

Mildred Ave

finish
start

Ocean Front Walk

Speedway

Carroll Canal

Linnie Canal

Dell Ave

Linnie Ave

Ocean Ave

Harbor St

Grand Canal

Howland Canal

Venice
Beach

Sherman Canal

28th Ave

PACIFIC
OCEAN

Pacific Ave

Washington Blvd

0	100	200	300 yards
0	100	200	300 meters

4 VENICE BEACH: OLD WORLD ITALY MEETS FUNKY SOCAL BEACH CULTURE

BOUNDARIES: **Abbot Kinney Blvd., Pacific Ave., Washington Blvd.**
THOMAS GUIDE COORDINATES: **Map 671; H6**
DISTANCE: **Approx. 2 miles**
DIFFICULTY: **Easy**
PARKING: **Free street parking is available on Ocean Ave.**

Venice Beach is probably the most distinctive beach town in all of Southern California, made all the more unique by its charming canals, which were built by Abbot Kinney in 1904 as an homage to the city's forebear in Italy. Here you'll find none of the snootiness that you might encounter in Malibu or Palos Verdes; Venice is undoubtedly more funky than fussy. That's not to say that the people who live there, particularly in the neighborhoods that line the canals and the oceanfront, aren't affluent. But Venice is still more affordable than next-door Santa Monica, and one might argue that it has a good deal more personality, as well.

Note: This walk can be particularly fun for both you and your pooch, provided he doesn't get overexcited at the sight of ducks. If you do bring him along, resist the temptation to remove his leash during the canal portion of the walk. Toward the end of the route, you'll come to the Westminster off-leash dog park, where Rover can get footloose and fancy-free with his canine pals.

● **This excursion begins in the South Venice neighborhood, just south of Venice Blvd. Begin by walking south on Ocean Ave. toward Linnie Ave. Notice that the houses along this stretch of Ocean are all relatively modest in size and style—some even have the appearance of one-room shacks.**

● **Turn right on Linnie Ave.**

- Cross the bridge arching over the Eastern Canal, pausing on top to admire the interesting mix of homes lining the waterway. The houses here are decidedly grander than those on Ocean Ave., ranging in architectural style from American Colonial Revival to modern to Tudor Revival.

- On the other side of the bridge, make an immediate left to follow the sidewalk alongside the canal.

- Follow the sidewalk as it turns to the right, taking you along Howland Canal. Ducks are everywhere, quackily going about their business, and small boats and canoes are parked at mini-docks in front of some of the houses. The homes along this waterway are all beautifully maintained and distinct from one another. Notable architectural styles here include Craftsman, Spanish Colonial Revival, Cape Cod, and modern stucco beach homes with huge picture windows.

- Cross Dell Ave. and then pause in the shade of the giant pine tree to bask in the tranquil, salt-tinged air of this remarkable neighborhood. You can't help but envy the residents and their Old-World-Italy-meets-funky-SoCal-beach-culture lifestyle. Unlike in most Los Angeles neighborhoods, there are virtually no homes for sale here, and only a few available for lease.

- Follow the sidewalk as it turns right at the corner of Grand Canal.

- Cross the pedestrian bridge on your left and then turn right to continue along the walkway on the other side of Grand Canal. You'll pass by a canoe rental facility on your left.

- Follow the pedestrian walkway up to South Venice Blvd. and turn right. The Venice Farmers Market sets up in the parking lot on the northeast corner of Dell Ave. and South Venice Blvd. every Friday from 7 to 11 A.M.

- Continue on South Venice Blvd. for a little under half a mile to Abbot Kinney Blvd.

- Turn left on Abbot Kinney.

- You'll continue along Abbot Kinney for three quarters of a mile. If you're in the mood for shopping, you'll be pleased to find vintage clothing, chic couture, art, furniture, custom perfumes, surfboards, and myriad other trinkets for sale on this lively street. This stretch of Abbot Kinney also offers numerous dining options. At the intersection of California Ave. are Abbot's Habit, a popular local hangout offering deli sandwiches and a salad bar, and Tortilla Grill, an excellent and inexpensive "fresh mex" eatery. Stroh's Gourmet sandwich and coffee shop sits a few short blocks farther down the street, just past Cadiz Ct.

- Just before you reach Westminster Ave, notice the low brick structure on your left with a faded metal sign that reads IRV'S FAMILY MARKET. The distinguished old building now houses art galleries and a travel agency.

- On the final block of Abbot Kinney between Westminster and Main St., you'll see Lilly's, an elegant French restaurant, as well as a gelato shop and restaurant-critic fave Joe's Restaurant on your right. The Westminster Avenue School is on your left.

- Turn left on Main St. This leg of the walk is a little drab compared to the thriving consumer mecca you've just left behind on Abbot Kinney, but does feature a few points of interest. As you approach the corner of Westminster Ave., you'll see the Westminster off-leash dog park on your right. This is a good place to stop if you've brought Fido along.

- Cross Westminster and continue on Main St. for about two blocks to the Windward Circle rotary, which was a picturesque lagoon back in Abbot Kinney's day, when over 16 miles of canals snaked through "Venice of America."

Venice canals

- At this point, you may choose to turn right on Windward Ave., which will take you the few short blocks to the Venice Beach Boardwalk. Also known as Ocean Front Walk, this is a popular destination with tourists where rollerbladers and cyclists coast along the waterfront, and sidewalk vendors hock wares of questionable value. If you do take this detour, return the way you came to the corner of Main St. and Windward.

- Walk along the west side of the rotary to remain on Main St.

- Turn left on Venice Way. You'll pass the Foundation yoga and dance studio on the corner.

- Walk one block to Riviera Ave. and turn right. As Riviera crosses Mildred Ave., it becomes Dell Ave.

- Turn left immediately before the auto and pedestrian bridge, and follow the sidewalk alongside Carroll Canal. At 421 Carroll Canal, you'll notice a whimsical metal sculpture garden.

- Continue straight along the sidewalk, pausing one last time to admire the unique and lovely homes on either side of the canal before crossing Eastern Ct. and returning to your starting point on Ocean Ave.

Back Story: Venice of America amusement park

The area now known as Venice was originally founded as "Venice of America" by real estate magnate Abbot Kinney in the fledgling years of the 20th century. This idealistic beach community was built on reclaimed marshland and featured an amusement park, a heated indoor saltwater "plunge," a miniature railroad, and over 16 miles of canals, complete with Venetian gondolas and gondoliers. Unfortunately, expensive upkeep and the rise of the automobile meant that most of the canals were paved over by 1929, and the remaining six eventually fell into disrepair. Fortunately, those six were restored in the early '90s, and today the neighborhood built around the canals is affluent and idyllic. Come to think of it, we suppose this sidebar might have more appropriately been named "Backwater."

POINTS OF INTEREST:

Venice Beach Farmers Market Corner of Dell Ave. and South Venice Blvd., Venice, CA 90291. Fridays 7 A.M. to 11 A.M.

Abbot's Habit 1401 Abbot Kinney Blvd., Venice, CA 90291, 310-399-1171

Tortilla Grill 1357 Abbot Kinney Blvd., Venice, CA 90291, 310-581-9953

Stroh's Gourmet 1239 Abbot Kinney Blvd., Venice, CA 90291, 310-450-5119

Joe's Restaurant 1023 Abbot Kinney Blvd., Venice, CA 90291, 310-399-5811

Lilly's 1031 Abbot Kinney Blvd., Venice, CA 90291, 310-314-0004

Foundation Yoga 1720 Main St., Venice, CA 90291, 310-305-1888

Westminster Off-Leash Dog Park 1234 Pacific Ave., Venice, CA 90291, 310-301-1550

ROUTE SUMMARY:

1. Head south on Ocean Ave.
2. Turn right on Linnie Ave.
3. Cross the bridge and immediately turn left to follow the sidewalk alongside Eastern Canal.
4. Follow the sidewalk as it turns right alongside Howland Canal.
5. Cross Dell Ave.
6. Turn right to follow the sidewalk alongside Grand Canal.
7. Cross the first bridge on the left and immediately turn right to follow the sidewalk on the other side of Grand Canal.
8. Follow the walkway up to South Venice Blvd. and turn right.
9. Turn left on Abbot Kinney Blvd.
10. Turn left on Main St.
11. Walk along the west side of the Windward Circle rotary to remain on Main St.
12. Turn left on Venice Way.
13. Turn right on Riviera St. Riviera turns into Dell Ave.
14. Turn left just before the bridge to follow the walkway alongside Carroll Canal.
15. Continue straight across Eastern Ct. and end back at Ocean Ave.

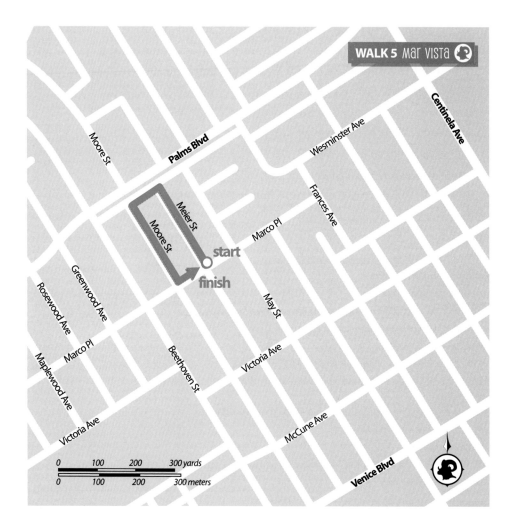

Moore St

Palms Blvd

Wesminster Ave

Centinela Ave

Meier St

Moore St

Frances Ave

Marco Pl

start

finish

Greenwood Ave

Rosewood Ave

Marco Pl

Maplewood Ave

Victoria Ave

Beethoven St

May St

Victoria Ave

McCune Ave

Venice Blvd

| 0 | 100 | 200 | 300 yards |
| 0 | 100 | 200 | 300 meters |

5 Mar Vista: a Utopian Vision of Modern Living

BOUNDARIES: **Palms Blvd., Beethoven St., Venice Blvd., Centinela Ave.**
THOMAS GUIDE COORDINATES: **Map 672; B4**
DISTANCE: **Approx. ¾ mile**
DIFFICULTY: **Easy**
PARKING: **Free street parking is available on Marco Pl.**

One of 1940s modernist architect Gregory Ain's finest achievements is a tract of houses in Mar Vista. This two-block housing project of 52 homes was marketed as the "Modernique Homes" when it was completed in 1948. The neighborhood embodies the now-kitschy 1940s perception of progressive architecture; the one-story houses are modest in size and style, with low, flat roofs and high rectangular windows. Nearly all of the structures in this neighborhood are uniform in design, but Ain gave each home its own look with carefully chosen interior and exterior color combinations. He also worked closely with Garrett Eckbo, a visionary of modern landscape design who created a rustic community landscape to further distinguish this zone from the surrounding neighborhood.

This very short walk will explore Ain's successful handiwork; the Mar Vista tract remains to this day a peaceful, well maintained collection of modest homes for middle-income homeowners in the rarefied air of Los Angeles' west side. Some of these homes may even look vaguely familiar, as they've served as shooting locations for several modern-day television commercials.

● Begin at the corner of Meier St. and Marco Pl. and head north, away from Marco Pl. The house on the northeast corner of Meier and Marco is a fine example of how Ain and Eckbo combined contemporary and rustic elements; the design of the home is unmistakably modern, but the unfinished-wood picket fence and thriving garden lend a country feel to the property.

This harmonious juxtaposition is echoed all along Meier St., with mature magnolia trees shading rows of homogenous houses, each with its own distinct color scheme and landscape design. The palette is muted: pale blues and greens, olive and mustard—nothing so jarring as to interfere with the neighborhood's cohesiveness. You will notice some variance of design between the homes, however. For example, some houses have overhanging roof extensions supported by diagonal stilts, while others have no such ornamentation to interfere with their boxy regularity. And the house at 3500 Meier is built on a slight incline at the end of the street, so it is a little larger than the rest, with the living space extended over a sunken garage.

- Turn left on Palms Blvd. While Palms is a fairly busy thoroughfare, this short portion of the street is separated from the main boulevard by a thickly landscaped meridian in order to shield the neighborhood from some of the traffic noise.

- Turn left on Moore St. Part of Eckbo's original vision for this neighborhood's landscape architecture was to give each street its own look with a particular species of tree, so while Meier got magnolias, Moore is trimmed with melaleucas, distinguished by their towering stature and peeling bark. At 3501 Moore is an elegant home with polished wood trim and glass brick windows. This is one of very few houses in this area that was not originally designed by Gregory Ain, although it does blend in nicely with its low flat roof and simple rectangular shape. Across the street at 3508 is the original model house created by Ain,

DESIGNER NAME: GREGORY AIN

Gregory Ain was a second-generation modernist architect, influenced by first-wave modernists like Rudolph Schindler and Richard Neutra. In fact, one of Ain's greatest architectural influences was Schindler's Kings Road house in West Hollywood (See Walk 15). Ain's noble goal was to create a utopian residential life for people who couldn't afford large, ostentatious homes, so he designed apartments and houses for low- to middle-income families that were stylish, dignified, and utilitarian.

identified by the pink diagonal stilts supporting the roof extension above the front walkway.

You'll notice that all of the houses in Ain's development are set close to one another, and there is a sense of communal living in the way the front yards flow into one another; very few homes along this street are separated by hedges or fences. The community landscaping is lush and shady, and the many varieties of palm trees give the neighborhood an almost tropical feel.

● Turn left on Marco Pl. to head back to your starting point. Note that at the intersection with Marco Pl., both Moore St. and Meier St. are slightly offset from their continuation to the south, as if Gregory Ain's careful study in modern community living was purposefully set apart from its less carefully planned surroundings.

route summary

1. Begin at the intersection of Marco Pl. and Meier St. and head north on Meier St.
2. Turn left on Palms Blvd.
3. Turn left on Moore St.
4. Turn left on Marco Pl.

Gregory Ain house

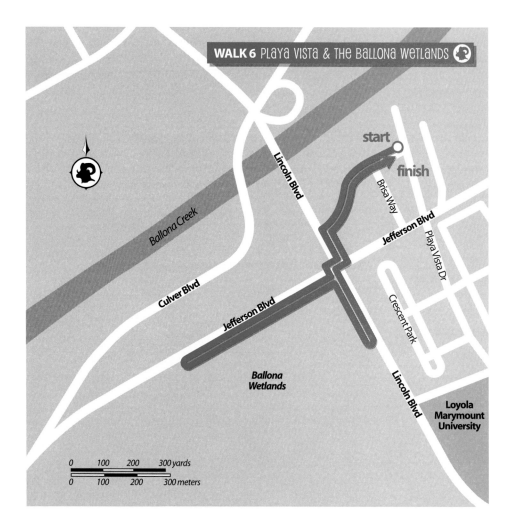

start

finish

Brisa Way

Lincoln Blvd

Jefferson Blvd

Playa Vista Dr

Ballona Creek

Culver Blvd

Jefferson Blvd

Crescent Park

Ballona
Wetlands

Lincoln Blvd

Loyola
Marymount
University

| 0 | 100 | 200 | 300 yards |
| 0 | 100 | 200 | 300 meters |

6 Playa Vista and the Ballona Wetlands: a carefully engineered slice of nature

BOUNDARIES: **Culver Blvd., Centinela Ave., Manchester Ave.**
THOMAS GUIDE COORDINATES: **Map 702; D1**
DISTANCE: **Approx. ½ mile**
DIFFICULTY: **Easy**
PARKING: **There is a free parking lot for the Playa Vista Visitor Center located at the corner of Fountain Park Dr. and Playa Vista Dr., north of Jefferson Blvd and east of Lincoln Blvd.**

One of the most fascinating, and sometimes disheartening, aspects of Los Angeles is the stark juxtaposition of urban development and nature. Perhaps the most illustrative example of this phenomenon is Playa Vista, a new housing development that lies just south of Marina del Rey. This luxury apartment complex encroaches on the Ballona Wetlands, which activists have been struggling to revitalize and preserve for many years now.

Fortunately, the conservationists got their wish (sort of). The Playa Vista complex has been completed, but not at the expense of the wetlands...or at least a portion of the wetlands. The company behind the development claims to be committed to respecting the natural environment through sustainable development, which places an emphasis on recycling, energy efficiency, and pollution control. Let's hope they stick to their word.

Across the street from this innovative residential complex lie the Ballona wetlands, an open expanse of freshwater marsh that has been restored as part of the Playa Vista development project. Our walk will begin at the Playa Vista Visitor Center before crossing busy Lincoln Blvd. to the serene and aromatic trail bordering the preserved ecosystem.

● **After parking in the Playa Vista visitor lot, head west toward Lincoln Blvd and the Visitor Center. If you'd like, you can poke around inside the building to learn more about the Ballona wetlands through dioramic exhibits, but you may be subject to a sales pitch from a "Playa Vista ambassador."**

- Continue through the Visitor Center courtyard to Lincoln Blvd. and turn left toward the intersection with Jefferson Blvd.

- Cross Lincoln Blvd., and then cross over to the southwest corner of Jefferson and Lincoln, where the nature trail begins.

- At this point, you may choose to head in whichever direction your heart desires. The nature trail doesn't make a loop or actually venture into the wetlands, but rather runs along two sides of the marsh, immediately adjacent to Lincoln and Jefferson Blvds.

   Posted signs along the trail educate visitors about the wildlife indigenous to the marsh ecosystem and discuss how the wetland preservation project works in synchronicity with the nearby housing development to filter runoff and curb pollutants in the water before it reaches the ocean.

   Despite the occasional distant roar of jets in the distance (LAX is located a few miles south of here), this is a peaceful stroll; the scent of wood chips mingled with marshland saturates the cool ocean-kissed air. The ungraceful, high-rise blocks of the Playa Vista development loom on the other side of Lincoln Blvd., and the crowded mansions of Playa del Rey teeter on the cliffs above the wetlands. These luxury residences of questionable taste mar the view somewhat, but the wetlands themselves are picturesque, a carefully cultivated slice of ecosystem that sits quietly at the junction of two major west side thoroughfares.

- After spending some time observing the native herons, terns, sparrows, and butterflies of the freshwater marsh, retrace your steps back to the Playa Vista visitor lot.

route summary

1. Park in the Playa Vista visitor lot at the corner of Fountain Park Dr. and Playa Vista Dr. and head west toward the Visitor Center.
2. Continue through the Visitor Center courtyard to Lincoln Blvd. and turn left toward the intersection with Jefferson Blvd.
3. Cross Lincoln Blvd., and then cross over to the southwest corner of Jefferson and Lincoln.
4. Walk along the nature trail that runs along the southwest corner of Jefferson and Lincoln.
5. Retrace your steps back to the Playa Vista visitor lot.

Ballona Wetlands

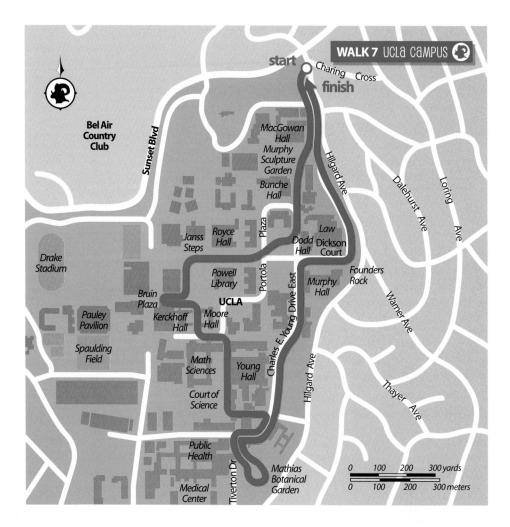

start

Charing Cross

finish

MacGowan Hall

Murphy Sculpture Garden

Bunche Hall

Bel Air Country Club

Sunset Blvd

Hilgard Ave

Dalehurst Ave

Loring Ave

Plaza

Law

Janss Steps

Royce Hall

Dodd Hall

Dickson Court

Drake Stadium

Portola

Founders Rock

Warner Ave

Powell Library

UCLA

Murphy Hall

Bruin Plaza

Charles E. Young Drive East

Pauley Pavilion

Kerckhoff Hall

Moore Hall

Thayer Ave

Spaulding Field

Hilgard Ave

Math Sciences

Young Hall

Court of Science

Public Health

Tiverton Dr

Mathias Botanical Garden

Medical Center

| 0 | 100 | 200 | 300 yards |
| 0 | 100 | 200 | 300 meters |

7 UCLA Campus: Ivy League Style with a West Coast Twist

BOUNDARIES: **Sunset Blvd., Hilgard Ave., Le Conte Ave., Gayley Ave.**
THOMAS GUIDE COORDINATES: **Map 592; B1**
DISTANCE: **Approx. 1¾ miles**
DIFFICULTY: **Easy**
PARKING: **Limited street parking is available on Hilgard Ave. south of Sunset Blvd. Paid parking is available on campus.**

UCLA is one of the most well known campuses in the state's famed public University of California system. Renowned for its challenging academic programs as well as for its gorgeous, ideally situated campus, UCLA represents the mythical undergraduate experience that many of us wish we had had.

This route will explore the most scenic spots of this massive campus, taking in innovative artwork, classically beautiful architecture, and a lovely botanical garden that's evolved over several decades.

● **Begin on Hilgard Ave. just south of Sunset Blvd. Look for Charles E. Young Dr., which splits off from Hilgard to the right. Follow Young Dr. into the UCLA campus.**

● **Turn right at the semicircular driveway to head into the Franklin D. Murphy Sculpture Garden. You'll pass a shallow fountain on your right as you descend the short stairway into the sunken grassy area. Notice the two columns topped with bronze sculptures of nude dancers by Robert Graham. The sculpture garden spans over five acres of UCLA's north campus and includes an eclectic blend of naturalistic and sleekly modern pieces from artists such as Alexander Calder, Henri Matisse, Jacques Lipchitz, and Auguste Rodin. It is the largest outdoor sculpture garden on the West Coast and one of the prettiest, with its rolling green lawns and feathery jacaranda trees. After taking some time to admire the sculptures and bas-reliefs (there are over 70 in total), return to the eastern end of the garden and follow the sidewalk heading south.**

- As you head south along the sidewalk, you'll come to Bunche Hall on your right, which features an innovative indoor palm garden in its central atrium. Continue to head south along the sidewalk, passing Luvalle Commons on your left.

- When you reach Dodd Hall, turn right to follow the diagonal path through the sunken, shady lawn of Dickson Plaza, which is shaded by mature sycamore and fig trees.

- After crossing the street, you'll find yourself in the university's Historic Quad. This wide, open grassy area runs between the four original buildings of the Westwood campus, all of which were built in 1929 in the Italian Romanesque style. You'll pass Haines Hall on your right and Kinsey Hall on your left before coming to the campus's two most well known landmarks. On your right is Royce Hall, which was designed by architect David Allison after a basilica in Milan. Powell Library is on your left, and while it bears some architectural resemblance to Royce Hall, it was designed by another architect, George Kelham. Powell's octagonal tower and main entrance are modeled after two different churches in Italy. Part of what makes the northeast portion of the UCLA campus so beautiful is its architectural integrity; the red brick, Italianate buildings lend a distinguished, Old World feel to the College of Humanities.

- Continue westward through the quad and you'll come to the semicircular Royce Hall fountain on Janss Terrace. Descend the Janss Steps, which provided the original entrance to the university, leading up from Westwood Blvd. Admire the expansive view of the intramural fields stretched out in the distance. To your right you'll see the Fowler Museum of Cultural History. The Student Activities Center lies on the south side of lawn below, with Kaufman Hall sitting opposite. On this side of campus, the university's newer buildings with their red brick and tan stone exteriors integrate beautifully with the original architecture.

- Turn left at the bottom of the stairs and follow the pathway heading south. Kerkhoff Hall lies straight ahead. Tree-shaded lawns roll gently alongside the sidewalk, yet another idyllic place for scholars to engage in or rest from their academic pursuits.

- At the end of the sidewalk, turn right to follow the Bruin Walk into Bruin Plaza, home of the Bruin Bear himself, a two-tone bronze statue of a ferocious-looking grizzly. At the southeast corner of the plaza is Ackerman Union, a modern building distinguished by ship-like arched wooden beams atop the roof. The UCLA store occupies the first floor of the building and offers just about anything a student would need to purchase, from groceries to designer apparel to Macintosh computers, as well as a diverse collection of dining options.

- Head back the way you came on Bruin Walk, past Ackerman Union, and you'll come back to Kerkhoff Hall (est. 1931), the only building on campus to be built in the Collegiate Gothic style. Continue straight ahead up the steps and then turn right (following the sign pointing toward the Kerkhoff Coffeehouse). Cross through the outdoor dining patio between Kerkhoff Hall and Moore Hall, which is on your left.

- Turn left on Portola Plaza; the Mathematical Sciences building is on your right. You are now entering into the more technical side of campus, which is not nearly as pretty as the Humanities section in terms of architecture.

- Just after you've passed the Math Sciences building, turn right to cross through the Court of Sciences. Boelter Hall is on your right, the Geology building, Young Hall, and Boyer Hall are on your left.

Author's Note: The remainder of this walk was recorded at a time of ongoing construction in the southern part of campus, so we were forced to make our way around the mess. The situation may be different at the time of publication, but as long as you make your way east back to Charles E. Young Dr., you'll be able to find your way to the next point of interest on the walk, the botanical gardens.

- Just after passing Boyer Hall, turn left and follow the path toward the

Royce Hall

Molecular Sciences building. Make your way through the outdoor patio of this building so that you emerge back onto Charles E. Young Dr.

● Turn right on Young Dr. and follow it as it curves to the right, passing the curving brick façade of the newly constructed building on your right.

● Turn left on Tiverton Dr. You'll see the sign for the Mildred E. Mathias Botanical Gardens on your left.

● Follow the driveway entrance to the botanical gardens, just across the street from the School of Dentistry, and then enter the actual gardens through the North Gate on your right.

Follow the gently sloping path that descends into the sunken gardens, taking the time to explore at your leisure, or perhaps simply sit and relax in the green shade on one of the many benches. This seven-acre oasis features plant life from all over the world, including many species of tropical and subtropical flora. The topography of UCLA's botanical gardens is a remnant of the ravine that used to run across the entire campus. Today, a water pump feeds the river that runs down the center of the gardens.

● After spending some time in the gardens, make your way back toward the point where you entered at the north end, and exit back out onto Tiverton Dr. Turn right on Tiverton.

● Turn right on Charles E. Young Dr. and follow it back the way you came, and then continue along the perimeter of campus. After crossing Westholme, you'll notice the barn-like structure of the Faculty Center on your right.

● Just past Murphy Hall, turn right (instead of continuing straight, which will take you back to the sculpture garden). This path will take you past the School of Law on your left.

● Turn left to continue on Charles E. Young Dr., following it all the way back to the intersection with Hilgard Ave., where you began.

POINT OF INTEREST

Mildred E. Mathias Botanical Gardens University of California, Los Angeles, Los Angeles, CA 90095, 310-825-1260. Please call ahead to make sure the gardens are open at the time of your visit.

ROUTE SUMMARY

1. Begin on Hilgard Ave. just south of Sunset Blvd. and turn right on Charles E. Young Dr., which leads into the UCLA campus.
2. Turn right at the semicircular driveway to head into the Franklin D. Murphy Sculpture Garden.
3. Turn left to cut across the garden and continue straight along the sidewalk that heads south.
4. When you reach Dodd Hall, turn right to follow the diagonal path through Dickson Plaza.
5. Cross the street to continue straight into UCLA's Historic Quad.
6. Cross the quad to the Janss Steps and descend.
7. Turn left at the bottom of the stairs and follow the pathway.
8. At the end of the sidewalk, turn right to follow the Bruin Walk into Bruin Plaza.
9. Head back the way you came on Bruin Walk. Continue straight ahead up the steps and then turn right. Cross through the patio between Kerkhoff Hall and Moore Hall.
10. Turn left on Portola Plaza; the Mathematical Sciences building is on your right.
11. Just after you've passed the Math Sciences building, turn right to cross through the Court of Sciences.
12. Just after passing Boyer Hall, turn left and follow the path toward the Molecular Sciences building. Make your way through the building's patio and back to Charles E. Young Dr.
13. Turn right on Young Dr. and follow it as it curves to the right.
14. Turn left on Tiverton Dr.
15. Follow the driveway entrance to the botanical gardens on your left, and then enter the actual gardens through the North Gate on your right.
16. Exit the gardens back out onto Tiverton Dr. and turn right.
17. Turn right on Charles E. Young Dr. and follow it back the way you came, and then continue along the perimeter of campus.
18. Turn right just past Murphy Hall.
19. Turn left to continue on Charles E. Young Dr., following it all the way back to your starting point at the intersection with Hilgard Ave.

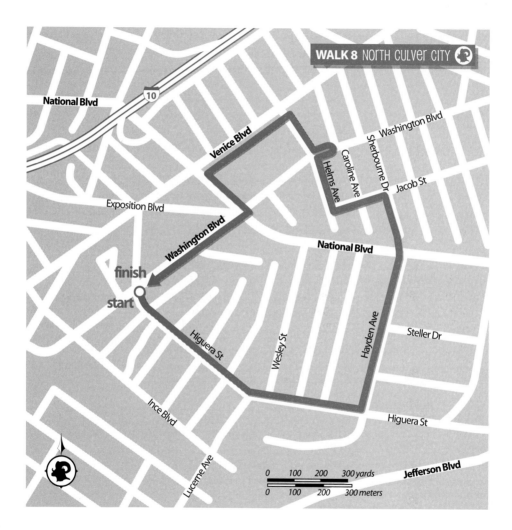

National Blvd

10

Venice Blvd

Washington Blvd

Washington Blvd

Sherbourne Dr

Caroline Ave

Helms Ave

Jacob St

Exposition Blvd

National Blvd

finish

start

Washington Blvd

Higuera St

Wesley St

Hayden Ave

Steller Dr

Ince Blvd

Higuera St

Luceme Ave

0   100   200   300 yards
0   100   200   300 meters

Jefferson Blvd

8 NOrTH CULVer CITY:
HIDDEN Treasure ON THE WesT SIDe

BOUNDARIES: Venice Blvd., Higuera St., Jefferson Blvd., La Cienega Blvd.
THOMAS GUIDE COORDINATES: Map 672; H1
DISTANCE: Approx. 1½ miles
DIFFICULTY: Easy
PARKING: Free street parking is available on Higuera St.

Culver City is truly a gem on LA's West Side, and this route uncovers those characteristics that make it such a desirable place to live. Beginning in the picturesque neighborhood known as Rancho Higuera, this walk takes in some of the most innovative industrial-style architecture in all of Los Angeles, and then visits the trendy area around the historic Art Deco Helms Bakeries buildings, which are now home to chic eateries and upscale furniture stores.

● Begin on Higuera St., just south of Washington Blvd. Head southwest on Higuera, away from Washington. This is the main thoroughfare through the Rancho Higuera neighborhood, popular with commuters cutting between Washington and Jefferson Blvds. For this reason, residents had mini rotaries installed at each of the cross streets, which effectively cause motorists to slow down. The homes on this street are modest in size and carefully maintained. Higuera is lined with flowering trees and bushes, with Baldwin Hills forming a pastoral backdrop.

● After several short blocks, turn left on Hayden Ave. (Hayden Pl. heads into an office park to the right). You'll notice a brick building with a unique stepped roofline on your left. This is the Debbie Allen (of *Fame* fame) Dance Academy, and it spans the length of a city block. Most of the buildings on this street are industrial warehouses, some of which are more worn down than others, yet it manages to retain the safe feel of the residential neighborhood you just left behind. At 3599 Hayden Ave. you'll see J.J.'s Café, a decent little lunch spot marked with a green awning.

As you draw closer to National Blvd., you'll pass two extraordinary buildings, one on either side of the street. On your left at 3535 is a massive, free-form structure in light gray stucco, punctuated by sharp points and odd outcroppings. On the right is a collection of structures identified as "Conjunctive Points." The dominant building looks like something Darth Vader might like to call home. It looms over the street, all sharp angles in faded black metal and glass. On your right at the corner of National and Hayden is an America Online building, its most interesting feature is a sort of brick bubble with three off-kilter windows that looks as if it was tacked on to the otherwise featureless gray wall. This has got to be one of the most striking collections of buildings in LA.

● When you reach National Blvd. cross at the crosswalk and then continue straight on the sidewalk that passes through the oleander hedge on the other side of the railroad tracks.

● Continue straight ahead onto Sherbourne Dr., another shady residential street much like Higuera.

● Turn left on Jacob St. and continue across Caroline Ave.

● Turn right on Helms Ave. When you reach the corner of Helms Ave. and Washington Blvd., you'll leave the residential neighborhood behind. Cross Washington and then walk a few yards to your right to take a peek at the colorful public art piece depicting a Helms Bakeries truck crashing into a movie studio backdrop of Culver City. A knocked-over fire hydrant spurts water, completing the comical effect.

Continue north on Helms Ave. On your left is the sprawling Art Deco Helms Bakeries complex. Built in 1930 and then closed in 1969, the bakery warehouses have been kept in pristine condition and are now home to many businesses, mostly upscale furniture and antique stores. La Dijonaise, a top-notch French bakery and café, occupies the southeast corner of the building. In addition to fresh, tasty food, this eatery offers reasonable prices and a pleasant, airy atmosphere, making it a great place to stop for lunch, coffee, dessert, or all three. Next door to La Dijonaise is the Jazz Bakery, one of LA's premier spots to hear talented jazz and blues artists. And Beacon, a hip

Asian eatery serving beautifully prepared and flavorful fusion cuisine ranging from pad thai to sashimi, is across the street on the east side of Helms Ave.

- Turn left on Venice Blvd. H.D. Buttercup, a huge, airy showroom where customers can purchase furnishings directly from over 50 manufacturers, sits on the corner of Venice and Helms. This diverse and upscale furniture mart has received a great deal of buzz since opening in early 2005 and also features a restaurant, bar, and Helms Bakery Museum.

- Turn left on National Blvd. You may catch a whiff of the pungent aromas drifting from the candle outlet on the southwest side of the street.

- Turn right on Washington Blvd. You'll notice The Jungle, a tropical plants nursery, on the northwest corner of National and Washington. The next couple of blocks are populated almost exclusively with new and used car dealers.

- Turn left on Higuera St. (the street is named Robertson Blvd. heading in the other direction) to return to your starting point. On your right, you'll notice a neighborhood market by the name of Jerry's Market Deli on the corner of Poinsettia Ct., a quiet little alley of charming, closely set Spanish-style homes. This peaceful lane captures the spirit of Rancho Higuera, which is a pretty, safe, diverse, and utterly unpretentious neighborhood in a wonderfully central location.

Helms Bakeries sign

POINTS OF INTEREST

J.J.'s Cafe 3599 Hayden Ave., Culver City, CA 90232, 310-837-3248

New School of Cooking 8690 Washington Blvd., Culver City, CA 90232, 310-842-9702

La Dijonaise 8703 Washington Blvd., Culver City, CA 90232, 310-287-2770

Jazz Bakery 3233 Helms Ave., Culver City, CA 90034, 310-271-9039

Beacon 3280 Helms Ave., Culver City, CA 90034, 310-838-7500

H.D. Buttercup 3225 Helms Ave., Culver City, CA 90034, 310-558-8900

route summary

1. Begin on Higuera St. just south of Washington Blvd and head southwest on Higuera St.
2. Turn left on Hayden Ave.
3. Cross National Blvd. and continue straight through the pedestrian passageway onto Sherbourne Dr.
4. Head north on Sherbourne Dr.
5. Turn left on Jacob St.
6. Turn right on Helms Ave.
7. Turn left on Venice Blvd.
8. Turn left on National Blvd.
9. Turn right on Washington Blvd.
10. Turn left on Higuera St.

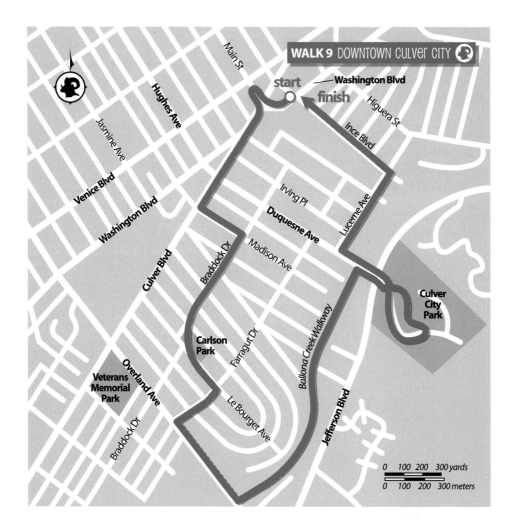

start

finish

Washington Blvd

Main St

Higuera St

Ince Blvd

Hughes Ave

Jasmine Ave

Venice Blvd

Washington Blvd

Irving Pl

Duquesne Ave

Luceme Ave

Culver Blvd

Braddock Dr

Madison Ave

Culver
City
Park

Farragut Dr

Ballona Creek Walkway

Carlson
Park

Overland Ave

Veterans
Memorial
Park

Le Bourget Ave

Jefferson Blvd

Braddock Dr

0   100 200   300 yards

0   100 200   300 meters

9 DOWNTOWN CULVER CITY: HOLDING ONTO ITS PLACE IN MOVIE-MAKING HISTORY

BOUNDARIES: **Venice Blvd., Overland Ave., Jefferson Blvd., Ince Blvd.**
THOMAS GUIDE COORDINATES: **Map 672; H1**
DISTANCE: **Approx. 3½ miles**
DIFFICULTY: **Moderate**
PARKING: **Free street parking is available on Ince Blvd.**

A quiet town on Los Angeles' otherwise high-profile west side, Culver City is home to sprawling Sony Pictures Studios, as well as historic Culver Studios. While it is said to have been a notorious spot for nightlife during Prohibition, downtown Culver City is now at its most bustling on weekdays, when purposeful young executives and interns from the studios run errands and enjoy lunch at its many charming dining establishments.

● Begin at Culver Studios, on the corner of Ince Blvd. and Washington Blvd. The studio façade resembles a grand colonial mansion, and will be instantly recognizable to film buffs from the opening credits of *Gone With the Wind*. Culver Studios was built by Thomas H. Ince in 1919, and has also been home to RKO, DeMille, and Desilu studios during its lifetime. Today it is owned by Sony Entertainment. Head northwest on Washington Blvd., away from Ince Blvd.

Immediately northwest of Culver Studios is the Culver Hotel, a six-story, triangular brick building situated at the junction of Washington, Culver Blvd., and Main St. Another historic landmark, this establishment opened as the Hotel Hunt in 1924 to accommodate the many actors who filmed at the studios across the street. In fact, the "munchkins" from *The Wizard of Oz* had such a good time here that they held a reunion of the surviving cast members at the hotel in 1997. As a tribute, the hotel restaurant is called Munchkins. This charming indoor/outdoor eatery serves lunch and dinner; menu choices include a diverse array of upscale fare with an emphasis on Asian flavors and sushi.

- As long as you're here, you should head north to stroll up Culver City's one-block Main Street—locals like to brag that it's the shortest main drag in the U.S. The Culver City Farmers Market sets up here every Tuesday from 3 to 7 P.M., later in the day than most of LA's farmers markets. Main Street is also home to the Massage Garage, where you can get a one-hour massage for only $45, and the Grand Casino Bakery, an Argentinean bakery and sandwich shop, as well as various other eateries, a thrift shop, and a hardware store. The sleepy feel of Culver City's diminutive Main Street contrasts sharply with the frantic commercial hubbub immediately to the north on Venice Boulevard.

- After grabbing a bite at Munchkins or one of downtown's many other casual restaurants, head southwest on Culver Blvd. for about a quarter of a mile. At the corner of Culver and Duquesne Ave. is City Hall, a collection of attractive white-stucco Spanish-style buildings. Take a moment to wander under the freestanding arched entryway through the courtyard and admire the fountains.

  Continue to head southwest on Culver and you'll notice an imposing stepped granite and glass structure across the street on your right at the intersection of Madison Ave. This is Sony Pictures Plaza. Directly opposite the entrance to the plaza on Madison is one of the gates to Sony Pictures Studios. You can't miss the signature water tower rising from the back lot. You can arrange a tour of the studios by calling 323-520-TOUR (there is a moderate fee).

- Turn left on Madison Ave. This will take you into a quiet residential neighborhood of mostly modest houses. Culver City showcases an interesting assortment of architecture, and this neighborhood in particular features everything from tidy bungalows to larger and, for the most part, uninspired, contemporary homes.

- Walk one block on Madison and then turn right on Braddock Dr. Continue for five short blocks on Braddock and you come to Dr. Paul Carlson Park.

- Cut diagonally across the shady park to Le Bourget Ave. and turn left.

- Walk one block on Le Bourget and then turn right on Farragut Dr.

- After three quiet residential blocks you arrive at busy Overland Ave. Turn left on Overland.

- After about a third of a mile, you'll come to the pedestrian entrance to the Ballona Creek walkway and bike path. Ballona Creek is a concrete-sided waterway that empties into the ocean in Marina del Rey, but today you will follow it inland. Take the pedestrian ramp down to the creek and continue to head east along the pathway. Depending on the time of year, there may be either a sad little trickle or a healthy stream burbling through the channel.

- Follow the river walkway for just under a mile to Duquesne Ave. You can't miss the exit to the street, as it is marked by a whimsical metallic structure in the shape of a giant water urn, which stands next to the Culver City Transportation Center on the opposite side of the creek.

- Turn right on Duquesne and walk to the intersection of Jefferson Blvd. Cross Jefferson and you're at the entrance to Culver City Park.

- Follow the road as it curves uphill, passing a playground on your right, and then turn left into the parking lot. This will take you to the base of a zig-zagging wooden walkway that leads to the top of the hill. Once you reach the summit, take a few minutes to enjoy the panoramic view of West Los Angeles and the Pacific Ocean. Also take a second to check out the giant sundial sculpture, which proclaims itself to be an "Homage to Ballona Creek." The mosaic-tiled base of the sundial is decorated with the

Culver Studios façade

49

words "Time is a River" in several different languages. It seems like a bit of a stretch on the part of the artists to relate the sundial to the paved waterway, but this is an interesting work of art nonetheless.

- Turn right at the top of the ramp and walk around the perimeter of the baseball field. Descend the stairway behind the snack bar.

- Turn right on the service road at the bottom of the stairs and follow it to where it intersects with Duquesne. Continue down the hill on Duquesne to return to the intersection at Jefferson Blvd.

- Cross Jefferson and head north on Duquesne back in the direction of downtown Culver City.

- Turn right on Lucerne Ave., a quiet, tree-lined street that leads through an unassuming residential neighborhood.

- After about a third of a mile, you reach Ince Blvd. Turn left here. As you make your way down Ince, you'll notice a studio back lot on your left. This is the utilitarian lot that resides behind Culver Studios' ostentatious façade. On the right side of the street at the intersection of Poinsettia is a low industrial-style building, cartoonishly ornamented with short orange columns. One column is intentionally crooked, giving the illusion that it is buckling under the weight of the roof. The name "Paramount Laundry Company" is engraved over the entrance. We suspect that this is no longer a laundry facility, but the building is otherwise unidentified. We have noticed well-dressed twenty-somethings milling around here, however, so we presume it is somehow connected to the studios across the street.

- Return to your starting point at the intersection of Ince Blvd. and Washington Blvd.

POINTS OF INTEREST

Culver Hotel 9400 Culver Blvd., Culver City, CA 90232, 888-328-5837
Massage Garage 3812 Main St., Culver City, CA 90232, 310-202-0082

Grand Casino French Bakery 3826 Main St., Culver City, CA 90232, 310-202-6969

Sony Pictures Studios 10202 West Washington Blvd., Culver City, CA 90232, 323-520-TOUR

Culver City Farmers Market Main St. between Culver Blvd. and Venice Blvd. Tuesdays 3:00 to 7:00 P.M.

route summary

1. Begin on the corner of Ince Blvd. and Washington Blvd. and head northwest on Washington Blvd., away from Ince Blvd. to the intersection with Culver Blvd. and Main St.
2. Head north to stroll along one-block Main St. and then return to Culver Blvd.
3. Turn right to head southwest on Culver Blvd.
4. Turn left on Madison Ave.
5. Turn right on Braddock Dr.
6. Cut diagonally across Dr. Paul Carlson Park to Le Bourget Ave. and turn left.
7. Turn right on Farragut Dr.
8. Turn left on Overland Ave.
9. Take the pedestrian entrance on your left down to the Ballona Creek walkway and bike path.
10. Follow the river walkway for just under a mile and then exit at Duquesne Ave.
11. Turn right on Duquesne and then cross Jefferson Blvd. to reach the entrance to Culver City Park.
12. Follow the road as it curves uphill, and then turn left into the parking lot and ascend the wooden walkway that leads up the hill from the parking lot.
13. Turn right at the top of the ramp and walk around the perimeter of the baseball field, and then descend the stairway behind the snack bar.
14. Turn right on the service road at the bottom of the stairs and follow it to where it intersects with Duquesne, and then continue down the hill to return to Jefferson Blvd.
15. Cross Jefferson and head north on Duquesne.
16. Turn right on Lucerne Ave.
17. Turn left on Ince Blvd.
18. Return to your starting point at the intersection of Ince Blvd. and Washington Blvd.

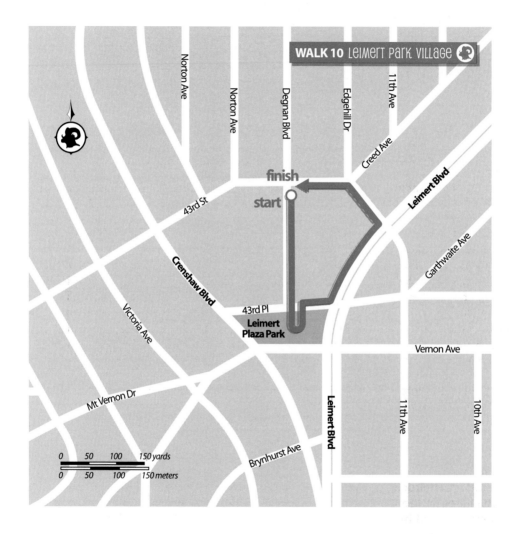

Norton Ave

Norton Ave

Degnan Blvd

Edgehill Dr

11th Ave

Creed Ave

Leimert Blvd

43rd St

finish

start

Garthwaite Ave

Crenshaw Blvd

Victoria Ave

43rd Pl

Leimert Plaza Park

Vernon Ave

Mt Vernon Dr

Leimert Blvd

11th Ave

10th Ave

| 0 | 50 | 100 | 150 yards |

| 0 | 50 | 100 | 150 meters |

Brynhurst Ave

10 Leimert Park Village: Preserving African American Business and Culture

BOUNDARIES: **Crenshaw Blvd, 43rd St., Leimert Blvd.**
THOMAS GUIDE COORDINATES: **Map 673; F3**
DISTANCE: **Less than ½ mile**
DIFFICULTY: **Easy**
PARKING: **Metered parking is available on Degnan Blvd. south of 43rd St. and in a parking lot on the southeast corner. Free street parking is available on Degnan north of 43rd St.**

Leimert Park Village is truly a treasure in South Los Angeles. A revitalization effort started over 10 years ago has been dedicated to preserving this area for small African American business owners who place an emphasis on cultural enrichment. Due to the success of this movement, Leimert Park has become Los Angeles' main destination for Afrocentric dining, shopping, art, and entertainment, particularly dance, poetry, jazz, and blues. While the Village is a fine place to visit during the day, especially if you want to enjoy some authentic soul food or browse the shops for ethnic clothing, jewelry, and gifts, it really comes alive at night, when the sidewalks are crowded with enthusiastic patrons of the arts and the air is saturated with the sounds of drum circles, jazz, blues, and passionate spoken word performances.

● **Begin at the intersection of 43rd St. and Degnan Blvd. To the north, Degnan is a shady residential street bordered by attractive, well maintained duplexes. To the south, it is the bustling commercial focal point of Leimert Park Village. On the northeast corner at 3351 W. 43rd St. is the Lucy Florence Coffee House/ Le Florence Gallery, an architecturally innovative multiuse space that includes a café, art gallery, and live performance theatre. Lucy Florence also offers a buffet at 10 A.M. every Saturday; patrons get to settle into comfortably furnished sitting rooms where they can listen to the radio or watch television while they eat—talk about making your customers feel at home! Twin brother proprietors Ron and Richard Harris named the establishment after their mother, and the company logo is a heartbreakingly lovely** sepia reproduction of her solemn wedding photo. The Harris brothers are fierce advocates of multicultural creative arts, so they've opened their doors to all manner of performance art and art exhibitions. Stop in at Lucy Florence to grab a cuppa joe and pick up some fliers about forthcoming shows and exhibitions—if you're lucky, you might even catch an interesting performance in progress.

● Head south on Degnan Blvd. At 4317 you'll come to M&M Soul Food Restaurant. This destination for authentic Southern-style cooking has expanded beyond South LA in recent years due to its popularity. A permanent sign declares this shop to be an "LAPD Stopping Location." This brings up an interesting fact about Leimert Park— though it's smack dab in the middle of an area of Los Angeles that sees its fair share of crime, this enclave feels safe and vibrant, both day and night, as it has thrived as a positive community gathering place since its revitalization. The Dance Collective at 4327 Degnan offers workshops in West African, Brazilian, tap, ballet, and jazz dance to the accompaniment of live drummers and musicians. So many people gather to watch the rehearsals that they often spill out onto the sidewalk. You'll come across the truly unique Museum in Black at 4331 Degnan, where you can check out hundreds of specimens of traditional African art and artifacts set under a verdant canopy of tropical plants.

Across the street at 4334 Degnan is Zambezi Bazaar, an eclectic gift shop selling a vast selection of ethnic jewelry and clothing, as well as African American greeting cards, figurines, tapestries, and posters. Next door is the Elephant Walk Restaurant, which serves adventurous California-French cuisine. You're likely to hear jazz, blues, or even spoken word drifting out of the World Stage Performance Gallery at 4344 Degnan—the plain interior set up with folding chairs sums up the low-key vibe in the Village.

● At the end of Degnan Blvd, cross 43rd Pl. to visit Leimert Plaza Park, a narrow greenway set around a circular fountain. Public restrooms are available in the park, and benches set underneath the trees make an excellent place to sit and chow down on carryout from one of Leimert Park Village's many casual eateries.

● Cross back to the north side of 43rd Pl. and turn right, passing by an old Art Deco building that now houses 5th Street Dick's Coffee Company at 3347, a hot spot for live jazz at night, as well as Sunny's Spot Coffee House, Kitchen on 43rd Place (another excellent nighttime jazz venue), and a barber shop.

- Turn left on Leimert Blvd. Babe Rickey's Inn at 4339 Leimert Blvd. is the spot for "World Famous Blues." Continue for one block back to 43rd St.

- Turn left on 43rd St. Tantalizing, smoky smells emanate from Phillip's BBQ, located on the southwest corner of Leimert Blvd. and 43rd St. Continue on 43rd St. around the corner. The Regency West Theatre, located at 3339 43rd St., shares the same building as Lucy Florence—a large, pale green structure painted with the silhouettes of what appear to be ancient African warriors armed with spears. This supper club hosts all types of theatrical performances, but is best known as a venue for urban poetry and comedy. Next you'll come back to the Lucy Florence Coffee House and the starting point of your walk.

M&M Soul Food

POINTS OF INTEREST

Lucy Florence Coffee House and Le Florence Gallery 3351 W. 43rd St., Los Angeles, CA 90008, 323-293-1356

M&M Soul Food Restaurant 4317 Degnan Blvd., Los Angeles, CA 90008, 323-298-9898

The Dance Collective 4327 Degnan Blvd., Los Angeles, CA 90008, 323-291-1538

Museum in Black 4331 Degnan Blvd., Los Angeles, CA 90008, 323-292-9528

Zambezi Bazaar 4334 Degnan Blvd., Los Angeles, CA 90008, 323-299-6383

Elephant Walk Restaurant 4336 Degnan Blvd., Los Angeles, CA 90008, 323-299-1765

World Stage Performance Gallery 4344 Degnan Blvd., Los Angeles, CA 90008, 323-293-2451

5th Street Dick's Coffee Company 3347 W. 43rd Pl., Los Angeles, CA 90008, 323-296-3970

Kitchen on 43rd Place 3347½ W. 43rd Pl., Los Angeles, CA 90008, 323-299-7799

Babe Rickey's Inn 4339 Leimert Blvd., Los Angeles, CA 90008, 323-295-9112

Phillip's BBQ 4307 Leimert Blvd., Los Angeles, CA 90008, 323-292-7613

Regency West Theatre 3339 W. 43rd St., Los Angeles, CA 90008, 323-292-5143

route summary

1. Begin at the intersection of 43rd St. and Degnan Blvd.
2. Head south on Degnan Blvd.
3. At then end of Degnan Blvd, cross 43rd Pl. to visit Leimert Plaza Park.
4. Cross back to the north side of 43rd Pl. and turn right.
5. Turn left on Leimert Blvd.
6. Turn left on 43rd St. Continue around the corner on 43rd St. to return to your starting point at the intersection of Degnan Blvd.

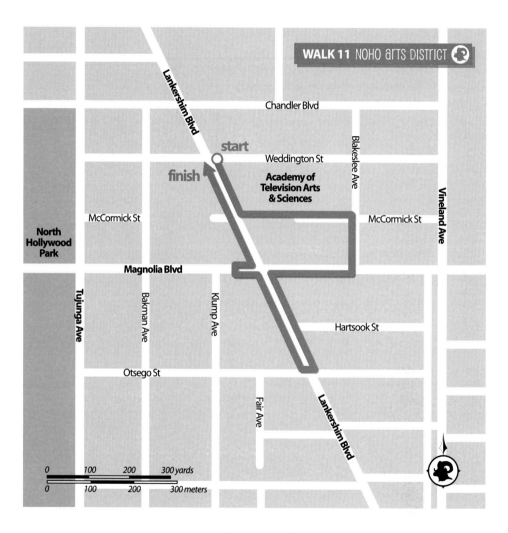

Chandler Blvd

Lankershim Blvd

Blakeslee Ave

start

Weddington St

finish

**Academy of
Television Arts
& Sciences**

Vineland Ave

McCormick St

McCormick St

**North
Hollywood
Park**

Magnolia Blvd

Tujunga Ave

Bakman Ave

Klump Ave

Hartsook St

Otsego St

Fair Ave

Lankershim Blvd

| 0 | 100 | 200 | 300 yards |
| 0 | 100 | 200 | 300 meters |

11 NOHO arts District: creativity Blooms in the most unlikely places

BOUNDARIES: **Chandler Blvd., Vineland Ave., Tujunga Ave., Otsego St.**
THOMAS GUIDE COORDINATES: **Map 562; J2**
DISTANCE: **Approx. ¾ mile**
DIFFICULTY: **Easy**
PARKING: **Metered parking is available on Lankershim Blvd. south of Weddington St.**

North Hollywood hardly seems like a walking destination, but the birth of the NoHo Arts District makes it a neighborhood worth exploring. A stroll up and down Lankershim Blvd. reveals a gaggle of art galleries, theatre companies, and dance studios, as well as an eclectic collection of outdoor public art works that you wouldn't expect to encounter on this otherwise anonymous suburban thoroughfare deep in the San Fernando Valley.

- Begin on the east side of Lankershim Blvd. just south of Weddington St. and head south.

- At 5220 you'll come to the Academy of Television Arts and Sciences complex. Enter the main plaza, passing by the colorful whirligigs that adorn the lawn next to the driveway entrance. The plaza is surrounded by somewhat creepy-looking bronze busts of famous personalities such as Red Skelton, Bill Cosby, and Walt Disney, along with the unfamiliar faces of numerous company executives. The centerpiece is a massive, burnished statue of the Emmy award itself, which sits atop a circular tiered fountain.

- Exit the Academy plaza via Blakeslee Ave, which heads south out to Magnolia Blvd. Carefully cross Magnolia, a fairly busy street. The south side of Magnolia is home to several small theatres. The NoHo Arts Center (formerly the American Renegade Theatre) located at 11136 devotes itself to multicultural performance art and theatre. The vintage Avery Schreiber Theatre is located a few steps east of Blakeslee at

11050 Magnolia. After picking up performance schedules at the theatres, head west on Magnolia back toward Lankershim.

- Turn left to head south on Lankershim. After passing the ubiquitous Starbucks on the corner, you'll come to the long black awning and big neon signs marking the entrance to the Eclectic Café, a neighborhood eatery that serves California cuisine and showcases the work of local artists. At 5100 Lankershim, the international head-quarters for paint-your-own-pottery chain Color Me Mine shares space with the NoHo Ceramics Gallery behind a quaint brick-and-wood storefront.

- Cross Hartsook St. and continue south on Lankershim, passing under the giant retro sign for the North Hollywood Gym on the corner. You'll pass the Meisner Center for the Arts at 5124 before coming to the cool 1950s-style marquee for the Deaf West Theatre at 5112. This theatre company is a member of the Mark Taper Foundation that caters to deaf and hard of hearing performers and audiences throughout the country. The Lankershim Arts Center occupies a former Department of Water and Power office building with the DWP's trademark Art Deco exterior next door at 5108. The Center is home to both the Road Theatre Company and the Lankershim Art Gallery. Gallery curator Dover Abrams is a former graffiti artist who has worked closely with the Community Redevelopment Agency to foster the burgeoning arts community in North Hollywood.

- When you reach Otsego St., carefully cross Lankershim to head north back up the other side of the boulevard. The Citibank building on the southwest corner of Otsego and Lankershim catches the eye—a towering edifice of various geometric shapes, surface materials and colors, it looks more like another art project than a financial institution. At 5113 Lankershim, you'll pass the Millennium Dance Complex.

- Turn left on Magnolia to explore a few of the galleries that lie just off of the main drag. Pit Fire Pizza Co. occupies an industrial-looking concrete building with an airy interior of exposed brick and corrugated metal on the northwest corner of Lankershim and Magnolia. A sign proclaims the pizza joint's mission of "Feeding a Hungry Nation." This is an excellent place to stop for a bite, serving mouth-watering wood-fired pizzas with innovative toppings, as well as delectable soups and sand-wiches. You can dine either inside, enjoying the aroma of fresh-baked pizza crust emanating from the hot ovens, or outside on the pleasant patio. Next door to Pit Fire is another public art display—a colorful mural depicting an idyllic park scene by artist Tim Fields. The Magart Mexican Furnishings gallery sits at 11221 Magnolia. Directly across the street are Sunny Meyer Fine Art and NoHo Modern, a gallery showcasing postwar decorative furnishings and accessories.

- Retrace your steps back to Lankershim and turn left to continue north, remaining on the west side of the street. The shops, galleries, and restaurants lining this block feature colorful neon and metal signs that seem to compete for the attention of passers-by. The NoHo Actors Studio sits at 5215 Lankershim—founded in 1993, this was one of the first performance spaces to open in the NoHo Arts District. The delightfully garish entrance to Tokyo Delve's Sushi Bar at 5239 features squiggly neon letters and metal cut-outs of classic Cadillacs. The kooky exterior design is an indicator of the crazy dining experience that awaits within—where diners are encouraged to dance on their chairs as everyone joins in on '80s sing-alongs.

- As you approach Weddington, look toward the northeast corner of Lankershim and Weddington to catch a glimpse of another mural. This depiction of various masks on a blue-sky background overlooking an empty lot was created by the Ryman Program for Young Artists. Carefully cross Lankershim to return to your starting point on the east side of the street near the entrance to the Academy of Television Arts and Sciences.

Emmy statue

POINTS OF INTEREST

Academy of Television Arts and Sciences 5220 Lankershim Blvd., North Hollywood, CA 91601, 818-754-2800

NoHo Arts Center 11136 Magnolia Blvd., North Hollywood, CA 91601, 866-811-4111

Avery Schreiber Theatre 11050 Magnolia Blvd., North Hollywood, CA 91601, 818-761-0704

Eclectic Café 5156 Lankershim Blvd., North Hollywood, CA 91601, 818-760-2233

NoHo Ceramics Gallery 5100 Lankershim Blvd., North Hollywood, CA 91601, 818-505-2100

Deaf West Theatre 5112 Lankershim Blvd., North Hollywood, CA 91601, 818-762-2998

Lankershim Arts Center 5108 Lankershim Blvd., North Hollywood, CA 91601, 818-760-1278

Pit Fire Pizza Co. 5108 Lankershim Blvd., North Hollywood, CA 91601, 818-980-2949

Magart Mexican Furnishings 11221 Magnolia Blvd., North Hollywood, CA 91601, 818-755-3904

Sunny Meyer Fine Art 11223 Magnolia Blvd., North Hollywood, CA 91601, 818-985-6630

NoHo Modern 11225 Magnolia Blvd., North Hollywood, CA 91601, 818-505-1297

Tokyo Delve's Sushi Bar 5239 Lankershim Blvd., North Hollywood, CA 91601, 818-766-3868

route summary

1. Begin on the east side of Lankershim Blvd. just south of Weddington and head south.

2. Enter the Television Arts and Sciences plaza at 5220 Lankershim.

3. Exit the Academy plaza via Blakeslee Ave, which heads south out to Magnolia Blvd. Carefully cross Magnolia Blvd. and head west back toward Lankershim.

4. Turn left to head south on Lankershim.

5. Cross Hartsook and continue south on Lankershim.

6. When you reach Otsego St., carefully cross Lankershim to head north back up the other side of the boulevard.

7. Turn left on Magnolia to explore a few of the galleries that lie just off of Lankershim.

8. Retrace your steps back to Lankershim and turn left to continue north, remaining on the west side of the street.

9. Cross the street to return to your starting point just south of Weddington on Lankershim.

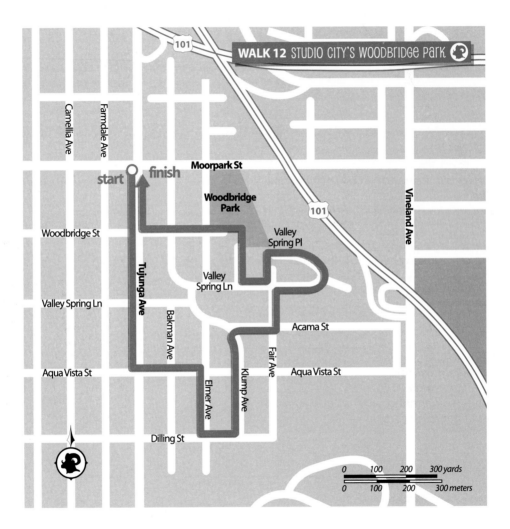

101

Camellia Ave

Farmdale Ave

Moorpark St

start **finish**

Woodbridge Park

Woodbridge St

Valley Spring Pl

Tujunga Ave

Valley Spring Ln

Valley Spring Ln

Bakman Ave

Acama St

Aqua Vista St

Fair Ave

Aqua Vista St

Elmer Ave

Klump Ave

Dilling St

Vineland Ave

101

0   100   200   300 yards

0   100   200   300 meters

12 STUDIO CITY'S WOODBRIDGE PARK: AN UNCANNILY FAMILIAR NEIGHBORHOOD

BOUNDARIES: Moorpark St., Tujunga Ave., Ventura Blvd, Vineland Ave.
THOMAS GUIDE COORDINATES: Map 562; J4
DISTANCE: Approx. 1½ miles
DIFFICULTY: Easy
PARKING: Metered street parking is available on Tujunga Ave.

Woodbridge Park is a preternaturally idyllic residential neighborhood in the Valley Village section of Studio City. The streets are shaded with mature trees and lined with meticulously maintained traditional homes. Bordered by the Los Angeles River on the south, the 101 Freeway on the northeast and Tujunga Ave. on the west, this charismatic slice of affluent small-town America is effectively isolated from the anonymous sprawl of the surrounding Valley. Further, the collection of shops, salons and restaurants in nearby Tujunga Village and a neighborhood park ensure that residents have little reason to leave their bucolic surroundings. It's no wonder the Brady Bunch chose to settle down here...

● Begin at the corner of Tujunga Ave. and Moorpark St. and head south toward Woodbridge St. You are in the midst of Tujunga Village, a collection of neighborhood restaurants, shops, and salons that retains a distinctly small-town vibe. The Aroma coffeehouse and bookstore, situated at 4360 Tujunga, is a big draw on this stretch; its ample patio seating makes it a great spot for dog owners, and the sandwiches, pastries, and coffee served by the friendly young staff are usually quite tasty. But for really good food, Caioti Pizza Café might be the better bet—chef-owner Ed LaDou is famed for inventing California Pizza (thin-crust pies with non-standard toppings), but the restaurant is best known for its Maternity Salad, a concoction of gorgonzola, balsamic vinegar, and walnuts said to induce labor in moms-to-be. Tujunga Village also features numerous boutiques and salons, a yoga studio, Spoiled: A Day Spa, and the Two Roads Theatre.

- After you cross Woodbridge St., Tujunga Ave. becomes a residential street lined with a mix of old and new apartment buildings. Tujunga is a main thoroughfare between Moorpark Ave. and Ventura Blvd., so traffic can be steady during rush hour.

- Turn left on Aqua Vista St., leaving the traffic of Tujunga behind as you enter into an orderly suburban paradise of quiet, smoothly paved streets, carefully manicured lawns, and charming cottage-style homes. The dominant architectural styles are traditional ranch homes and wooden farmhouses, but Woodbridge Park also features a number of English cottages and Spanish-style homes.

- Turn right on Elmer Ave. You'll notice a colorful Southwest-style house on the southeast corner of Elmer and Aqua Vista. This vibrant home, sheltered by pine trees and innovatively adorned with abstract metal sculptures, stands out from the more traditional homes on this block. Continue to head south on Elmer Ave. Straight ahead, you can see the low green hills of Studio City.

- When you reach the end of Elmer, turn left on Dilling St. At 11222 Dilling you'll come upon a familiar house—despite a new paint job and the addition of a low wall around the front yard, this home will be instantly recognizable by members of a certain generation as the Brady Bunch abode. Dilling is cut off from surrounding streets to the south and the east by the concrete-paved aqueduct that is somewhat misleadingly referred to as the Los Angeles River.

- Turn left to head north on Klump Ave., the street just opposite the Brady house. The ignobly named street is trimmed with eucalyptus, sycamore and magnolia trees, whose ample shade provides a welcome relief during the hot Valley summer. A quaint stone cottage catches the eye at 4146 Klump. After crossing Aqua Vista, look for the owl statue perched atop the low peaked roof of the garage at 4208 Klump.

- Turn right on Acama St. and continue for one block to Fair Ave. On the northeast corner of Fair and Acama is a home with a beautiful abstract stained glass window facing Acama.

- Turn left on Fair Ave. A very 60s-style apartment building resides at 4252 Fair, its colorful façade a jarring combination of stucco, wood, and stone.

- Turn right on Valley Spring Ln. At this point, the neighborhood starts to have a more rustic feel as the sidewalks disappear and the foliage becomes a little overgrown. The rural vibe is somewhat spoiled by the noise of the adjacent 101 Freeway, however, as you continue to head east.

- Follow the road as it curves to the left, becoming Valley Spring Pl. When you reach the dead end, you'll see a low white fence on the left, constructed to prevent cars from trying to cut through the narrow passageway leading to Fair Ave. Cut through here, and continue to head south on Fair Ave.

- Turn right on Valley Spring Ln. and continue for one short block to Klump Ave.

- Turn right on Klump. At the end of the street, continue to head straight along the footpath that passes through a picket fence.

- The path emerges into the park for which this neighborhood is named. Woodbridge Park is a good-sized community gathering place complete with a playground, recreation center, and jogging trails. Cut through the park, heading toward the southeast corner, where you will come upon the intersection of Elmer Ave. and Woodbridge St.

- Head west on Woodbridge, back toward Tujunga Ave. At the intersection of Bakman Ave., you'll come upon a magnificent English cottage that looks like it sprung from the pages of a children's storybook.

- Turn right on Tujunga Ave., returning to your starting point in Tujunga Village.

POINTS OF INTEREST

Aroma Coffee and Tea Co. 4360 Tujunga Ave., Studio City, CA 91604, 818-508-6505

Caioti Pizza Café 4346 Tujunga Ave., Studio City, CA 91604, 818-761-3588

Spoiled: A Day Spa 4338 Tujunga Ave., Studio City, CA 91604, 818-508-9772

Scentsabilities Gift Boutique 4336 Tujunga Ave., Studio City, CA 91604, 818-761-7727

Two Roads Theatre 4348 Tuhunga Ave., Studio City, CA 91604, 818-762-7488

route summary

1. Begin on Tujunga Ave., between Moorpark St. and Woodbridge St. and head south toward Woodbridge.
2. Turn left on Aqua Vista St.
3. Turn right on Elmer Ave.
4. Turn left on Dilling St.
5. Turn left on Klump Ave.
6. Turn right on Acama St.
7. Turn left on Fair Ave.
8. Turn right on Valley Spring Ln.
9. Turn left on Valley Spring Pl.
10. Follow the pedestrian path on left and then head south on Fair Ave.
11. Turn right on Valley Spring Ln.
12. Turn right on Klump Ave. and follow the pedestrian path into Woodbridge Park.
13. Cut across to southwest corner of Woodbridge Park.
14. Head west on Woodbridge St.
15. Turn right on Tujunga Ave.

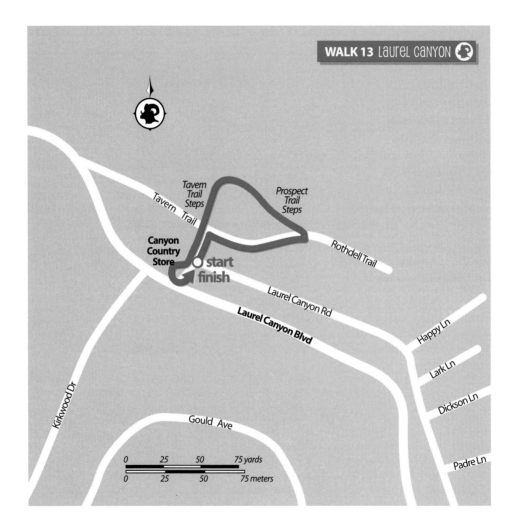

Tavern Trail Steps

Tavern Trail

Prospect Trail Steps

Rothdell Trail

Canyon Country Store

start finish

Laurel Canyon Rd

Laurel Canyon Blvd

Happy Ln

Lark Ln

Dickson Ln

Kirkwood Dr

Gould Ave

Padre Ln

| 0 | 25 | 50 | 75 yards |
| 0 | 25 | 50 | 75 meters |

13 Laurel Canyon: Strolling Along "Love Street"

BOUNDARIES: **Laurel Canyon Blvd, Mt. Olympus Dr.**
THOMAS GUIDE COORDINATES: **Map 593; A3**
DISTANCE: **About ¼ mile**
DIFFICULTY: **Strenuous**
PARKING: **Free street parking is available on Laurel Canyon Rd.**

Note: This is a short but interesting trek that includes a very brief hike through brush-covered, uneven dirt terrain, so be advised to wear comfortable closed-toe shoes and long pants.

Any self-respecting Doors fan knows that all four band members took up residence at one time or another in Laurel Canyon, the rustic bohemian enclave that lies north of the Sunset Strip. Today, the face of Laurel Canyon has changed considerably as more and more wealthy professionals have been drawn to this peaceful oasis in the center of Los Angeles. But the lower canyon in particular has managed to retain its artsy vibe, thanks to the aging hippies who still reside in shabby hillside homes and the endurance of establishments like the Canyon Country Store and the former home of Mr. Mojo himself.

● **Begin at the intersection of Laurel Canyon Rd. and Rothdell Tr., about 1 mile north of Sunset Blvd. Laurel Canyon Rd. runs parallel to Laurel Canyon Blvd., and Rothdell Tr. branches off from the northeast side of the street (the street is called Kirkwood Dr. heading southwest). The former residence of Jim Morrison and his girlfriend Pamela Courson stands in all its glory at 8021 Rothdell Tr., facing outward toward Laurel Canyon Blvd. The two-story wooden home is distinguished by a large bell that can be seen through the window of the top floor, below a peaked roof. Bougainvillea spills over the retaining wall of the small front yard. According to Doors lore, Rothdell Tr. is actually the "Love Street" from the song of the same name, and the Canyon Country Store across the street is the very same "store where the creatures meet."**

- Head uphill on Rothdell, following the road as it curves to the right. The rarefied country air is saturated with the scent of eucalyptus.

- You'll soon come to the Prospect Trail steps on your left, marked with a street sign at 2100 N. Prospect. Ascend the stairway past the quaint but dilapidated wooden homes on either side. Watch your step, as these stairs are no longer maintained by the city and are broken and crumbling in some places. The staircase is also over-grown in spots where the residents haven't been diligent about trimming their shrubbery. The Prospect Trail steps end abruptly at a vacant dirt lot. Turn around at the top of the stairway to catch a view of LA's flatlands through the hills rising on either side of Laurel Canyon Blvd.

- At the top of the stairway, look for the vague path that has been worn through the brush and follow it uphill slightly and then to the left, watching out for cactus plants. The path runs alongside the wire fence behind the houses on your left—follow the path back downhill so that you remain next to this fence. After several more steps you'll come to another stairway known as Tavern Trail—a century plant makes it easy to spot.

- Descend the Tavern Trail stairway, again taking care to avoid cracks and holes in the steps. You'll pass more wood-paneled hillside homes, some more worn down than others. Follow the stairs all the way back down to Rothdell, where you'll emerge next door to the local dry cleaning shop.

- Continue across the street to the old brick building that is home to Pace, a funky upscale Italian bistro, as well as the fabled Canyon Country Store. Continue to the front of the store, which sits facing Laurel Canyon Blvd. at the intersection with Kirkwood. Ascend the short flight of steps to the market's spacious tiled patio, which offers locals plenty of seating on which to plop down and sip espresso from the out-door coffee counter. The store itself sells standard convenience market fare, as well as an ample selection of wine, and also features a newsstand and a deli counter.

- After grabbing a sandwich or a cold drink at the store, return down to street level and cross back over to the intersection of Laurel Canyon Rd. and Rothdell Tr. where you started.

POINTS OF INTEREST

Pace 2100 Laurel Canyon Blvd., Los Angeles, CA 90046, 323-654-8583

Canyon Country Store 2100 Laurel Canyon Blvd., Los Angeles, CA 90046, 323-654-8583

ROUTE SUMMARY

1. Begin at the intersection of Laurel Canyon Rd. and Rothdell Tr.
2. Head uphill on Rothdell, following the road as it curves to the right.
3. Ascend the Prospect Trail staircase on your left at 2100 N. Prospect.
4. At the top of the stairs, continue up into the empty lot and follow the dirt path that runs alongside the fence on your left.
5. Descend the Tavern Trail stairway, which is marked by a century plant on your left. Follow the steps all the way back down to Rothdell.
6. Cross Rothdell, passing Pace Italian restaurant on your right, and then follow the short flight of steps up to the Canyon Country Store, which occupies the front of the large brick building.
7. Return to street level and cross back over to the intersection of Laurel Canyon Rd. and Rothdell Tr. where you started.

Jim Morrison's former home

WALK 14 SUNSET STRIP

Hillside Ave

Marmont Ave

Laurel Canyon Blvd

Monteel Rd

start

Sunset Blvd

finish

Harold Way

Kings Rd

Sunset Blvd

Havenhurst Dr

Crescent Heights

Laurel Ave

Queens Rd

De Longpre Ave

La Cienega Blvd

Olive Dr

Flores St

Sweetzer Ave

Harper Ave

Fountain Ave

Fountain Ave

Norton Ave

| 0 | 100 | 200 | 300 yards |
| 0 | 100 | 200 | 300 meters |

14 SUNSET STRIP: WHERE THE BEAUTIFUL PEOPLE COME TO PLAY

BOUNDARIES: **Sunset Blvd., Crescent Heights Blvd., La Cienega Blvd., Fountain Ave.**
THOMAS GUIDE COORDINATES: **Map 593; A5**
DISTANCE: **Approx. 1 mile**
DIFFICULTY: **Easy**
PARKING: **Free street parking is available on Havenhurst Dr. before 6 P.M. Metered parking is available on Sunset Blvd.**

West Hollywood's Sunset Strip is considered a tribute to Hollywood's colorful history by some, a den of iniquity to others, and a horrific traffic jam for us east-west commuters. One thing's for sure, you can't drive along this stretch of Sunset Blvd. without being distracted by provocative billboards, giant flashing video screens, and an endless stream of very attractive people, either dining on restaurant patios or, in some cases, shooting a scene for a movie. All this adds up to a fender bender waiting to happen, so better to park the car and walk a portion of this glitzy stretch of road so often identified with the City of Angels. This route will also afford a peek at what lies just below the Strip and off the neon-lit path.

● **Begin at the intersection of Havenhurst Dr. and Sunset Blvd. On the northwest corner, mysteriously shrouded behind dense foliage, is the notorious Chateau Marmont. We've all heard the stories of John Belushi's overdose and the Lizard King's leap from a balcony, but the seven-story white castle and its tight-lipped staff continue to play impeccable hosts to a steady parade of present-day Hollywood A-listers and their indecorous shenanigans.**

Head west on Sunset—your attention is caught by endless billboards and a string of partying/dining establishments, like trendy Japanese restaurant Miyagi's at 8225, and the Cabo Cantina, a funky outdoor margarita and taco joint at 8301. Speaking of indecorous behavior, the Body Shop strip club sits on the southwest corner of Sunset and Harper Ave.

- Cross Sweetzer Ave., and you'll come to the relentlessly hip Standard Hotel (note the quirky upside-down sign). Take a minute to wander through the retro-space-age-themed lobby outside to the poolside bar, which affords a spectacular view of the city below.

- Head back out to the street and continue west, passing Carney's Restaurant (housed in a train car) at 8351. The Saddle Ranch Chop House also sits on the north side of the street—notice the disheveled-looking mannequins of Old West characters leaning out over the balconies. It gets even rowdier inside, where a mechanical bull completes the *Urban Cowboy* scene. Soon you'll come to the loveliest structure on Sunset—the Argyle Hotel. This Art Deco landmark opened its doors as the Sunset Tower apartments in 1929, and past residents include John Wayne, Bugsy Siegel, and Howard Hughes.

  As you approach Olive Dr., you'll come to the ramshackle, Deep South-themed shanty that is the House of Blues. Bankrolled by one of the original Blues Brothers, Dan Aykroyd (along with John Belushi's brother Jim), this high-profile but relatively intimate venue gives concertgoers the chance to get up close and personal with their favorite musicians. If you're so inclined, drop into the Porch Restaurant upstairs for some stick-to-your-ribs soul food. The Comedy Store is directly across the street.

- Turn left on Olive Dr., passing by the House of Blues box office and main entrance as you head downhill away from the glitz of the Strip and into a more residential neighborhood.

- Turn left on Fountain Ave., a popular alternative driving route to the constantly congested boulevard above.

- After one block, turn left on De Longpre Ave. and follow the road as it curves to the right, passing behind the Argyle Hotel before you come to William S. Hart Park on your left.

- Follow the path up to this popular gathering spot for neighborhood residents, which includes an off-leash dog park, an AIDS memorial garden, and the quaint shingled house that has long been the West Coast headquarters of the Actors Studio. Descend the stairs back down to De Longpre and continue to head east.

- When the street ends, turn right on Sweetzer Ave., and then take an immediate left to get back on De Longpre. This peaceful residential street is lined with small, distinctive apartment buildings that appear to have been designed and built in the 1950s and 60s.

- Turn left on Harper Ave. Several gorgeous Spanish-style apartment buildings line the east side of the street. Casa Real at 1354 Harper is particularly interesting, with its muted tile work and copper fixtures that have turned a lovely slate-green with age. "7 Fountains" at 1414 features a sculpture of an angel overlooking the front steps and is prettily embellished with colorful tile work.

- Turn right on Sunset Blvd., retracing your steps back to your starting point at the corner of Havenhurst.

Argyle Hotel

POINTS OF INTEREST

Chateau Marmont 8221 W. Sunset Blvd, West Hollywood, CA 90046, 323-656-1010

Miyagi's 8225 W. Sunset Blvd, West Hollywood, CA 90046, 323-650-3524

Cabo Cantina 8301 W. Sunset Blvd, West Hollywood, CA 90069, 323-822-7820

Standard Hotel 8300 W. Sunset Blvd, West Hollywood, CA 90069, 323-650-9090

Carney's Restaurant 8351 W. Sunset Blvd, West Hollywood, CA 90069, 323-654-8300

Saddle Ranch Chop House 8371 W. Sunset Blvd, West Hollywood, CA 90069, 323-656-2007

Argyle Hotel 8358 W. Sunset Blvd, West Hollywood, CA 90069, 323-654-7100

House of Blues/Porch Restaurant 8430 W. Sunset Blvd, West Hollywood, CA 90069, 323-848-5100

Comedy Store 8433 W. Sunset Blvd, West Hollywood, CA 90069, 323-656-6225

William S. Hart Park 8341 DeLongpre Ave., West Hollywood, CA 90069, 323-848-6308

route summary

1. Begin at the intersection of Havenhurst Dr. and Sunset Blvd. and head west on Sunset.
2. Cross Sweetzer Ave. and then check out the lobby/poolside bar of the Standard Hotel at 8300 W. Sunset.
3. Continue west on Sunset Blvd.
4. Turn left on Olive Dr.
5. Turn left on Fountain Ave.
6. Turn left on De Longpre Ave. and follow the road as it curves to the right.
7. Follow the path up into Hart Park and then head down the stairs back to De Longpre and continue east.
8. Turn right on Sweetzer Ave., and then take an immediate left to get back on De Longpre.
9. Turn left on Harper Ave.
10. Turn right on Sunset Blvd., retracing your steps back to Havenhurst.

Chateau Marmont

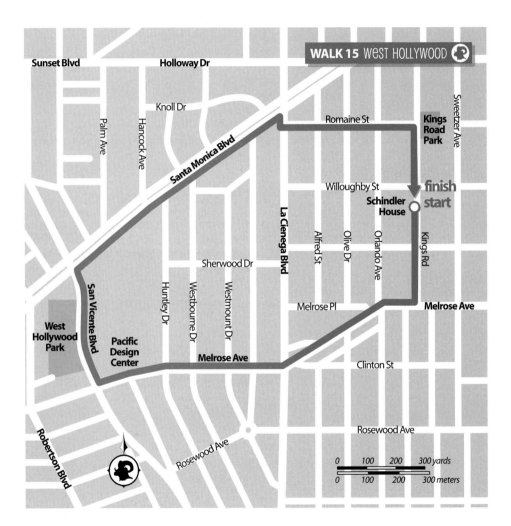

Sunset Blvd

Holloway Dr

Knoll Dr

Palm Ave

Hancock Ave

Santa Monica Blvd

Romaine St

Kings Road Park

Sweetzer Ave

Willoughby St

finish
start

Schindler House

La Cienega Blvd

Alfred St

Olive Dr

Orlando Ave

Kings Rd

Sherwood Dr

San Vicente Blvd

Huntley Dr

Westbourne Dr

Westmount Dr

Melrose Pl

Melrose Ave

West Hollywood Park

Pacific Design Center

Melrose Ave

Clinton St

Robertson Blvd

Rosewood Ave

Rosewood Ave

| 0 | 100 | 200 | 300 yards |
| 0 | 100 | 200 | 300 meters |

15 WeST HOLLYWOOD: a STUDY IN INTERIOR AND EXTERIOR DESIGN

BOUNDARIES: **Melrose Ave., San Vicente Blvd., Santa Monica Blvd., Kings Rd.**
THOMAS GUIDE COORDINATES: **Map 593; A6**
DISTANCE: **Approx. 2 miles**
DIFFICULTY: **Easy**
PARKING: **Free street parking is available on Kings Rd.**

This tour of the best West Hollywood has to offer begins at the Schindler House, an early modern architectural gem and home of LA's MAK Center for Art and Architecture. The walk then goes on to explore the *tres chic* stretch of Melrose Ave. that is home to countless home furnishing galleries and antique stores, as well as Eastern-influenced establishments like Elixir Tonics and Teas and the Bodhi Tree Bookstore.

Easily the most dramatic destination on this journey is the Pacific Design Center, a colossal structure of blue and green glass colloquially known as the "Blue Whale" that houses over a hundred interior design showrooms. From there, you'll pass through the commercial center of West Hollywood along Santa Monica Blvd. before returning to your starting point on Kings Rd.

● **Begin on Kings Rd., just south of Willoughby Ave. The Schindler House sits at 835 Kings Rd., hidden from view by a tall bamboo hedge. Proceed along the dirt path to the MAK Center office and bookstore, where you can submit a donation before exploring the building. The Schindler House is a building like no other. Composed of unadorned concrete and dark-stained wood, the one-story building manages to feel airy and light despite the low, wood-beamed ceilings. Furnishings are modern and sparse, and a couple of rooms feature copper-topped fireplaces. The indoor and out-door space is seamlessly integrated; clear plastic curtains separate the rooms of the house from the peaceful green gardens, which are shrouded from the surrounding area by more bamboo.**

- After leaving the Schindler House, continue south on Kings Rd. toward Melrose Ave.

- Turn right on Melrose. Across the street is the Mel & Rose Wine Store, which is graced by a delightfully tacky giant wine bottle with a neon sign. Citrine Restaurant, a sophisticated and pricey destination for "California cuisine" sits at 8360 Melrose. And next door is Sweet Lady Jane, a family-owned dessert shop and bakery that offers a staggering array of sweets that have been celebrated by everyone from *Zagat* to *W Magazine*.

- Keep to the left at the fork in the road to avoid wandering onto Melrose Pl., which is home to a cache of snooty designer boutiques, and continue along Melrose Ave. Both sides of the street are lined with an interesting collection of furniture stores, antique shops and galleries.

- Cross La Cienega Blvd. At this point, you can see the Pacific Design Center looming ahead, and it's obvious why it came to be known as the "Blue Whale." On the southwest corner of La Cienega and Melrose is a singularly ugly strip mall structure composed of black and white, horizontally striped marble. At 8540 Melrose, you'll pass the Heritage Book Shop, where you can purchase rare first-edition tomes.

DESIGNER NAME: RUDOLF M. SCHINDLER

The Schindler House located on Kings Road in West Hollywood is considered an icon of early modern architecture. Built in the early 1920s, the minimalist structure is an example of what Rudolf M. Schindler described as "space architecture," and functioned as his home and studio until he died in 1953. The space communicates a singular blend of old and new; while the design of the building is undoubtedly modern, the low ceilings and organic, unadorned materials reveal the influence of indigenous architecture.

After crossing Westmount Dr., you'll find yourself in West Hollywood's ultra-hip enclave of Far East influence. At 8565 Melrose is Urth Caffe, an ostensibly healthy eatery that is invariably crowded with beautiful people looking to indulge in rich foods made with guilt-free ingredients. Next door at 8585 is the Bodhi Tree Bookstore, which sells incense, candles, and other spiritual paraphernalia in addition to new and used books on topics ranging from Zen Buddhism to Women's Health. Across the street at 8612 is Elixir Tonics and Teas, which sells an array of proprietary herbal beverages. Behind the teahouse is a large botanical garden that provides a serene respite for patrons with its trickling central fountain and comfy wicker chairs. Elixir also features an on-site licensed herbalist, as well as bodywork services in the "mini spa" behind the garden.

At 8687 Melrose Ave., just before San Vicente Blvd., you'll finally come upon the Pacific Design Center. Up close, the massive blue glass structure is striking...almost intimidating. At night, the effect is even more dramatic, as the tall, pod-shaped spotlights bathe the building's exterior in a red glow. The Design Center is home to 130 showrooms displaying furniture and interior design pieces from an array of designers and manufacturers, ranging in style from traditional to contemporary. The Center also frequently hosts exhibitions, lectures, and special events. The Museum of Contemporary Art (MOCA) even has a satellite gallery on the Pacific Design Center premises.

● The main entrance to Pacific Design Center is located around the corner on San Vicente. You'll pass by a giant metal sculpture of a chair as you turn the corner. The entryway is situated off of a large open courtyard, which is dominated by a spectacular dancing fountain. Security is heavy

Schindler House interior

around the Center, adding to the somewhat daunting persona of this remarkable edifice. Do call ahead or visit www.pacificdesigncenter.com to see if there is an exhibit worth seeing either at MOCA or in the Design Center at the time of your visit. Across the street at 647 N. San Vicente you'll notice West Hollywood Park, which features a public swimming pool and tennis courts.

- After exploring the Design Center, continue north on San Vicente, passing the sheriff's station on your right at the corner of Santa Monica Blvd.

- Turn right on Santa Monica. You are now in the heart of gay West Hollywood, as evidenced by the names of the stores, bars, and restaurants along this stretch (Don't Panic!, Rage, Trunks) and the rainbow flags lining the boulevard. To the north, you can spot the hotels and oversized billboards of the elevated Sunset Strip.

- Continue east along Santa Monica for just under three-quarters of a mile. This stretch is populated with a multitude of spots to grab a snack or refreshment—coffeehouses, juice bars, frozen yoghurt shops. Santa Monica Blvd. also reflects West Hollywood's residents' profound sense of self-preservation with its collection of gyms, Pilates and yoga studios, UV-free tanning salons, and massage centers.

- When you reach La Cienega Blvd., turn right and then take an immediate left on Romaine St. You have now left the hustle and bustle of the boulevard behind and entered a quiet residential neighborhood. The shady street is lined with the ubiquitous Spanish-style apartments and houses, as well as a few Norman-style cottages.

- After four blocks, Romaine St. ends at Kings Road Park, a delightful, dog-friendly haven tucked between two apartment buildings. The shady little park features benches arranged around a burbling fountain, a small playground and public restrooms, as well as dog waste bags to ensure that owners clean up after their pooches.

- After visiting the park, head south on Kings Rd. toward your starting point. The street is lined with unprepossessing courtyard apartment buildings; a narrow, dark-shingled complex labeled as "The Tree House" stands out from the rest at 906 N. Kings Rd.

- Cross Willoughby Ave. to return to your starting point near the Schindler House at 835 Kings. Rd.

POINTS OF INTEREST

Schindler House and MAK Center for Design 835 North Kings Road, West Hollywood, CA 90069, 323-651-1510

Citrine Restaurant 8360 Melrose Ave., West Hollywood, CA 90069, 323-655-1690

Sweet Lady Jane 8360 Melrose Ave., West Hollywood, CA 90069, 323-653-7145

Urth Caffe 8565 Melrose Ave., West Hollywood, CA 90069, 310-659-0628

Bodhi Tree Bookstore 8585 Melrose Ave., West Hollywood, CA 90069, 310-659-1733

Elixir Tonics and Teas 8612 Melrose Ave., West Hollywood, CA 90069, 310-657-9300

Pacific Design Center 8687 Melrose Ave., West Hollywood, CA 90069, 310-657-0800

Heritage Bookshop 8540 Melrose Ave., West Hollywood, CA 90069, 310-659-3674

ROUTE SUMMARY

1. Begin at the Schindler House at 835 Kings Rd., just south of Willoughby Ave.
2. Head south on Kings Rd.
3. Turn right on Melrose Ave.
4. Keep left on Melrose Ave. to avoid Melrose Pl.
5. Cross La Cienega Blvd. and continue on Melrose.
6. Turn right on San Vicente Blvd. to reach the entrance of the Pacific Design Center.
7. Continue north on San Vicente Blvd.
8. Turn right on Santa Monica Blvd.
9. Continue east along Santa Monica for just under three quarters of a mile.
10. Turn right on La Cienega and then take an immediate left on Romaine St.
11. At the end of Romaine St., enter Kings Road Park.
12. Exit the park and head south on Kings Rd.
13. Cross Willoughby Ave. to reach starting point at 835 Kings Rd.

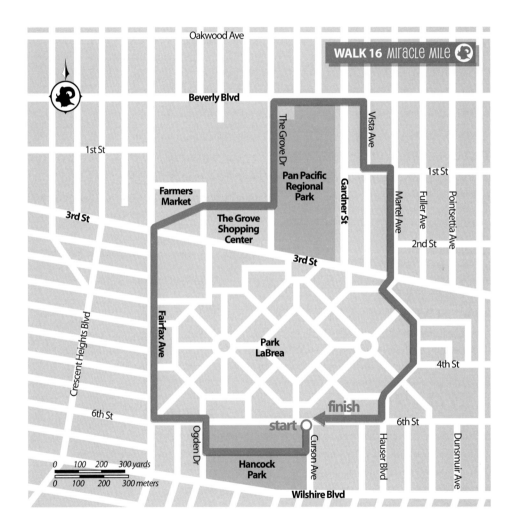

Oakwood Ave

Beverly Blvd

1st St

The Grove Dr

Vista Ave

1st St

Pan Pacific
Regional
Park

Martel Ave

Fuller Ave

Pointsettia Ave

Farmers
Market

Gardner St

3rd St

The Grove
Shopping
Center

2nd St

3rd St

Park
LaBrea

4th St

Crescent Heights Blvd

Fairfax Ave

6th St

finish

start

6th St

Hauser Blvd

Dunsmuir Ave

0   100   200   300 yards

0   100   200   300 meters

Ogden Dr

Curson Ave

Hancock
Park

Wilshire Blvd

16 MIRACLE MILE: 40,000 YEARS IN THE MAKING

BOUNDARIES: Wilshire Blvd., Fairfax Ave., Beverly Blvd., Martel Ave./Hauser Blvd.
THOMAS GUIDE COORDINATES: Map 633: C2
DISTANCE: Approx. 2½ miles
DIFFICULTY: Easy
PARKING: Free parking is available on the north side of 6th St. Metered parking is available on the south side.

The Miracle Mile district is a prized area in Los Angeles, in large part due to its central location and proximity to just about anyplace one might want to go. This neighborhood itself is home to the Los Angeles County Museum of Art (LACMA), the historic Farmers Market, and—unlikely as it may seem in the middle of this bustling city—one of the world's most famous fossil sites. The La Brea Tar Pits, located adjacent to LACMA, is said to have the largest and most diverse collection of animal and plant fossils from the last Ice Age, tens of thousands of years ago. After exploring the tar pits and fossil excavation sites, you'll get a strong dose of modern-day Los Angeles at the Grove, an enormously popular outdoor mall that seems to have been inspired by Disneyland's Main Street USA.

● **Begin at the corner of 6th St. and Curson Ave. and head south on Curson (toward Wilshire Blvd.).**

● **Just before you reach Wilshire, you'll see an entrance to Hancock Park on your right. This park is home to the tar pits and the Page Museum, which oversees the preservation, study, excavation, and cleaning of fossils from the tar pits. The Los Angeles County Museum of Art also resides on these grounds.**

● **Enter Hancock Park (there are public restrooms near the entrance, should you need them) and notice the Page Museum on your right. Take a few minutes to follow the steps to the roof of the building and you'll be rewarded with a view down into the museum's lush tropical garden and koi pond. It's peaceful up here, with the sound of a trickling waterfall and birds flitting in and out of the oasis below. The garden is topped with an intricate, open ironwork cage of sorts, the sides of which are decorated with a bas-relief of prehistoric creatures.**

- Return to ground level and walk south across the park to observe the largest of the tar pits on the premises, where the smell of liquid asphalt is reminiscent of hot days on the playground. The Page Museum has erected a heartbreaking sculptural tableau of a baby mammoth accompanied, presumably, by its father on the shore of the pond, wailing in agony as it watches its mother get sucked into the muck. You can still see evidence of geologic activity on these grounds with the occasional bubbling up of gases through the water's murky surface.

- Head west through the park, away from Curson. Hancock Park is a popular place for locals to walk their dogs, play Frisbee, or simply stroll across the hilly green lawns. You'll pass the Pavilion for Japanese Art on your left; this swoopily designed building is part of LACMA. Continue along the walking path, passing a fossil excavation site on your right, and the concrete- and slate-sided LACMA structure on your left. As you near the exit to the park onto Ogden Dr., take a minute to peek into the observation pit on your left, where you might catch a glimpse of the Page Museum's latest discovery.

- Exit onto Ogden Dr. and turn right.

Back Story: rancho La Brea Tar Pits

The Page Museum located at the site of Rancho La Brea gives visitors a taste of Los Angeles as it was 10,000 to 40,000 years ago, during the final Ice Age of the Pleistocene Epoch. The source of the asphalt pits that serve as the museum's excavation sites is a large underground petroleum reservoir located a short distance to the north of the park.

This extraordinarily sticky piece of land was the site of roughly 10,000 creatures' demise over the span of 30,000 years. The unlucky victims included small and large mammals, birds, and insects (but no dinosaurs, which were long since extinct during the Pleistocene Epoch). After an animal, such as a saber-toothed cat or dire wolf, became stuck in the goo, it would fall prey to carnivorous mammals and birds, some of which would themselves get caught in the mire. Today, the resulting collection of Ice Age fossils is one of the largest and most diverse in the world.

- Turn left on 6th St.

- Walk one block to Fairfax Ave. and turn right. Continue on Fairfax for about half a mile. The western side of the massive Park La Brea apartment complex occupies several blocks on your right. You'll pass Molly Malone's Irish Pub at 575 Fairfax on your left. Mani's Bakery, a health food café and bakery specializing in all-natural, wholesome desserts (which are actually quite tasty, if a bit dry at times) sits at 519 Fairfax. And you won't miss the four-story Art Deco building that's home to Samy's Camera at 431 Fairfax.

- Cross 3rd St. and enter the Farmers Market right next to the sign that reads "Meet me at Third and Fairfax."

- Walk in to the market through the entrance near DuPar's restaurant and make your way through the maze of food stands, coffee shops, butchers, bakeries, produce counters, and souvenir shops that comprise this popular destination for locals and tourists alike. Needless to say, this is a great place to grab a bite. Notable eateries include Loteria, a Mexico City-style taco stand, The Gumbo Pot for Cajun food, and The French Crepe Company. As you make your way through the Farmers Market, head toward the northeast corner, where you will exit straight into The Grove.

- Finding your way through The Grove is easy, as it's pretty much laid out in a straight line. It might not be so easy to make it through without blowing your paycheck, however. Most of the stores here are on the pricey side, with an emphasis on men and women's clothing. There are also

Rancho La Brea Tar Pits

several nice restaurants, a huge movie theatre, an Apple computer store, and a Barnes and Noble. The Grove distinguishes itself from Southern California's other outdoor malls with an old-fashioned trolley (a rather silly attraction, as this shopping center can't be more than a third of a mile long), and a large fountain shooting streams of water that "dance" to the tune of old standards by the likes of Dean Martin and Frank Sinatra. It all makes for quite a spectacle, and it draws people in droves.

● After passing the Gap, turn left to exit the mall onto The Grove Dr. and turn left.

● On your right is Pan Pacific Park. This sunken expanse of rolling green lawns, play-grounds, playing fields and jogging paths that is relatively hidden from view of the surrounding streets is a delightful discovery for anyone who's never been here before. You should take some time to explore the park, which is usually filled with with picnicking families and young athletes.

● Continue north on The Grove Dr. to the corner of Beverly Blvd. On the southwest cor-ner of the intersection is Erewhon Natural Foods Market. This oddly named store (it *almost* spells "nowhere" backwards, but not quite) is the destination for any sort of vegetarian, vegan, organic, Kosher, macrobiotic, herbal, gluten-free, or dairy-free deli-cacy you could desire. The market also includes an extensive prepared foods counter that it likes to refer to as a "healthy-catessan" and a juice bar. If you've managed to hold out this long without stopping at one of the many eateries on this walk, you may want to pick up a wrap or sandwich to take on a picnic in the park across the street.

● Turn right on Beverly Blvd., passing the post office on the south side of the street before you come to the Pan Pacific Park Recreation Center, which is constructed of red- and green-painted bricks—its curvy outer wall lends the structure a pleasing, organic quality. Across the street at 7619–21 Beverly Blvd. is Brooks Massage Therapy, an affordable, back-to-basics massage center with a natural-rock eucalyptus steam room and no-nonsense massage therapists.

● Turn right on Vista St. You have now entered the Historic Preservation Overlay Zone (HPOZ) known as Miracle Mile North. Continue along Vista for one block, taking note of the variety of residential architectural styles. The modest-sized homes on this street are beautifully maintained, their preservation carefully overseen by the HPOZ board. The predominant styles are Spanish Colonial Revival, Tudor Revival, and American Colonial Revival. The home at 116 N. Vista catches the eye, its white stucco façade adorned with pale blue frescos of ivy leaves that match the wooden trim of the eaves. A sculpture of an owl sits atop the roof.

- Turn left on 1st St., noticing the striking Norman cottage on the southeast corner.

- After one short block, turn right on Martel Ave. Here you'll spot a classic example of the American Colonial Revival architectural style on the southeast corner at 100 S. Martel. Continue to head south on Martel. After you cross 2nd St., notice the collection of distinctive Spanish duplexes on your right from 187 to 217 S. Martel. The congruity of layout and the intricate wrought iron details on each building suggests that they were all designed by the same talented architect.

- Cross 3rd St. At this point, Martel Ave. becomes Hauser Blvd. Continue on Hauser for several blocks through the Park La Brea apartment complex. On your left you'll see the relatively new, Italian-influenced Palazzo division of the complex. On your right are the original Park La Brea high-rises, which resemble an inner-city housing project more than an high-priced apartment complex.

- Turn right on 6th St. and then cross Curson to return to the start of your walk.

POINTS OF INTEREST

Page Museum 5801 Wilshire Blvd., Los Angeles, CA 90036, 323-934-7243

Los Angeles County Museum of Art 5905 Wilshire Blvd., Los Angeles, CA 90036,
323-857-6000

Mani's Bakery 519 S. Fairfax Ave., Los Angeles, CA 90036, 323-938-8800

Farmers Market 6333 West 3rd St., Los Angeles 90036, 323-933-9211

The Grove 189 The Grove Dr., Los Angeles, CA 90036, 888-315-8883

Erewhon Natural Foods Market 7660 Beverly Blvd., Los Angeles, CA 90036,
323-937-0777

Brooks Massage Therapy 7619-21 Beverly Blvd., Los Angeles, CA 90036, 323-937-8781

Pan Pacific Park 7600 Beverly Blvd., Los Angeles, CA 90036, 323-939-8874

route summary

1. Begin at the corner of 6th St. and Curson Ave. and head south on Curson Ave. toward Wilshire Blvd.
2. Enter Hancock Park on your right and, once inside the park, explore the Page Museum to your right.
3. Visit the main tar pits on the south side of the park opposite the Page Museum.
4. Head west through Hancock Park.
5. Exit the park onto Ogden Dr. and turn right.
6. Turn left on 6th St.
7. Turn right on Fairfax Ave.
8. Cross 3rd St. and enter the Farmers Market.
9. Cut through the Market, heading toward the northeast corner.
10. Exit the Farmers Market and enter the Grove shopping complex.
11. Exit the Grove to the left after passing the Gap and turn left onto The Grove Dr.
12. Head north on The Grove Dr. toward Beverly Blvd.
13. Turn right on Beverly Blvd.
14. Turn right on Vista St.
15. Turn left on 1st St.
16. Turn right on Martel Ave.
17. Cross 3rd St., where Martel Ave. becomes Hauser Blvd.
18. Turn right on 6th St. and then cross Curson Ave. to return to your starting point.

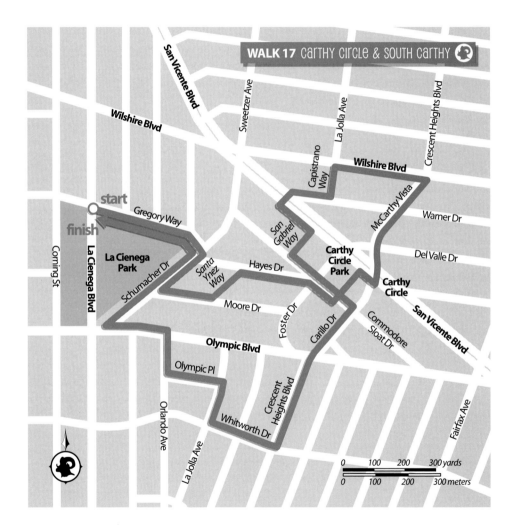

San Vicente Blvd

Wilshire Blvd

Sweetzer Ave

La Jolla Ave

Crescent Heights Blvd

Capistrano Way

Wilshire Blvd

start

Gregory Way

finish

San Gabriel Way

McCarthy Vista

Warner Dr

Corning St

La Cienega Blvd

La Cienega Park

Schumacher Dr

Santa Ynez Way

Hayes Dr

Carthy Circle Park

Del Valle Dr

Moore Dr

Foster Dr

Carillo Dr

Carthy Circle

Commodore Sloat Dr

San Vicente Blvd

Olympic Blvd

Olympic Pl

Crescent Heights Blvd

Orlando Ave

Whitworth Dr

La Jolla Ave

Fairfax Ave

0	100	200	300 yards
0	100	200	300 meters

17 Carthay Circle and South Carthay: an Oasis of Domestic Harmony

BOUNDARIES: La Cienega Blvd, Wilshire Blvd., Fairfax Ave., Whitworth Dr.
THOMAS GUIDE COORDINATES: Map 632; J2
DISTANCE: Approx. 2 miles
DIFFICULTY: Easy
PARKING: Metered parking is available on La Cienega Blvd. and Gregory Way.

This walk explores the neighborhoods of Carthay Circle and South Carthay in Los Angeles' bustling Miracle Mile district, just southeast of Beverly Hills. Carthay Circle and South Carthay, while they are right next to each other, have been designated as two separate Historic Preservation Overlay Zones by the city of Los Angeles due to the architectural integrity and cohesiveness of their houses and apartment buildings. Carthay Circle is composed of mostly Spanish Colonial Revival-style homes, with a few Tudor Revival and American Colonial Revival houses thrown in. The homes of South Carthay are a little more cohesive, consisting almost entirely of Spanish Colonial Revival structures. Both neighborhoods are well maintained and relatively isolated from the busy surrounding boulevards, making this a peaceful respite smack dab in the middle of one of LA's most thriving business districts.

- The first part of this walk covers Carthay Circle, which features a mix of single-family homes and duplexes in an appealing variety of architectural styles, ranging from Spanish Colonial Revival to Tudor. Begin at La Cienega Park, situated on the east side of La Cienega Blvd. between Olympic Blvd. and Gregory Way. Head east on Gregory Way along the northern border of the park.

- Turn right on Schumacher Dr. At 865 Schumacher is an interesting stone house with parapets atop the roof, giving it the incongruous look of a medieval castle.

- Turn left on Moore Dr. Notice the pair of Spanish-style homes on the northeast and southeast corners, each of which is dominated by a squat, tower-like structure.

- After less than a block, turn left on Santa Ynez Way, a narrow, slightly overgrown sidewalk alley.

- Santa Ynez way emerges onto Hayes Dr. Turn right here.

- Hayes Dr. boasts an interesting variety of homes. At 6518 Hayes is a shingle-covered residence that echoes the Cape Cod architectural style. A unique, low-lying brick house covered with ivy is located at 6513, and at 6444 Hayes is a lovely Spanish Colonial Revival home, dominated by three perfect arches above the front patio and driveway.

- At the three-way intersection with Commodore Sloat Dr. and Foster Dr., bear right onto Commodore Sloat.

- After about half a block, you'll see Carthay Circle Park—a narrow greenway between two office buildings—on your left. Turn left to cut through the park to San Vicente Blvd. At the end of the park, facing San Vicente, you'll notice the sculpture of Juan Bautista de Anza, who led the first settlers from Sonora, Mexico to California, according to the inscription.

- Turn right on San Vicente and cross Carrillo Dr. to the crosswalk that will take you safely across San Vicente.

Back Story: Miracle Mile's Auspicious Beginning

The conceit of the Miracle Mile district is that there doesn't appear to be anything miraculous about it. It's a vibrant and pleasant neighborhood, to be sure, with its museums, tall buildings and charming residential neighborhoods. But it doesn't appear to be any grander than most of LA's other affluent districts.

The stretch of Wilshire Blvd. between La Brea Ave. and Fairfax Ave. was dubbed Miracle Mile when developer A.W. Ross decided to transform the dusty 18-acre expanse of land into a prestigious shopping and business district in the 1920s. To this day, many of the original commercial buildings along Wilshire continue to bustle with corporate activity, a dream come true for Mr. Ross. His original designation stuck, and the surrounding area has come to be known as the Miracle Mile district.

- Continue to go straight on the street that is now called McCarthy Vista for two short blocks to Wilshire Blvd.

- On the southeast corner of Wilshire Blvd. and McCarthy Vista is Wahoo's Fish Taco, a convenient place to stop for a bite. Originally founded in San Diego, Wahoo's locations now dot Los Angeles County. It's a popular eatery, as the food is fresh, quickly served, and inexpensive.

- After noshing on a taco or two, turn left to head west on Wilshire.

- At La Jolla Ave., you'll see an alley cutting between two tall office buildings on your left—turn here. This drab alley turns into Capistrano Way, a peaceful sidewalk trimmed with bougainvillea.

- As you emerge from Capistrano Way, you're faced with a remarkably lovely yellow Spanish-style home at 6354 Warner Dr. Turn right on Warner.

- Warner ends at San Vicente Blvd. Carefully cross San Vicente (a grassy island dividing this busy street makes jaywalking easy, but not necessarily legal, so keep an eye out for cops).

- Once across San Vicente, you'll see a sign for San Gabriel Way to your left; this is yet another charming sidewalk alley. Follow San Gabriel Way through to Commodore Sloat Dr. Notice the striking American Colonial Revival house opposite the alley at 6440 Commodore Sloat.

- Turn left and follow Commodore Sloat for about two blocks.

- Turn right on Carrillo Dr. Carthay Circle Elementary School is on your right.

- When you reach the intersection with Olympic Blvd., cross the street using either the crosswalk or the underground tunnel (thoughtfully built for the safety of the schoolchildren, we presume). At this point, you have entered the neighborhood of South Carthay.

- Continue to go straight on what is now Crescent Heights Blvd. This block is distinguished by gorgeous, immaculately maintained Spanish-style duplexes and small apartment buildings.

- Turn right on Whitworth Dr. and continue for two blocks to La Jolla Ave.

- Turn right on La Jolla. Here the residences are primarily one-story, single-family homes. The predominant architectural style is Spanish Colonial Revival, identified by its low-pitched red-tile roofs and arched doorways and windows. Notice that many of these Spanish Colonial houses feature stained-glass details in the windows, just one example of the many decorative accents that distinguish this timelessly elegant architectural style. It is evident why the city of Los Angeles chose to designate this as a historic district.

- Turn left on Olympic Pl. and continue for one block to Orlando Ave.

- Turn right on Orlando and walk one block to Olympic Blvd.

- Turn left on Olympic. On the south side of Olympic, you'll notice several apartment buildings that mimic the French Normandy architectural style, which makes them stand out from the other residences in the area.

- Turn right on Schumacher Dr. and continue for two blocks back to Gregory Way.

- Turn left on Gregory Way and you're back at the beginning. At this point, you may need to use the facilities. Rest assured that there are public restrooms nearby in La Cienega Park.

POINTS OF INTEREST

La Cienega Park Community Center 8400 Gregory Way, Beverly Hills, CA 90211, 310-550-4625

Wahoo's Fish Taco 6258 Wilshire Blvd., Los Angeles, CA 90048, 323-933-2480

route summary

1. Begin at the corner of La Cienega Blvd. and Gregory Way and head east on Gregory Way.
2. Turn right on Schumacher Dr.
3. Turn left on Moore Dr.
4. Turn left on Santa Ynez Way
5. Turn right on Hayes Dr.
6. Bear right onto Commodore Sloat Dr.
7. Turn left to cut through Carthay Circle Park.
8. Turn right on San Vicente Blvd., cross Carrillo Dr. to reach crosswalk, and then cross San Vicente Blvd.
9. Continue straight on McCarthy Vista.
10. Turn left on Wilshire Blvd.
11. Turn left into alley opposite La Jolla Ave. This becomes Capistrano Way.
12. Turn right on Warner Dr.
13. Cross San Vicente Blvd.
14. Continue straight through the San Gabriel Way alley.
15. Turn left on Commodore Sloat Dr.
16. Turn right on Carrillo Dr.
17. Cross Olympic Blvd.
18. Continue straight on Crescent Heights Blvd.
19. Turn right on Whitworth Dr.
20. Turn right on La Jolla Ave.
21. Turn left on Olympic Pl.
22. Turn right on Orlando Ave.
23. Turn left on Olympic Blvd.
24. Turn right on Schumacher Dr.
25. Turn left on Gregory Way.

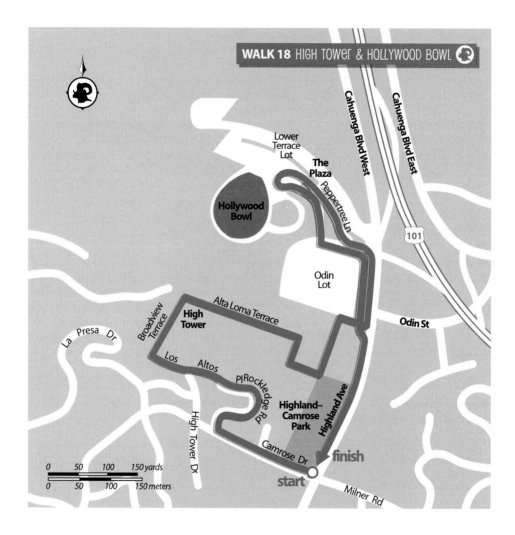

Cahuenga Blvd West

Cahuenga Blvd East

Lower
Terrace
Lot

**The
Plaza**

Peppertree Ln

101

Hollywood
Bowl

Odin
Lot

Odin St

Alta Loma Terrace

Broadview
Terrace

**High
Tower**

La Presa Dr

Los Altos

Pl Rockledge Rd

Highland Ave

High Tower Dr

**Highland–
Camrose
Park**

Camrose Dr

finish

start

Milner Rd

0   50   100   150 yards
0   50   100   150 meters

18 HIGH TOWER AND THE HOLLYWOOD BOWL: HIDEAWAY IN THE HILLS

BOUNDARIES: **Highland Ave., Camrose Dr., 101 Freeway**
THOMAS GUIDE COORDINATES: **Map 593; E3**
DISTANCE: **Approx. 1 mile**
DIFFICULTY: **Moderate**
PARKING: **Free street parking is available on Camrose Dr. Please be aware that parking anywhere in this vicinity on summer evenings can be problematic due to Hollywood Bowl parking restrictions.**

Hollywood is bordered to the north by hills that provide a haven for those residents who crave privacy and quiet but still wish to remain close to the action, so to speak. The neighborhood that lies adjacent to the Hollywood Bowl is one such retreat—a cozy, peaceful collection of homes, many of which are accessible only by stairway or by the elevator tower, known as "High Tower," for which the area is known. This excursion will provide a rare glimpse into the hidden sanctuary sometimes referred to as Hollywood Heights.

● Begin at the northwest corner of Highland Ave. and Camrose Dr. at Highland-Camrose Park. If the corner entrance is unlocked, you can enter here; otherwise, use the main entryway on Camrose Dr. This sanctuary is walled off from busy Highland Ave. to provide a convenient picnic area for patrons of the Hollywood Bowl, which lies just to the north. It's an interesting spot; in addition to rows of picnic tables and shaded lawns, the park features several offices housed in colorful little bungalows and a small police station. Public restrooms are also available here.

● Exit the park through the main gateway onto Camrose and turn right, passing a retirement home and several apartment buildings on your left, and cute single-family bungalows on your right.

● Turn right on Rockledge Rd. The cottage-style house on the northeast corner of Camrose and Rockledge boasts a meticulously tended rose garden out front. Straight ahead on Rockledge you'll see a gorgeous white stucco Spanish-style home with extensive blue tile work and a long balcony of arches overlooking the front courtyard.

- Follow the road as it curves and heads uphill. The Mediterranean houses are increasingly ornate and colorful as you continue upward, some even have castle-like architectural flourishes.

- When you reach the cul-de-sac you'll come to Los Altos Pl., a pedestrian walkway. Descend the short flight of stairs and continue along the narrow path between homes. The atmosphere is tranquil with the sound of trickling fountains.

- Cross High Tower Dr., which is lined with stand-alone garages for the residents of the neighborhood's hilltop homes. To the right you'll see the Bolognese-style tower for which the street is named. This structure houses a locked elevator to which only residents have a key. Continue along the slightly overgrown path on the other side of High Tower Dr.

- Turn right on Broadview Terr., another pedestrian path, and continue up the stairs. The homes along this stretch run the gamut from your typical Hollywood Mediterranean architecture to modern eclectic. As you approach the tower, you'll notice a raised clearing on your right. This overgrown patch of land appears to be too small to accommodate another house and provides a nice vantage point from which to admire the view of Hollywood to the southeast. The hills of Whitley Heights lie straight ahead with the spire of the Capitol Records building poking up on the other side.

- Ascend the stairs next to High Tower. An interesting multistory modern home sits at 2184 Broadview Terr., next door to the tower.

- Turn right on Alta Loma Terr. This path is shady and peaceful, and slopes downward at about a 30-degree angle. The houses on either side are accessible only by way of this pathway, hence the detached rows of garages on the street below. Architectural styles range from Mediterranean to Japanese to rambling clapboard farmhouse. This bucolic residential enclave is surrounded by hills, providing isolation from the urban hustle and bustle of the city.

- Turn right to continue along Alta Loma Terr. You'll come to a charming fairy-tale like house with miniature doors and windows at 6840.

- Turn left to descend the stairs.

- At the bottom of the stairs you'll find yourself in a private fenced-off parking lot for the residents of Alta Loma Terr. Turn left to head toward the black iron gate exiting onto Highland Ave.

- On the other side of the gate, turn left toward the Hollywood Bowl parking lot. Follow the sidewalk adjacent to the lot until you reach the main entrance to the Bowl.

- Turn left to follow the pathway identified as Peppertree Lane uphill to the amphitheatre. On your left you'll see the Hollywood Bowl Museum. It's worth stopping in to see blown-up panoramic photos of how the outdoor theatre looked when it was first incorporated into its natural canyon surroundings in 1922, and to admire exhibits about the many legendary performers who have graced its stage over the decades.

- You'll eventually come to a circular plaza surrounded by snack bars, the box office and the Hollywood Bowl gift shop. If there is a concert in session (and you don't have tickets), you won't be able to explore much farther. If not, continue up the hill through the turnstiles and enter the massive nearly 18,000-seat outdoor venue. If you're lucky, you might even be able to catch an artist in the middle of sound check. A summer evening at the Bowl is a quintessential LA experience that every resident should try to enjoy at least once a year.

High Tower

- To leave the Hollywood Bowl complex, return to the plaza in front of the box office and then follow the signs for the Odin Lot Path/Museum Terrace, which will take you along the elevated walkway that runs behind the museum and eventually deposits you in the massive parking lot. Just before you descend the stairs to the parking lot, you'll pass the Museum Terrace patio on your left—this looks like a lovely spot for evening cocktail gatherings of LA's literati.

- Turn left to cut through the parking lot back to Highland Ave. and then turn right to follow the sidewalk back toward Highland-Camrose Park, where you began your walk.

POINTS OF INTEREST:

Hollywood Bowl Museum 2301 N. Highland Ave, Los Angeles CA 90068, 323-850-2058

route summary:

1. Begin at the northwest corner of Highland Ave. and Camrose Dr. at Highland-Camrose Park.

2. Exit the park through the main gateway onto Camrose and turn right

3. Turn right on Rockledge Rd.

4. Follow the road as it curves and heads uphill.

5. At the cul-de-sac you'll come to Los Altos Pl., pedestrian walkway. Descend the stairs.

6. Cross High Tower Dr. and continue on Los Altos Pl.

7. Turn right on Broadview Terr.

8. Ascend the stairs next to High Tower.

9. Turn right on Alta Loma Terr.

10. Turn right to continue along Alta Loma Terr.

11. Turn left to descend the stairs.

12. Turn left into the parking lot and then exit through the gate on the right onto Highland Ave.

13. Turn left on Highland Ave. Follow the sidewalk until you reach the main entrance to the Hollywood Bowl.

14. Turn left at the main entrance to the Bowl and follow the pathway identified as Peppertree Lane uphill to the plaza near the box office.

15. Continue uphill to explore the amphitheatre if there isn't a concert in session.

16. Return to the plaza in front of the box office and then follow the signs for the Odin Lot Path/Museum Terrace.

17. Turn left to cut through the parking lot back to Highland Ave. and then turn right to follow the sidewalk back toward Highland-Camrose Park.

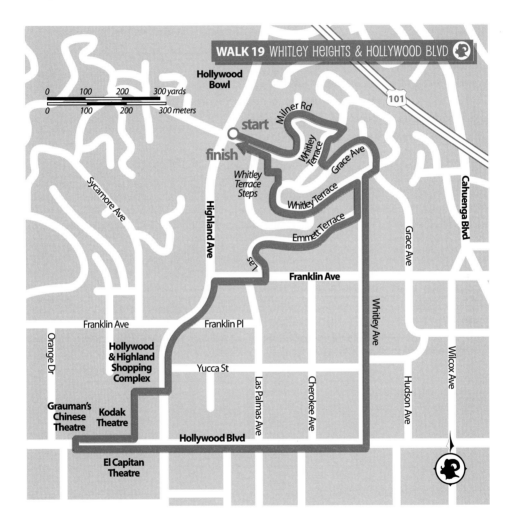

Hollywood
Bowl

0   100   200   300 yards
0   100   200   300 meters

Milner Rd

start

finish

Whitley Terrace

Grace Ave

Whitley
Terrace
Steps

Whitley Terrace

Sycamore Ave

Emmett Terrace

Highland Ave

Las

Franklin Ave

Cahuenga Blvd

101

Grace Ave

Whitley Ave

Wilcox Ave

Franklin Ave

Franklin Pl

Hollywood
& Highland
Shopping
Complex

Orange Dr

Yucca St

Las Palmas Ave

Cherokee Ave

Hudson Ave

Grauman's
Chinese
Theatre

Kodak
Theatre

Hollywood Blvd

El Capitan
Theatre

WHITLEY HEIGHTS AND HOLLYWOOD BOULEVARD: A HOLLYWOOD renaissance?

BOUNDARIES: **Hollywood Blvd., Orange Dr., Wilcox Ave., 101 Freeway**
THOMAS GUIDE COORDINATES: **Map 593; E3**
DISTANCE: **Approx. 2 miles**
DIFFICULTY: **Moderate**
PARKING: **Street parking is available on Milner Rd. (pay attention to posted signs), and there's also a parking lot for the Hollywood Heritage Museum just north of Milner on Highland Ave. Please be aware that parking anywhere in this vicinity on summer evenings can be problematic due to Hollywood Bowl parking restrictions.**

Whitley Heights is a charming Mediterranean-style residential neighborhood tucked into the hills just east of the Hollywood Bowl. Most of the homes were built between 1918 and 1928, and the predominant architectural style is Spanish Colonial Revival. The seclusion and beauty of this neighborhood attracted such stars as Rudolph Valentino, Judy Garland, and Charlie Chaplin during Hollywood's heyday. Alas, the construction of the 101 Freeway in 1946–1947 divided the hill in two, demolishing 40 historic homes in the process. In order to preserve what's left, the Historic Preservation Overlay Zone (HPOZ) alliance has granted the neighborhood protected status. Today, Whitley Heights is still home to many industry professionals, and many of the original Mediterranean homes still stand lovely as ever, but the address doesn't hold the same prestige it once did.

From Whitley Heights, this route will travel down to Hollywood Boulevard and the Hollywood & Highland shopping complex to get a glimpse of the still-in-progress revitalization of the heart of Hollywood.

● **Begin on Milner Rd., just east of Highland Ave. and head east away from Highland. A park that is home to shady picnic areas for Hollywood Bowl patrons, as well as the Hollywood Heritage Museum, is on your left. Pass the Whitley Terrace Steps next door to 6776 Milner (you'll descend these later), and follow the road as it curves to the left, past romantic Mediterranean houses built up against the hill on your right,** and charming cottage-like homes on your left. A posted sign signals that you've entered the Whitley Heights Historical Preservation area.

- Continue heading uphill, and bear right to stay on Milner at the split in the road—you'll notice a stunning white Spanish home on the corner with dark-stained wood and a huge arched picture window. Two more Spanish Colonial Revival homes catch the eye at 6708 and 6718 Milner; both have a slightly imposing Old World beauty.

- Turn right on Whitley Terr. Several more elegant Spanish-style homes adorn the hill on your right. Many of the newer homes in Whitley Heights maintain the Spanish Colonial Revival architectural style, integrating nicely into the old neighborhood. As Whitley Terr. curves to the left, you'll notice an interesting castle-like home at 6697 with unique floral tile murals and stained glass.

- Ascend the hidden wooden staircase on your left just past 6681 Whitley Terr. You'll notice a row of stand-alone garages on the other side of the steps; most of Whitley Heights' homes were built in the 1920s with single-car garages, so the row garages were built to accommodate the extra household vehicles.

- Turn left at the top of the steps onto Grace Ave. You're now approaching the upper-most portion of Whitley Heights, where the homes have a peaceful secluded quality. As you approach the top of the hill, you get a lovely view of Griffith Observatory in the distance. You'll notice a gated-off road off to your left when Grace Ave. turns to your right. This is Kendra Ct., the only street in the neighborhood that's closed to the public. Continue to follow Grace down the hill.

- When you reach Whitley Terr., cross the street and continue down Whitley Ave. This is a tricky 4-way intersection, so pay attention to the street signs. Whitley Ave. heads sharply downhill, and features a mix of old and new apartment buildings. Cross Franklin Ave. and continue to head south on Whitley as the street levels out. You'll pass numerous lovely old apartment buildings on this stretch, including the Havenhurst on the southwest corner of Franklin and Whitley, and the blue-tiled Hollywood Ardmore across the street on the southeast corner; the historic Fleur de Lis apartments at 1825; the self-proclaimed "legendary" Fontenoy Apartments at 1811; and the La Leyenda building at 1737. Many of these historic structures feature intricate wrought iron fire escape designs and ornately carved stone facades; they recall an elegance that is altogether missing in the modern mixed-use residential/commercial developments popping up all over Hollywood today.

● Turn right on Hollywood Blvd. and proceed west along the Walk of Fame. While it's true that the boulevard has fallen far from its legendary status of the 1920s and 30s, it is currently in the midst of a renaissance of sorts. A spattering of notable new attractions combined with the revitalization effort being applied to many Golden Age landmarks has made Hollywood a viable tourist destination once again.

Hollywood Toys & Costumes, a large shop featuring frightful wigs, sexy costumes, and various props and novelties, is directly ahead at the end of Whitley Ave. The legendary Frederick's of Hollywood Lingerie Museum is right next door; drop in to have a peek at bustiers worn by the likes of Madonna and Cher. Jimi Hendrix's star resides just in front of Book City Collectibles (6631 Hollywood Blvd.), Hollywood's venerable used bookshop. Located at 6667, Hollywood's oldest restaurant, the Musso & Frank Grill, serves steaks and martinis in a darkened old-fashioned setting. Built in 1922 as one of Hollywood's original themed movie palaces, the Egyptian Theatre (located at 6712 Hollywood Blvd.) is now owned by non-profit film organization American Cinematheque. Next door, the Pig n' Whistle restaurant and bar offers trend-seeking patrons the opportunity to drink and dine on canopied beds.

On the north side of the street at the intersection of McCadden Pl. you'll come to "Artisans Patio," a narrow alley lined with galleries and arts and crafts shops. The relatively new

Hollywood and Highland's Babylon Court

Erotic Museum sits at 6741 Hollywood Blvd.; note that its doors are only open to adults over the age of 18.

● Cross Highland Ave. The Hollywood & Highland shopping complex occupies half a block on the north side of the street. The brilliantly lit marquee of the El Capitan theatre (est. 1926) is directly across the street. Today the former live performance venue shows Disney films, often preceded by a live stage show, making it an exciting destination for kids.

Take a quick detour west on Hollywood Blvd. to see the Kodak Theatre, which is part of the Hollywood & Highland complex and current home of the Academy Awards, and the famous Grauman's Chinese Theatre next door. Built in 1927 and recently revamped to look a little more contemporary, the lavishly designed (inside and out) theatre frequently hosts star-studded movie premieres. The home of the very first Academy Awards ceremony back in 1929, the Hollywood Roosevelt Hotel, is just west of the Chinese Theatre on the south side of the street.

● Make your way back to the Hollywood & Highland steps and ascend the wide stairway entrance, which was positioned to provide a view of the Hollywood sign in the hills beyond. You'll emerge into Babylon Court, the whimsically named circular plaza at the center of the mall. The bizarre architecture was inspired by D.W. Griffith's 1916 *Intolerance*, and features Egyptian imagery from the film, including giant elephants perched on columns high above Babylon Court. It all makes for a very innovative but slightly bewildering shopping environment. Dining options include Vert, Wolfgang Puck's version of a French brasserie; Trastevere Italian restaurant; and The Grill on Hollywood, a fancy steakhouse, as well as numerous casual eateries. Of course, Hollywood & Highland also features the usual assortment of fashionable clothing and beauty supply and gift stores, as well.

Continue straight through the central plaza and pass under the massive archway, which is decorated with a bas-relief of Egyptian figures, continue past California Pizza Kitchen and descend the stairs, which will place you in front of the Renaissance Hotel on Highland Ave.

- Turn left to head north on Highland back toward the hills. If you look ahead and to your left, you'll see the Japanese-themed Yamashiro restaurant peeking through the trees atop a hill. And if you look up at the hill just to the right of the big church on the northwest corner of Franklin and Highland, you'll catch a glimpse of one of Frank Lloyd Wright's distinctive Mayan-style textile-block houses.

- Turn right on Franklin Ave. (which comes *after* Franklin Pl.) passing by the corner mall that is home to Whitley Market, a small neighborhood grocery store, an upscale flower shop, and, of course, a Starbucks.

- Turn left on Las Palmas Ave. Follow the road as it turns right and becomes Emmet Terr., a quaint street cozily tucked halfway up the hill. You're now back in Whitley Heights, as evidenced by the abundance of Mediterranean-style hillside homes.

- Turn left on Whitley Ave, ascending the same steep hill you walked down earlier.

- Turn left on Whitley Terr. A couple of the houses on the left side of the street are modern in design, but most maintain the Mediterranean theme.

Nearby and Notable:

Just northwest of Hollywood & Highland you'll find two distinctive Hollywood institutions. Yamashiro Japanese restaurant was built in 1911. Its grounds were modeled after a palace near Kyoto, and feature acres of lush gardens, as well as a breathtaking view of the city below. The Magic Castle is located below Yamashiro on the same hill. This members-only magic club hosts jaw-dropping performances by talented magicians, but you have to be invited by a member if you want to attend.

Yamashiro 1999 N. Sycamore Ave., Los Angeles, CA 90068, 323-466-5125

The Magic Castle 7001 Franklin Ave., Los Angeles, CA 90068, 323-851-0800

Located several blocks east of Hollywood & Highland on Hollywood Boulevard is the stunning Pantages Theatre. This 1929 Art Deco masterpiece is positively dripping with ornately carved, shimmering, and colorful artistic details—truly a sight to see. The former movie palace now hosts hit Broadway shows and musicals.

Pantages Theatre 6233 Hollywood Blvd., Los Angeles, CA 90028, 323-468-1770

While the homes on this side of the street appear modest in size compared to the stately homes on your right, they are actually quite grand, spilling down the hill on the other side and affording spectacular views of Hollywood and beyond.

● Look for the sign for the staircase on your left that reads 2000 N. Whitley Terr. Steps (just past 6666 Whitley Terr.), noticing the Hollywood sign in the distance. There is a black wrought iron gate at the top of the stairs, but it's always unlocked. Descend the long staircase past several homes, a couple of which are only accessible by the stairs, giving them a great feeling of privacy. As you head downward, admire the charming vista of the hills on the other side of Highland; the red tile roofs scattered among the treetops really do give the impression that you're in a Mediterranean town far from Los Angeles.

Note: At the time of publication, there was a neighborhood discussion about adding a locked gate to the bottom of the Whitley Terrace Steps. Should this come to pass, walkers can continue north on Whitley Terr., turn left on Milner Rd. and follow the street downhill to their starting point.

● Turn left on Milner Rd. at the bottom of the steps to return to your starting point.

POINTS OF INTEREST

Hollywood Heritage Museum 2100 N. Highland Ave., Los Angeles, CA 90068, 323-874-4005

Frederick's of Hollywood Lingerie Museum 6608 Hollywood Blvd., Los Angeles, CA 90028, 323-466-8506

Hollywood Toys & Costumes 6600 Hollywood Blvd., Los Angeles, CA 90028, 323-464-4444

Musso & Frank Grill 6667 Hollywood Blvd., Los Angeles, CA 90028, 323-467-7788

Egyptian Theatre 6712 Hollywood Blvd., Los Angeles, CA 90028, 323-466-3456

Pig n' Whistle 6714 Hollywood Blvd., Los Angeles, CA 90028, 323-463-0000

Erotic Museum 6741 Hollywood Blvd, Los Angeles, CA 90028, 323-463-7684

El Capitan Theatre 6838 Hollywood Blvd., Los Angeles, CA 90068, 323-467-7674

Hollywood & Highland 6801 Hollywood Blvd., Los Angeles, CA 90028, 323-960-2331

Grauman's Chinese Theatre 6925 Hollywood Blvd., Los Angeles, CA 90028, 323-464-6266

route summary

1. Begin on Milner Rd., just east of Highland Ave. and head east away from Highland.
2. Bear right to stay on Milner at the split in the road.
3. Turn right on Whitley Terr.
4. Ascend the hidden wooden staircase on your left just past 6681 Whitley Terr.
5. Turn left at the top of the steps onto Grace Ave.
6. Cross Whitley Terr. and continue down Whitley Ave.
7. Turn right on Hollywood Blvd.
8. Cross Highland Ave. and continue west for half a block to see Grauman's Chinese theatre before returning to the stairway leading into the Hollywood & Highland complex just west of Highland Ave.
9. Ascends the stairs into Hollywood & Highland's Babylon Court and continue straight through the mall, descending the stairs back down to Highland Ave.
10. Turn left to head north on Highland.
11. Turn right on Franklin Ave.
12. Turn left on Las Palmas Ave. and follow the road as it turns right and becomes Emmet Terr.
13. Turn left on Whitley Ave.
14. Turn left on Whitley Terr.
15. Descend the Whitley Terrace Steps on your left at 2000 N. Whitley.
16. Turn left on Milner Rd. at the bottom of the steps to return to your starting point.

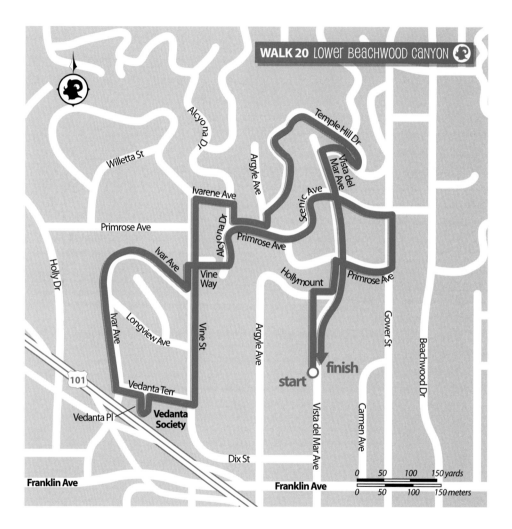

Alcyona Dr

Willetta St

Ivarene Ave

Argyle Ave

Temple Hill Dr

Vista del Mar Ave

Scenic Ave

Primrose Ave

Alcyona Dr

Primrose Ave

Ivar Ave

Vine Way

Primrose Ave

Hollymount

Holly Dr

Ivar Ave

Longview Ave

Vine St

Argyle Ave

Gower St

Beachwood Dr

start   finish

Vedanta Terr

Vedanta Pl

Vedanta Society

Vista del Mar Ave

Carmen Ave

Dix St

Franklin Ave

Franklin Ave

| 0 | 50 | 100 | 150 yards |
| 0 | 50 | 100 | 150 meters |

20 LOWER BEACHWOOD CANYON: REMNANTS OF ANCIENT SPIRITUALITY IN THE HOLLYWOOD HILLS

BOUNDARIES: **Franklin Ave., Ivar Ave., Gower St., Temple Hill Dr.**
THOMAS GUIDE COORDINATES: **Map 593; F3**
DISTANCE: **Approx. 2 miles**
DIFFICULTY: **Moderate**
PARKING: **Free street parking is available on Vista del Mar Ave.**

You can't get much more "Hollywood" than Beachwood Canyon. Situated in the hills immediately below the legendary sign, this neighborhood is home to rising young stars and accomplished entertainment industry professionals, as well as aging Hollywood burnouts and struggling actors. This disparate community is reflected in the buildings that line the narrow streets, an interesting juxtaposition of beautifully maintained million-dollar houses and run-down '60s-era apartment buildings.

A word of caution to dog-walkers: The narrow and winding streets of this hillside neighborhood can be fairly busy; vehicles tend to materialize around blind curves with little advance notice, and sidewalks are scarce. Therefore, it's wise to keep your wits about you and keep your furry friend on a short leash.

● Begin on Vista del Mar Ave. (north of Franklin Ave.), just before the road curves to the right. Straight ahead you'll see a wide double staircase.

● Ascend the stairway, which was once grand and lovely, but has become somewhat dilapidated over the years. At the top of the steps, you'll see a towering white stucco mansion across the street at 6215 Hollymont Dr. This is the former home of Golden Age actress Barbara Stanwyck. Like the stairway you just ascended, it appears to have fallen from its former glory, however it still stands in reasonably good condition (although the current resident does assert that it is "very haunted").

- Turn right on Hollymont and follow it a short distance to where it connects with Vista del Mar.

- Turn left on Vista del Mar. At 2117–2121 is an apartment building with a sign displaying a pyramid symbol and the words "Krotona of Old Hollywood." This structure is one of several buildings in this area left over from the days of the Krotona Colony. This colony was a part of the Theosophical movement of the early twentieth century, which melded elements of spiritualism, Eastern religion, Masonic lore, and scientific speculation. Across the street is another remnant of the Krotona Colony; the former Krotona Inn incorporates elements of Moorish design, particularly in the domed house that is set back from the street amongst dense foliage.

- When you reach Primrose, notice the crèche containing a statue of the Madonna and Child on the northeast corner; the cavity has become blackened over the years with the smoke of many candles. Turn right on Primrose Ave. and continue for one short block to Gower St.

- Turn left on Gower. At 2122 Gower you'll spot a small modern house that incorporates rounded and rectangular shapes to unique effect. The front gate and garage door are painted in primary colors, completing the pleasingly kindergarten-like impression.

- Upon reaching Scenic Ave., notice the impressive French Normandy-style apartment complex on the northeast corner. Turn left on Scenic. You'll see that the homes on this street are consistently well maintained and attractive, encompassing a variety of architectural styles. A Tudor Revival house, partially obscured by bamboo, sits at 6111 Scenic; directly across the street is an English cottage with an undulating thatched roof.

- Cross Vista del Mar and continue uphill, following the road as it curves to the left. A flawless Spanish Colonial Revival home in dark-stained wood and pale stucco with intricate tile work catches the eye at 6220.

- Turn right on Primrose Ave., where you'll catch a view of the hills above Lake Hollywood, a neighborhood known as the Hollywood Knolls. Cross Argyle Ave. and follow the road as it heads downhill.

- Turn left on Alcyona Dr.—a NOT A THROUGH STREET sign makes it easy to spot.

- When you reach the end of the cul-de-sac, keep an eye out for the hidden stairway, and then descend the shady steps to Vine Way.

- Continue straight on Vine Way to Vine St.

- Turn left on Vine St. and follow it one block to Ivar Ave.

- Turn right on Ivar. At 2154 is a wooden, barn-like house that stands out from the other homes in this neighborhood. Follow Ivar as it curves around, The street is narrow here, and crowded with parked cars. The sound of rushing traffic indicates that you're approaching the 101 Freeway. At 2062 Ivar, you'll notice a towering home built in the style of a medieval castle.

- Continue past the intersection with Longview Ave. and then turn left on Vedanta Terr., immediately before the freeway overpass.

- When you reach the intersection with Vedanta Pl., turn right to take a quick detour to the Vedanta Society of Southern California complex, which features a bookstore and a white temple that looks like a mini Taj Mahal. The Vedanta Society is an ancient religious philosophy based on the sacred scriptures of India known as the Vedas. The temple is open to the public daily for meditation, classes, lectures, and seminars. After checking out the temple, return to Vedanta Terr. and turn right.

- Turn left on Vine St. If you look over your shoulder to the south, you'll see the top of the distinctive Capitol Records building on the other side of the freeway. At 2030 Vine is a lovely Spanish Mission-style home with a little bell set into the arch over the front gate. A fountain can be heard trickling inside the hidden courtyard. Another charming Spanish-style residence, the Monastery Gardens apartments, is situated a little farther up the street at 2062.

- Turn right on Ivarene Ave. A brilliant golden-colored stucco home sits at 6281 Ivarene.

- At the intersection of Alcyona Dr., notice the remarkable house constructed of weathered wooden boards to the left of the intersection at 2174 Alcyona—it has the look of a mountain ski lodge and is somewhat incongruous in the heavily Mediterranean-influenced Hollywood Hills. Turn right on Alcyona.

● Turn left on Primrose Ave., heading back up the steep hill you descended earlier.

● Turn left on Argyle Ave. at the top of the hill.

● Turn right on Temple Hill Dr. Notice the blue-shingled farmhouse on the northeast corner that is almost completely obscured by bushes and trees. Temple Hill Dr. has a rustic air; high in the hills as it is, the freeway and the sordid streets of Hollywood seem far away.

● As the road curves downhill, there are fewer houses, emphasizing the rustic feel. An unexpected view of downtown Los Angeles materializes as the road turns to head southeast.

● Turn right on Vista del Mar Ave., where Temple Hill ends. Continue downhill along the curving street, noticing the variety of architectural styles—Spanish, English, Tudor, Moorish, modern—the residents of the Hills have no compunction about mixing and matching their architectural styles, but the effect is more whimsical than tacky.

● At the intersection with Vista del Mar Pl., turn left to stay on Vista del Mar Ave. Cross Scenic Ave. and Primrose Ave., retracing your steps down to Hollymont. Instead of turning on Hollymont to descend the stairway from the beginning of the walk, remain on Vista del Mar as it curves to the right, taking you back to the beginning of your journey.

If you're feeling peckish by this time, you can continue one block south to the 101 Coffee Shop, a casual, vaguely retro-themed neighborhood eatery inside the motel on the corner of Vista del Mar and Franklin Ave.

POINTS OF INTEREST:

Vedanta Society of Southern California 1946 Vedanta Place, Hollywood, CA 90068, 323-465-7114

101 Coffee Shop 6145 Franklin Ave, Los Angeles, CA 90028, 323-467-1175

route summary:

1. Head north on Vista del Mar Ave. toward the staircase (don't follow the road as it curves to the right).
2. Ascend the stairs.
3. Turn right on Hollymont Dr.
4. Turn left on Vista del Mar Ave.
5. Turn right on Primrose Ave.
6. Turn left on Gower St.
7. Turn left on Scenic Ave.
8. Cross Vista del Mar and continue uphill on Scenic.
9. Turn right on Primrose Ave.
10. Turn left on Alcyona Dr.
11. Descend the stairway to Vine Way.
12. Continue straight on Vine Way.
13. Turn left on Vine St.
14. Turn right on Ivar Ave.
15. Turn left on Vedanta Terr.
16. Turn right on Vedanta Pl.
17. Return to Vedanta Terr. and turn left.
18. Turn left on Vine St.
19. Turn right on Ivarene Ave.
20. Turn right on Alcyona Dr.
21. Turn left on Primrose Ave.
22. Turn left on Argyle Ave.
23. Turn right on Temple Hill Dr.
24. Follow the road as it curves to the left, heading downhill.
25. Turn right on Vista del Mar Ave.
26. Turn left to stay on Vista del Mar Ave. (avoiding Vista del Mar Pl.)
27. Follow Vista del Mar Ave. as it curves to the right, taking you downhill to your beginning.

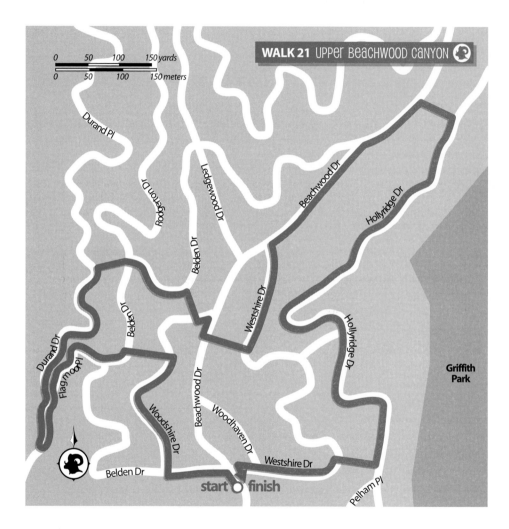

0   50   100   150 yards
0   50   100   150 meters

Durand Pl

Rodgerton Dr

Ledgewood Dr

Beachwood Dr

Hollyridge Dr

Belden Dr

Belden Dr

Westshire Dr

Hollyridge Dr

Durand Dr

Flagmoor Pl

Woodshire Dr

Beachwood Dr

Woodhaven Dr

Westshire Dr

Belden Dr

Griffith Park

start ○ finish

Pelham Pl

21 Upper Beachwood Canyon: a Little Place Hollywood Players Like to Call Home

BOUNDARIES: **Franklin Ave., 101 Freeway, Griffith Park**
THOMAS GUIDE COORDINATES: **Map 593; F1/G1**
DISTANCE: **Approx. 2 miles**
DIFFICULTY: **Strenuous**
PARKING: **Free parking is available on Beachwood Dr.**

Beachwood Canyon works hard to maintain its rural, small-town vibe, even though its population is about as Hollywood as you can get. The neighborhood's origins reflect this conceit; in 1923, developer S.H. Woodruff created the development in the rustic hills north of Hollywood and erected a garish, four-story sign proclaiming the development to be "Hollywoodland." The last four letters have since been removed, and the remainder of the sign has been treated to the occasional facelift over the past 80 years. Today the gleaming white letters remain one of the most recognizable landmarks in the world.

At the time of development, Woodruff hired European stonemasons to construct roadside walls and six long stairways out of wrought iron and stone to interconnect the residential streets of Hollywoodland. This walk will seek out and conquer every one of these steep flights, so be sure to bring plenty of water and wear comfy shoes.

● **Begin on Beachwood Dr., just south of Belden Dr. (Westshire Dr. to the right) and head north into the canyon. The original stone gates to Hollywoodland sit on either side of the road, and a street sign welcomes residents home while imploring them to "slow down and relax." To the right at 2700 Westshire Dr. is the original Hansel and Gretel-style cottage that still houses the Hollywoodland Realty Company.**

● **Turn left on Belden Dr. You'll walk past the neighborhood hub, where locals grab breakfast at the Village Coffee Shop, do light grocery shopping at the Beachwood**

Market, and stay up to date on the community happenings posted on the neighborhood bulletin board.

- Turn right on Woodshire Dr., which is narrow and windy with a pleasing rustic feel, and follow the road past flawless Spanish homes, many with stained glass details in the windows. An imposing Norman castle-style home at 2755 Woodshire catches the eye. Next door is an ivy-covered English cottage with a coat of arms painted over the front door. While the predominant architectural style in the canyon is Mediterranean, the Anglo influence is also readily apparent.

- Just before 2795 Woodshire, look for the first of the somewhat hidden Hollywoodland stairways on your left and ascend. You'll emerge back onto Belden Dr. Turn left here.

- When you reach the fork in the road, bear right to continue uphill on Flagmoor Pl. About halfway up the short street, a clearing on your left treats you to a great view of downtown's high-rises to the southeast. And as you approach the next intersection, you can catch an unobstructed view of Griffith Observatory directly to the east.

- At the intersection with Durand Dr., continue to head uphill on Durand. As you round the bend in the road, you'll notice a great stone wall on your right. As you approach the front of this magnificent castle-like home, which sits at 2869 Durand, you'll discover that it has been built in the style of a French chateau. This is another of the several homes you'll see today that seem to demonstrate the residents' perceived royal kinship.

- Cross in front of the entrance to 2869 Durand, and take a few steps down the dirt trail that lies next to the structure's small, private parking area. The Lake Hollywood reservoir sparkles below. If you're feeling adventurous, you can follow the dirt trail all the way down to the concrete jogging path encircling the reservoir and then return to this spot, but this is quite a hike, and you have many stairways yet to conquer.

- Retrace your steps back down Durand Dr., continuing to head straight on Durand past the intersection with Flagmoor. The Hollywood sign looms large directly ahead.

- Just past 2954 Durand, you'll come to stairway number two, which is broken up by pathways and landings. Follow the steps all the way down to the street below. Use caution, as some of the stairs have eroded over time. As you descend, you'll see an enormous rectilinear modern home dead ahead; this is another common architectural style in these hills. At the bottom of the steps, cross Rodgerton Dr. to continue straight on Belden Dr.

- Follow Belden as it curves around, looking for the next stairway just past 2950 Belden. This is perhaps the most recognizable of Beachwood Canyon's stairways, a straight, narrow flight divided by what used to be small ponds but are now sand-filled planters. Descend the steps and then turn left at the bottom. A bronze sign at the base declares Hollywoodland's granite retaining walls and interconnecting stairways to be historic cultural monuments by the City of Los Angeles Cultural Heritage Commission.

- Cross Beachwood Dr. and turn right on the other side of the street. Between 2800 and 2810 Beachwood is another very long stairway. Take a deep breath and ascend the 144 steps to Westshire Dr. Again, watch out for cracks and holes in the 80-year-old concrete.

- Turn left at the top of the stairs on Westshire and follow the road downhill to where it merges with Beachwood Dr. Continue north on Beachwood past vibrantly painted Spanish homes, charming traditional wood-and-brick houses, and more faux castles—the residence at 2925 even features a large mural of a medieval knight on the wall facing the street. As you approach the intersection with Belden Dr., notice the particularly

Hollywoodland Gates

adorable English cottage at 2958, complete with low stone walls and a thatched-style roof.

● Cross Belden Dr. and continue straight on Beachwood, keeping an eye out for the next staircase, which lies between 3020 and 3030 Beachwood. Begin your ascent up the longest stairway of this walk—176 steps—pausing as needed to catch your breath. Even though this is an especially long set of stairs, note that there are no "stairway homes" that aren't accessible from the street. Instead, the houses on either side have particularly large lots, lending a nice, open feel to this portion of the walk.

● At the top of the stairs, turn right on Hollyridge Dr. for the longest stairway-free stretch of today's route. Thankfully, the road slopes gently downhill here, providing some relief after the last grueling sets of stairs. Many of the homes on the hill to your left are concealed behind dense foliage, but you can catch glimpses of several interesting styles, including another stone castle and a few starkly modern residences. There's a fine line between eccentric and tacky, and you may agree that much of the architecture in the canyon walks that line. Continue straight on Hollyridge past the intersection with Lechner Pl.

● At the intersection with Pelham Pl., just past 2831 Hollyridge, turn right to descend the final stairway of your journey.

● At the bottom of the steps, turn left to follow Westshire Dr. for about a block back to Beachwood Dr., and then turn left to return to your starting point next to the stone gates marking the entrance to Hollywoodland.

POINTS OF INTEREST

Village Coffee Shop 2695 N. Beachwood Dr., Los Angeles, CA 90068, 323-467-5398
Beachwood Market 2701 Belden Dr., Los Angeles, CA 90068, 323-464-7154

route summary

1. Begin on Beachwood Dr., just south of Belden Dr. (Westshire Dr. to the right) and head north into the canyon.

2. Turn left on Belden Dr.

3. Turn right on Woodshire Dr.

4. Ascend the stairway just before 2795 Woodshire. At the top, turn left on Belden Dr.

5. Bear right to continue uphill on Flagmoor Pl.

6. At the intersection with Durand Dr., continue to head uphill on Durand.

7. Cross in front of the entrance to 2869 Durand, and take a few steps down the dirt trail that lies next to the building's small parking area for a view of the Lake Hollywood reservoir below.

8. Retrace your steps back down Durand Dr., continuing to head straight on Durand past the intersection with Flagmoor.

9. Just past 2954 Durand, descend the next set of stairs. At the bottom of the steps, cross Rodgerton Dr. to continue straight on Belden Dr.

10. Descend the stairway just past 2950 Belden and turn left at the bottom.

11. Cross Beachwood Dr. and turn right on the other side of the street. Ascend the stairway between 2800 and 2810 Beachwood Dr.

12. Turn left at the top of the stairs on Westshire Dr. and follow the road downhill to where it merges with Beachwood Dr. Continue north on Beachwood.

13. Ascend the staircase between 3020 and 3030 Beachwood Dr.

14. At the top of the stairs, turn right on Hollyridge Dr. Continue straight on Hollyridge past the intersection with Lechner Pl.

15. At the intersection with Pelham Pl., just past 2831 Hollyridge, turn right to descend the stairs.

16. At the bottom of the steps, turn left to follow Westshire Dr. for about a block back to Beachwood Dr., and then turn left to return to your starting point

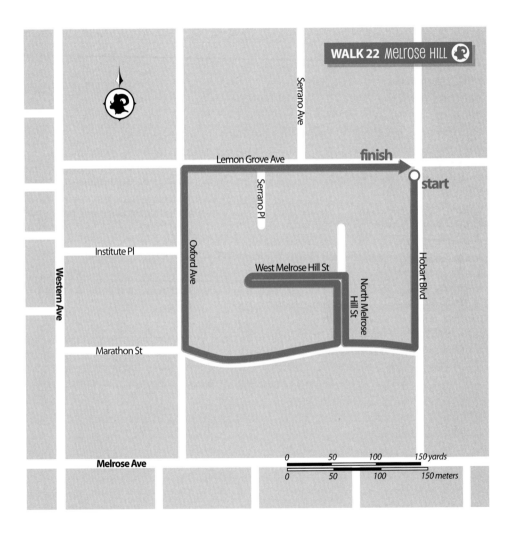

Serrano Ave

Lemon Grove Ave

finish

start

Serrano Pl

Institute Pl

Oxford Ave

West Melrose Hill St

North Melrose Hill St

Hobart Blvd

Western Ave

Marathon St

Melrose Ave

0	50	100	150 yards
0	50	100	150 meters

22 MELROSE HILL: DIAMOND IN THE ROUGH

BOUNDARIES: **Western Ave., Melrose Ave., Lemon Grove Ave., Hobart Blvd.**
THOMAS GUIDE COORDINATES: **Map 593: H6**
DISTANCE: **Approx. ½ mile.**
DIFFICULTY: **Easy**
PARKING: **Free street parking is available on Lemon Grove Ave. and Hobart Blvd.**

Melrose Hill is an easy place to miss, which is a shame. This small but notable neighborhood is situated in the heavily urban area just north of Melrose Ave. and east of Western Ave. This region's proximity to these busy thoroughfares, not to mention the adjacent 101 Freeway, contributes to the somewhat grimy atmosphere.

But the two cross streets that comprise Melrose Hill seem far removed from their surroundings and are worth exploring. Los Angeles' Historic Preservation Overlay Zone (HPOZ) Alliance thought so, which is why they designated this neighborhood an HPOZ. Historic preservation status was granted this neighborhood due to the architectural significance of its California bungalows, which incorporate elements of both Craftsman and Colonial Revival styles. No more than a half mile from start to finish, this trek essentially amounts to a walk around the block and focuses on the charming and distinctive homes atop the hill.

- Begin at the corner of Lemon Grove Ave. and Hobart Blvd. The Lemon Grove Park and Recreation Center sits on the northeast corner of this intersection, and you can catch a lovely view of the Griffith Park observatory to the north.

- Head south on Hobart Blvd. This street is home to mostly Latino families, and you're likely to see kids playing in their front yards as their parents look on.

- Turn right on Marathon St. In contrast to Hobart, which sees its share of traffic, this street is peaceful, becoming quieter still as it slopes gently uphill. The tidily kept bungalows on this block have a timeless beauty; they seem out of place here in the middle of Hollywood.

- Turn right on N. Melrose Hill. As is typical in Los Angeles, the houses are slightly larger as you move farther up the hill.

- Turn left W. Melrose Hill. On the southwest corner of 4900 W. Melrose Hill and 800 N. Melrose Hill is a gorgeous dark wood shingle and brick house.

- Continue to the end of the cul-de-sac, taking a minute to admire the classic Craftsman home at 4954 and the unique American Colonial Revival house next door at 4960.

- Make your way back to the intersection of N. Melrose Hill, and turn right to retrace your steps back down to Marathon.

- Turn right on Marathon. Part of what makes this neighborhood so delightful is the abundance of trees; the sidewalk is shaded with palms, jacaranda trees, and crepe myrtle.

- Turn right on Oxford Ave. The large wood-sided houses on your right appear to be older, or perhaps just not as well maintained, as the homes on Melrose Hill.

- Turn right on Lemon Grove Ave. You may want to take a short detour to peruse the attractive Spanish-style apartments at the end of the short cul-de-sac at Serrano Pl. Immediately after you cross Serrano Pl., as you continue to head east on Lemon Grove, you'll see a cute pueblo-style house on your right that features ironwork adorned with bunches of grapes. Most of the homes on this street have bars on the windows, a reminder that this isn't the safest neighborhood in LA. But it's by far not the most dangerous, either.

- You'll return to your starting point at the intersection of Lemon Grove and Hobart Blvd.

route summary:

1. Begin at the corner of Lemon Grove Ave. and Hobart Blvd.
2. Head south on Hobart Blvd.
3. Turn right on Marathon St.
4. Turn right on N. Melrose Hill.
5. Turn left on W. Melrose Hill.
6. Continue to the end of the cul-de-sac.
7. Return to N. Melrose Hill and turn right to retrace steps down to Marathon St.
8. Turn right on Marathon St.
9. Turn right on Oxford Ave.
10. Turn right on Lemon Grove Ave.
11. Return to start at the intersection of Lemon Grove Ave. and Hobart Blvd.

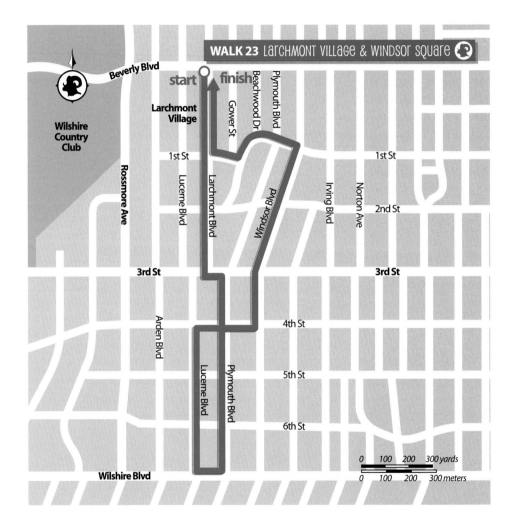

WALK 23 Larchmont Village & Windsor Square

Beverly Blvd

start   finish

Larchmont Village

Wilshire Country Club

Gower St

Beachwood Dr

Plymouth Blvd

1st St   1st St

Lucerne Blvd

Larchmont Blvd

Wilshire Blvd

Irving Blvd

Norton Ave

2nd St

Rossmore Ave

3rd St   3rd St

Arden Blvd

4th St

Lucerne Blvd

Plymouth Blvd

5th St

6th St

0   100   200   300 yards
0   100   200   300 meters

Wilshire Blvd

23 Larchmont Village and Windsor Square: a Welcome Dose of Small Town Charm

BOUNDARIES: **Beverly Blvd., Rossmore Ave., Wilshire Blvd., Windsor Blvd.**
THOMAS GUIDE COORDINATES: **Map 633; F1**
DISTANCE: **Approx. 2 miles**
DIFFICULTY: **Easy**
PARKING: **Free street parking is available on Larchmont south of 1st St. Metered parking is available north of 1st St.**

The Hancock Park/Windsor Square region lies just south of Hollywood and is considered one of the nicest areas in central Los Angeles. This area encompasses the posh Wilshire Country Club, as well as Larchmont Village, a collection of small, independently owned shops and restaurants (with a few commercial chain establishments thrown in) that is constantly teeming with residents and their canine companions. This route begins in the Village and heads south to explore the ostentatious homes of Windsor Square, a wealthy neighborhood that was very recently declared a Historic Preservation Overlay Zone by the city of Los Angeles.

● Begin at the corner of Beverly Blvd. and Larchmont Blvd., in the middle of Larchmont Village, which stretches for several blocks between Melrose Ave. and 3rd St. The Village is home to more restaurants than you can shake a stick at, ranging from Greek to Japanese to Caribbean. It also features such commercial staples as Starbucks, Baskin-Robbins, and Jamba Juice. Sartorial enthusiasts will be delighted to find a collection of fine boutiques along Larchmont, as well, although the names on some of the storefronts seem to change regularly. It's worth your time either before or after today's walk to explore Larchmont Village and grab a bite to eat, if you can make up your mind about where to dine, that is. Dependable eateries include Café du Village, Village Pizzeria, Le Petit Greek, and Chan Dara, a popular Thai restaurant that lies just north of Beverly Blvd.

● Head south on Larchmont Blvd., which turns into a residential street south of 1st St., populated with mostly Spanish and Norman one- and two-story homes. The street median is planted with flowering trees, lily of the Nile, and bird of paradise. On the southwest corner of 2nd St. and Larchmont, you'll notice a wood-shingled home with an eye-catching Polynesian-themed garden dominated by a red lacquered bridge and wishing well. Incongruously enough, the Japanese-looking wishing well is decorated with a picture of Snow White and the words "I'm wishing." The effect is eclectic and puzzling. As it turns out, this house was designed and built by Adriana Caselotti, who provided the voice of Snow White in the 1937 animated feature. After lending her voice to the raven-haired cartoon character (a tribute to her human counterpart, as Snow White was originally conceived to have blond hair), Adriana taught singing lessons in Hawaii and came to love Asian culture, hence the idiosyncratically designed home and garden.

As you near 3rd St., you'll see a stone column at the south end of the Larchmont median, erected by the Windsor Square Association. There was some dispute among the residents of Windsor Square as to whether or not the neighborhood should be declared a Historic Preservation Overlay Zone. This designation can be a blessing in that it protects the houses in a given area and ensures that the architectural integrity and cohesiveness of all the buildings in that area is carefully upheld, but it can also be limiting to residents who wish to impose their own unique mark on their property.

● Cross 3rd St. and then turn left, walking less than a block to Plymouth Blvd.

● Turn right on Plymouth, a quiet street lined with royal palms. The houses here are more appropriately deemed mansions, with expansive green lawns and self-conscious ornamentation such as diamond-paned windows and gingerbread trim. The primary architectural styles are those that work well on a grand scale, such as American Colonial Revival, Spanish Colonial Revival, and Tudor Revival. 425 Plymouth is notable for its pale green tile roof—a rare deviation from the typical red clay tiles— and Corinthian-style columns upholding the front entryway. After crossing 6th St., you'll pass the Windsor House at 606 Plymouth Blvd; the imposing brick Tudor building is securely gated off from the street.

● Turn right on Wilshire Blvd. The commanding structure of the Scottish Rite Masonic Temple sits on the northwest corner of Plymouth and Wilshire. The temple houses the American Heritage Masonic Museum, which celebrates the humanitarian and academic influence of Freemasons throughout history. On the south side of Wilshire is the Wilshire United Methodist Church; this beautiful building combines elements of Romanesque and Gothic design and has been declared a historic cultural monument by the city of Los Angeles. The Italian Renaissance-style headquarters for the Ebell of Los Angeles is just west of the church at the corner of Lucerne Blvd., encompassing the Wilshire Ebell Theatre and Club House. Founded in 1894, the Ebell of Los Angeles is one of the nation's oldest and largest women's clubs. The Wilshire theatre and clubhouse were built in 1927.

- Turn right on Lucerne Blvd. At 637 Lucerne you'll notice a Victorian mansion that looks a bit like a haunted house. Across the street at 630 is an elaborate Craftsman shingled in dark green wood. Apart from these two remarkable structures, most of the homes along Plymouth echo the same architectural styles on display along Plymouth.

- Turn right on 4th St., taking notice of the lovely gingerbread trim that adorns the white mansion on the southeast corner of Lucerne and 4th.

- Turn left on Windsor Blvd. A classic white American Colonial Revival home sits on the northeast corner at 354 Windsor.

- Carefully cross 3rd St.; the street is fairly busy and there's no crosswalk at Windsor. At 270 S. Windsor, a cheerful orange Spanish home with blue and white striped awnings catches the eye. As you continue along Windsor, you'll see many of the gardens planted with white roses and purple lily of the Nile; the landscaping along this street is impressively congruous. As you cross 2nd St., notice the magnificent live oak tree stretching its low, dense branches across the sidewalk on the northeast corner. Even in the dry heat of summer, Windsor Blvd. smells verdant, thanks to the blooming magnolia trees and amply watered lawns.

- Turn left on 1st St. The Spanish-style home on the northwest corner looks like a tropical resort, gorgeously landscaped with palms and exotic flowering plants. As you cross Plymouth Blvd. for the last time, look to the north to catch a glimpse of the water tower at Paramount Studios.

- When you come to the intersection of Beachwood Dr., veer left to remain on 1st St., crossing Gower St. and returning to the intersection of Larchmont Blvd.

- Turn right on Larchmont and head one block back to Beverly Blvd. where you started in Larchmont Village.

POINTS OF Interest

American Heritage Masonic Museum 4357 Wilshire Blvd., Los Angeles, CA 90010, 323-930-9806

Cafe Chapeau 236 N. Larchmont Blvd., Los Angeles, CA 90004, 323-462-4985

Café du Village 139½ N. Larchmont Blvd., Los Angeles, CA 90004, 323-466-3996

California Roll & Sushi 125 N. Larchmont Blvd., Los Angeles, CA 90004, 323-841-5458

Center for Yoga 230½ Larchmont Blvd., Los Angeles, CA 90004, 323-464-1276

Chan Dara Restaurant 310 N. Larchmont Blvd., Los Angeles, CA 90004, 323-467-1052

Chevalier's Books 126 N. Larchmont Blvd., Los Angeles, CA 90004, 323-465-1334

Espresso Roma Cafe 124 N. Larchmont Blvd., Los Angeles, CA 90004, 323-465-3461

La Bottega Marino 203 N. Larchmont Blvd., Los Angeles, CA 90004, 323-962-1325

La Luna Ristorante 113 N. Larchmont Blvd., Los Angeles, CA 90004, 323-962-2130

Landis General Store 142 N. Larchmont Blvd., Los Angeles, CA 90004, 323-465-7998

Larchmont Beauty Center 208 N. Larchmont Blvd., Los Angeles, CA 90004, 323-461-0162

Leonidas Belgian Chocolates 201 N. Larchmont Blvd., Los Angeles, CA 90004, 323-860-7966

Le Petit Greek 127 N. Larchmont Blvd., Los Angeles, CA 90004, 323-464-5160

Louise's Trattoria 232 N. Larchmont Blvd., Los Angeles, CA 90004, 323-962-9510

Prado Restaurant 244 N. Larchmont Blvd., Los Angeles, CA 90004, 323-467-3871

Village Pizzeria 131 N. Larchmont Blvd., Los Angeles, CA 90004, 323-465-5566

Z Pizza 123 N. Larchmont Blvd., Los Angeles, CA 90004, 323-466-6969

Ebell Club of Los Angeles 743 S. Lucerne Blvd., Los Angeles, CA 90005, 323-931-1277

route summary

1. Begin at the corner of Beverly Blvd. and Larchmont Blvd.
2. Head south on Larchmont Blvd.
3. Cross 3rd St. and then turn left.
4. Turn right on Plymouth Blvd.
5. Turn right on Wilshire Blvd.
6. Turn right on Lucerne Blvd.
7. Turn right on 4th St.
8. Turn left on Windsor Blvd.
9. Carefully cross 3rd St., and then continue across 2nd St.
10. Turn left on 1st St.
11. At the intersection of Beachwood Dr., veer left to remain on 1st St., crossing Gower St. and returning to Larchmont Blvd.
12. Turn right on Larchmont and head one block back to Beverly Blvd. where you started.

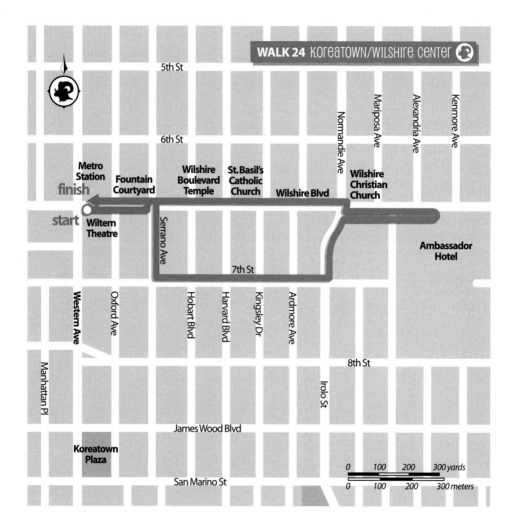

5th St

6th St

Mariposa Ave

Alexandria Ave

Kenmore Ave

Normandie Ave

Metro Station

finish

Fountain Courtyard

Wilshire Boulevard Temple

St. Basil's Catholic Church

Wilshire Blvd

Wilshire Christian Church

start **Wiltern Theatre**

Serrano Ave

7th St

Ambassador Hotel

Western Ave

Oxford Ave

Hobart Blvd

Harvard Blvd

Kingsley Dr

Ardmore Ave

8th St

Irolo St

Manhattan Pl

James Wood Blvd

Koreatown Plaza

San Marino St

0   100   200   300 yards

0   100   200   300 meters

24 Koreatown/Wilshire Center: Modern Korean Culture Meets Los Angeles History

BOUNDARIES: **Western Ave., Wilshire Blvd., Catalina St., 7th St.**
THOMAS GUIDE COORDINATES: **Map 633; H2**
DISTANCE: **Approx. 1½ miles**
DIFFICULTY: **Easy**
PARKING: **Metered street parking is available on Western Ave.**

The area known as Koreatown or Wilshire Center truly has it all—historical buildings, a plethora of dining and shopping options, a giant spa and sports club, and a sizzling nighttime scene. The neighborhood even features two convenient Metro stations—one at Wilshire and Western, where this walk begins, and another at Wilshire and Normandie, making it easy to get here and spend both day and night without worrying about parking fees (or designating a driver, should that become an issue). While the area is home to a mostly Korean-American population and many of the businesses primarily cater to Korean-speaking clientele, it has plenty to offer anyone else looking for an adventure, a dose of Los Angeles history, or a taste of authentic Korean culture.

● **Begin at the corner of Wilshire and Western boulevards. The Wilshire/Western Metro station is located at the northeast corner, and the striking Wiltern Theatre building is directly across the street. This green terra cotta Art Deco structure opened as an office building and movie theatre in 1931, and has since been renovated and declared a Los Angeles Historic Cultural Monument. Today the venue hosts a variety of performances, from comedians to garage bands. Take a minute to check out the underside of the flashy metal and neon marquee, which is decorated with an ornate sunburst design in plaster, and the beautiful carved mahogany doors that open into the theatre lobby.**

Head east on the south side of Wilshire, passing by Opus Bar & Grill, a posh new nightspot occupying the former space of retro-style jazz supper club, Atlas. Opus serves "modern California steak and seafood" and boasts one of the largest bars in Los Angeles.

The Aroma Spa and Sports Center occupies the southeast corner of the intersection with Serrano Ave.; its *Blade Runner*-esque electronic billboard lures passersby to try out the exclusive club's saunas, spa treatments, 4-story driving range, and other sports facilities.

● Cross back over to the north side of Wilshire Blvd. at Serrano and continue to head east. You'll pass the Wilshire Boulevard Temple on the northeast corner of Wilshire and Hobart. Built in 1929, this striking Byzantine-influenced structure is listed in the U.S. Register of Historic Places. The building's exterior is dominated by a massive dome 100 feet in diameter. If the synagogue is open to the public at the time of your visit, you should take time to explore the inside, which is decorated in gold and black Italian marble and features murals depicting the biblical story of creation.

After crossing Harvard Blvd. you'll come upon St. Basil's Catholic Church (1969), an imposing building whose vertical concrete panels are interspersed with jagged columns of colorful stained glass, giving it the slightly discordant feel of a Picasso painting.

BCD Tofu House is located on the southeast corner of Wilshire and Kingsley Dr. Here you can get a table full of *banchan* (assorted Korean salads and pickles) to go with your delicious bubbling bowl of *soon* (a flavorful stew served with tofu and your choice of meat, fish, or vegetables), all for under ten bucks...and it's even open 24 hours.

● At the northeast corner of Wilshire and Normandie Ave. is the Wilshire Christian Church, an ornate Romanesque structure built in 1927. Cross Normandie to the south side of Wilshire and continue to head east. From this side of the street, you have a better vantage point of the white Art Deco building just east of Wilshire Christian Church, which houses the Consulate General of the Republic of Indonesia. On your right, you'll pass by a variety of small, inexpensive eateries. This area is bustling with office workers on the weekdays; worthwhile lunch spots here include Wasabi for Japanese food, Mama Mia for Italian, and Café Metro for toasty sandwiches and hearty salads.

After crossing Mariposa Ave., you'll notice Wilshire Center's tallest structure, the Equitable building, towering on the opposite side of the boulevard. The Wilshire Center Farmers Market takes place on Mariposa north of Wilshire every Friday from 11:30 A.M. to 3:00 P.M., and is a wonderful place to pick up lunch, produce, nuts, flowers, and miscellaneous stuff such as handbags and designer jeans of questionable authenticity.

The northeast corner of Wilshire and Alexandria is the former site of the first of the legendary hat-shaped Brown Derby restaurants, but the site is now occupied by a cheesy-looking strip mall (named "Brown Derby Plaza" in honor of the former Hollywood Golden Age hot spot). Just east of the plaza are the 1920s-era Gaylord Apartments, named for Henry Gaylord Wilshire, the millionaire who developed what is now called MacArthur Park (located in what is now a high-crime neighborhood a little over a mile east of here). According to popular lore, Wilshire Blvd. was so-named because Mr. Wilshire would only allow a boulevard to bisect his property if it bore his name.

On the south side of the street is the Ambassador Hotel, former playground for Hollywood's rich and famous and the infamous site of Robert F. Kennedy's assassination. The hotel and its Cocoanut Grove nightclub opened in 1921 and enjoyed decades of fame as a beautiful people's mecca before Sirhan Sirhan killed Robert F. Kennedy there

Wilshire Boulevard

on June 5th, 1968. The now-shuttered hotel stands behind a chain link fence, the subject of a lawsuit filed by several Los Angeles preservation and neighborhood organizations. An elementary school is planned for the site, but the question remains as to how many of the Ambassador's original historic structures will be preserved. In front of the hotel, a sign on the median declares this stretch of Wilshire Blvd. to be the Robert F. Kennedy Memorial Parkway.

● Retrace your steps back to Normandie and turn left on Normandie Ave./Irolo St. Another historic apartment building, the Piccadilly, is located at 682 S. Irolo St.

● Turn right on 7th St. This residential street is occupied for the most part with anonymous apartment buildings. One notable exception is the cute courtyard apartment building at 3530 W. 7th St.—its rounded corners and retro 50s-style architecture bring to mind the fenders of a classic automobile.

● Turn right on Serrano Ave. You'll notice the netted driving range of Aroma Spa and Sports on your right. The Koreatown branch of the Los Angeles public library is on your left.

● Cross Wilshire Blvd. and turn left. The curved twin towers of the Wilshire Colonnade office complex on your right are built around a gorgeous circular fountain courtyard— a nice place to enjoy a sandwich or an iced coffee from the Starbucks across the street.

● Continue for two blocks to your starting point at the corner of Wilshire and Western.

POINTS OF INTEREST

Wiltern Theatre 3790 Wilshire Blvd, Los Angeles, CA 90010, 213-380-5005

Opus Bar & Grill 3760 Wilshire Blvd., Los Angeles, CA 90010, 213-738-1600

Aroma Spa and Sports 3680 Wilshire Blvd., Los Angeles, CA 90010, 213-387-0212

Wilshire Boulevard Temple 3663 Wilshire Blvd., Los Angeles, CA 90010, 213-388-2401

St. Basil's Catholic Church 3611 Wilshire Blvd., Los Angeles, CA, 213-381-6191

BCD Tofu House 3575 Wilshire Blvd., Los Angeles, CA 90010, 213-382-6677

Wilshire Christian Church 634 S. Normandie Ave., Los Angeles, CA 90005, 213-382-6337

Wilshire Center Farmers Market Mariposa Ave. just north of Wilshire Blvd.
Fridays 11:30 A.M. to 3:00 P.M.

Ambassador Hotel 3400 Wilshire Blvd., Los Angeles, CA 90010

ROUTE SUMMARY

1. Begin at the corner of Wilshire and Western boulevards and head east on the south side of Wilshire.

2. Cross to the north side of Wilshire Blvd. at Serrano Ave. and continue to head east.

3. Cross Normandie back to the south side of Wilshire and continue to head east.

4. Retrace your steps back to Normandie and turn left on Normandie Ave./Irolo St.

5. Turn right on 7th St.

6. Turn right on Serrano Ave.

7. Cross Wilshire Blvd. and turn left.

8. Continue for two blocks to your starting point at the corner of Wilshire and Western.

Wilshire Christian Church

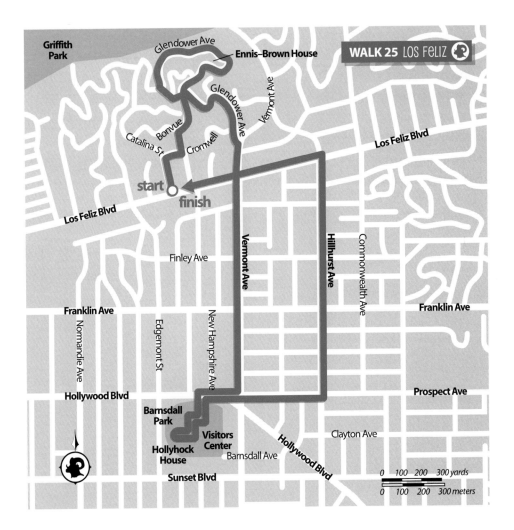

Griffith
Park

Glendower Ave

Ennis–Brown House

Glendower Ave

Vermont Ave

Bonvue

Cromwell

Catalina St

Los Feliz Blvd

start

finish

Los Feliz Blvd

Vermont Ave

Hillhurst Ave

Commonwealth Ave

Finley Ave

Franklin Ave

Franklin Ave

Normandie Ave

Edgemont St

New Hampshire Ave

Hollywood Blvd

Prospect Ave

Barnsdall
Park

Visitors
Center

Clayton Ave

Hollyhock
House

Barnsdall Ave

Hollywood Blvd

Sunset Blvd

0   100   200   300 yards

0   100   200   300 meters

25 LOS FELIZ: WRIGHT'S ARCHITECTURAL GEMS AND SWINGERS' FAVORITE NIGHT SPOTS

BOUNDARIES: **Edgemont St., Glendower Ave., Hillhurst Ave., Sunset Blvd.**
THOMAS GUIDE COORDINATES: **Map 594; A3**
DISTANCE: **Approx. 1½ to 3½ miles (depending on route chosen)**
DIFFICULTY: **Strenuous**
PARKING: **Free street parking is available on Catalina St.**

Los Feliz is a charming and vibrant neighborhood that lies just northeast of Hollywood. Much of the area, particularly the homes in the hills to the north, is very exclusive in terms of property values, and the rest of the region is quickly gentrifying as homebuyers come to appreciate the neighborhood's proximity to both the wilderness of Griffith Park and the action of Hollywood and Silver Lake. Fans of Doug Liman's 1996 movie *Swingers* will also recognize a couple of the night spots featured prominently in the film, the Dresden restaurant and bar, and the Derby swing club, along Los Feliz' main drags.

This neighborhood is also notable for its architecture, in particular Frank Lloyd Wright's Ennis-Brown house, which is tucked high in the hills, and the architect's Hollyhock house, which sits just over a mile south in the seedier part of town. This route winds up into Los Feliz's affluent hilly residential area before taking an optional detour south through Los Feliz Village to Barnsdall Art Park, home of the Hollyhock house.

● Begin at the corner of Los Feliz Blvd. and Catalina St. and head north on Catalina. The quiet, magnolia-lined street features attractive, expensive-looking homes. If you look up to your left you'll see that Griffith Observatory is surprisingly close in the hills above. Notice the home at 2220, which features elaborate outdoor metal sculptures of a Native American in a full headdress and a cactus.

● Turn right on Cromwell Ave. and then look for the Berendo stairway on your left, across the street from 2251 Berendo St.

- Ascend the long stairway, which is shaded in places by overhanging oleander and bougainvillea bushes. About two thirds of the way up, you'll come to a landing with thoughtfully provided built-in benches.

- At the top of the stairs, turn right on Bonvue Ave. and follow the narrow road as it winds higher into the hills, keeping an eye out for cars around each sharp bend. This street has a very Mediterranean feel, with magnificent, two- and three-story Spanish homes built into the hill on the left.

- Eventually, you'll come to a split in the road. Continue straight on what is now Glendower Ave. You'll pass by a Rudolf Schindler-designed home at 2567, but you can't see much of the building apart from the shimmering green outer wall. A few doors down at 2587 is another eye-catching house; composed of metal and gray-concrete, the industrial-looking structure towers over the road, supported by sturdy-looking cement columns. Finally, at 2607 Glendower, you'll reach the start of Frank Lloyd Wright's imposing and innovative Ennis-Brown House, one of several of the architect's textile block designs in the LA area. This massive structure overlooks the Los Angeles basin below and is composed of cinder blocks carved with Mayan designs, giving it the look of an ancient fortress. The magnificent building is currently in a state of disrepair, and a season of unusually heavy rains have recently exacerbated the situation. It remains to be seen whether the landmark's planned multimillion-dollar renovation will ever see the light of day.

- Follow Glendower as it curves around the Ennis-Brown house, eventually lending a view of the north-facing façade of the home. For a small fee, you can arrange a tour of the spectacular interior of the house, which is perhaps most recognizable as Harrison Ford's character's home in *Blade Runner*, although it's been featured in many other films as well. Call 323-668-0234 for more information. Continue west on Glendower. The eclectic, architectural mix of homes on this high, sunny street boast spectacular views of the city below.

- Just before you reach 2763 Glendower, you'll see a signpost reading PUBLIC WALK. Descend these stairs down to Bryn Mawr Rd., pausing to admire the stunning vista of the hills to the northeast, and of the Ennis-Brown house to your left.

- Cross the cul-de-sac and continue down the next set of steps to Bonvue Ave. This stairway is enhanced by a colorful tiled mural that was funded by the Los Feliz neighbors association.

- At the bottom of the steps, cross the street to go straight on Bonvue. Follow the winding road past more beautiful homes as it gently leads down the hill.

- The road curves sharply to the right, becoming Glendower Ave. once again (avoid Glendower Pl., which branches off to the left). Continue to follow Glendower down the hill.

- Glendower merges with Vermont Ave., which leads up to the Greek Theatre, a moderate-sized outdoor concert venue. Continue south on Vermont.

- At this point, you can either turn right on Los Feliz Blvd. and head a few blocks west back to your starting point at Catalina St., or you can continue through Los Feliz Village to the Barnsdall Art Park, home of Frank Lloyd Wright's Hollyhock House. This optional addendum route is detailed below.

Addendum:

- Cross Los Feliz Blvd., and continue south on Vermont Ave. into Los Feliz Village. The first few blocks along Vermont consist mostly of apartment buildings and a few houses of worship. But after you cross Franklin Ave., it becomes more interesting. The thriving collection of shops and restaurants along the next few blocks includes the Electric Lotus Indian restaurant and adjacent Psychobabble coffeehouse; House of

Looking west from Barnsdall Art Park

Pies, a middling family restaurant with a huge selection of doughy desserts; Palermo Italian restaurant, where vino flows freely in the waiting lounge on busy nights; Fred 62, a retro diner for hipsters; independent Skylight Books and the Skylight Theatre; the Los Feliz 3 movie theatre; Squaresville vintage clothing store, the legendary Dresden restaurant and bar; and several more casual and upscale eateries, chic clothing shops and home décor boutiques. It's amazing how many commercial points of interest are crammed into this short stretch of street.

- Turn right on Prospect Ave., which merges with Hollywood Blvd. You have now entered the neighborhood dubbed Little Armenia.

- Cross the street at New Hampshire Ave. to enter Barnsdall Art Park on the south side of Hollywood Blvd. This innovative community arts center sits atop Olive Hill and is virtually hidden from the streets below. In addition to the Los Angeles Municipal Arts Gallery and Junior Arts Center, the park is home to another Frank Lloyd Wright masterpiece, the Hollyhock House.

- Ascend the stairs up into the park. Turn right at the road (following the sign for the Gallery Theatre), and then ascend the

DESIGNER NAME: FRANK LLOYD WRIGHT

Born in 1867, Frank Lloyd Wright is probably America's best-known architect, renowned for masterpieces as diverse as the Guggenheim Museum in New York City and the Fallingwater residence in western Pennsylvania. Inspired by the wide-open prairies of his birthplace in Wisconsin, Wright innovated the idea of open floor plans and organic design in residential architecture.

In the early 1920s, Wright pioneered his concrete textile block style in Southern California. This innovative technique involved building out of pre-manufactured, engraved concrete blocks that were inset with glass to allow light to filter indoors. One advantage of this system was affordability, as concrete blocks made a cheap, modular building material. There are four examples of Wright's textile block architecture in the Los Angeles area—the Ennis-Brown house in Los Feliz, the Millard house in Pasadena, and the Samuel Freeman and John Storer houses in the Hollywood Hills.

next set of steps on your left. You'll find yourself in a beautiful grassy park dotted with pine trees.

- If you'd like to learn more about the art programs at the park or pick up literature about the Hollyhock House, you can do so at the visitor's center on the left. Otherwise, continue straight along the path through the park, and then turn right to reach the Hollyhock House itself. This was Frank Lloyd Wright's first project in Los Angeles, pre-dating the Ennis-Brown house you visited earlier. Wright used this project to create a regionally appropriate architectural style, which he referred to as "California Romanza." This style interweaves indoor and outdoor space, making extensive use of rooftop terraces and enclosed gardens. After many years of renovation, the Hollyhock House is finally open to the public; call 323-644-6269 if you'd like to arrange a tour.

- After exploring the park, return down to Hollywood Blvd. the same way you came.

- Cross the street at New Hampshire and turn right to retrace your steps along Prospect Ave.

- Cross Vermont Ave. and continue east on Prospect, passing several old wooden houses and a collection of slightly run-down apartment buildings.

- Turn left on Hillhurst Ave. This isn't exactly a pretty street, but it does feature numerous restaurants, bars and coffeehouses that are popular with both locals and out-of-towners looking for an authentic "eastsider" experience. At 1760 you'll pass Home, a—you guessed it—*home*-style outdoor eatery that offers a few healthy twists on your traditional diner

Frank Lloyd Wrights Hollyhock House

menu. At 1831, you'll pass by Ye Rustic Inn, a dive bar in a strip mall that has proven inexplicably popular with trend-seeking scenesters, as well as neighborhood drunks. As you near Los Feliz Blvd., you'll come to Mexico City, a decent middle-price range eatery that serves stiff margaritas; Tangiers Lounge, a relatively new exotic hot spot; and finally, The Derby, the swing-dancing club immortalized in *Swingers*, the film that provided a humorous glimpse into the nightlife of Hollywood's struggling actors on the brink of the late-'90s swing-dancing craze.

● Turn left on Los Feliz Blvd. After crossing Vermont Ave., the homes on either side of the street become increasingly opulent. Continue for three more short blocks back to your starting point at the corner of Los Feliz and Catalina St.

POINTS OF INTEREST

Ennis-Brown House 2607 Glendower Ave., Los Angeles, CA 90027, 323-668-0234 (Call to schedule a tour)

Barnsdall Art Park/Hollyhock House 4800 Hollywood Blvd., Los Angeles, CA 90027, 323-644-6269 (Call to schedule a tour)

Psychobabble 1866 N. Vermont Ave., Los Angeles, CA 90027, 323-664-7500

Electric Lotus 4656 Franklin Ave., Los Angeles, CA 90027, 323-953-0040

Palermo Italian Restaurant 1858 N. Vermont Ave., Los Angeles, CA 90027, 323-663-1178

Fred 62 1850 N. Vermont Ave., Los Angeles, CA 90027, 323-667-0062

Skylight Books 1818 N. Vermont Ave., Los Angeles, CA 90027, 323-660-1175

Dresden Restaurant and Bar 1760 N. Vermont Ave., Hollywood, CA 90027, 323-665-4294

Home Restaurant 1760 Hillhurst Ave., Los Angeles, CA 90027, 323-669-0211

Tangiers Lounge 2138 Hillhurst Ave., Los Angeles, CA 90027, 323-666-8666

Mexico City 2121 Hillhurst Ave., Los Angeles, CA 90027, 323-661-7227

The Derby 4500 Los Feliz Blvd., Los Angeles, CA 90027, 323-663-8979

route summary

1. Begin at the corner of Los Feliz Blvd. and Catalina St. and head north on Catalina.
2. Turn right on Cromwell Ave.
3. Ascend the stairway opposite 2251 Berendo St.
4. At the top of the stairs, turn right on Bonvue Ave.
5. Continue straight on Glendower Ave.
6. Follow Glendower as it curves around the Ennis-Brown House.
7. Descend the stairway next to 2763 Glendower.
8. Cross the cul-de-sac and continue down the next set of steps.
9. At the bottom of the steps, cross the street and continue straight on Bonvue.
10. Follow the road as it curves sharply to the right, becoming Glendower Ave.
11. Glendower merges with Vermont Ave. Continue south on Vermont.
12. Turn right on Los Feliz to return to starting point at Catalina St. or continue on the following optional addendum.

Addendum:

13. Cross Los Feliz Blvd., and continue south on Vermont Ave.
14. Turn right on Prospect Ave., which merges with Hollywood Blvd.
15. Cross the street at New Hampshire Ave. to enter Barnsdall Art Park on the south side of Hollywood Blvd.
16. Ascend the stairs up into the park. Turn right at the road, and then ascend the next set of steps on your left.
17. Continue straight along the path through the park, and then turn right to reach the Hollyhock House.
18. Return down to Hollywood Blvd. the same way you came.
19. Cross the street at New Hampshire and turn right to retrace your steps along Prospect Ave.
20. Cross Vermont Ave. and continue east on Prospect.
21. Turn left on Hillhurst Ave.
22. Turn left on Los Feliz Blvd. and walk several blocks back to your starting point at Catalina St.

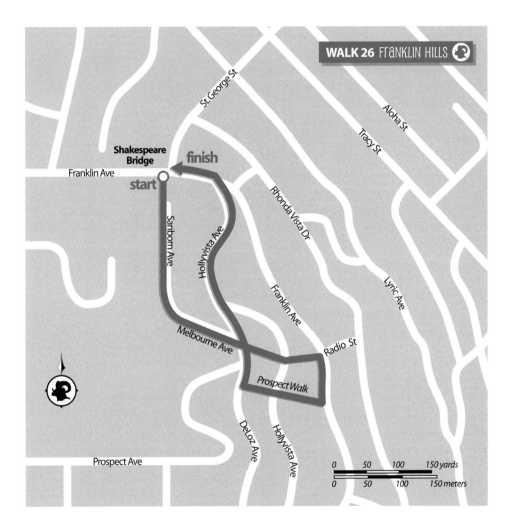

WALK 26 FRANKLIN HILLS

St. George St

Aloha St

Tracy St

Shakespeare
Bridge

finish

Franklin Ave

start

Sanborn Ave

Hollyvista Ave

Rhonda Vista Dr

Franklin Ave

Lyric Ave

Melbourne Ave

Radio St

Prospect Walk

DeLoz Ave

Hollyvista Ave

Prospect Ave

0   50   100   150 yards
0   50   100   150 meters

26 Franklin Hills:
what lies on the other side of the bridge

BOUNDARIES: **Franklin Ave., Fountain Ave., Talmadge St., Hyperion Ave.**
THOMAS GUIDE COORDINATES: **Map 594; B3**
DISTANCE: **Approx. ½ mile**
DIFFICULTY: **Moderate**
PARKING: **Free street parking is available on the north side of Franklin Ave. east of the Shakespeare Bridge.**

Nestled between Los Feliz and Silver Lake, Franklin Hills is another of central Los Angeles' endearing hilly neighborhoods. This residential area was developed in the 1920s as a quiet community centrally located in the midst of the sprawling metro area, and today retains an old-fashioned, neighborly quality that is lacking in many of LA's newer developments. This impression is reinforced by the two very long concrete stairways that connect the region's winding streets, giving neighbors relatively easy walking access to one another's homes, while at the same time keeping their hearts in great condition, no doubt.

● Begin just east of the Shakespeare Bridge on Franklin Ave. The distinctive white structure was built in 1926 and bridged the way, so to speak, for the charming residential neighborhood of Franklin Hills. On the south side of the street, just past the house that sits immediately east of the bridge, you'll notice steps leading down just beyond the sign for St. George St. Descend this staircase, which is shaded with ficus and bougainvillea.

● You'll emerge into the cul-de-sac at the north end of Sanborn Ave. Continue south on Sanborn; most of the homes on this street are simple and modern in design, and a few are painted in vibrant colors. You'll pass a community garden on your right, planted by the neighbors with a variety of vegetables. Behind the garden is a community picnic area and playground.

● Follow the road as it curves to the left, becoming Melbourne. Most of the homes here are modest and well maintained, and exhibit a variety of architectural styles—

traditional, Spanish Colonial Revival, English country cottage. The Spanish-style home at 3916 Melbourne is especially lovely, with cheerful yellow paint, gorgeous tile work and an elegant fountain in the front yard. Next door at 3912 is a dramatically different style of home—a fairy tale English cottage with a deeply sloping wood-shingled roof and diamond-pane windows.

- Continue straight across DeLoz Ave. and look for the sign for the Radio Walk steps just to the right of 1856 DeLoz. Ascend the long staircase, which is overgrown and covered with a thick layer of dead leaves, giving it the feel of a secret passage. Cross Hollyvista Ave. and continue up the next flight of steps, which is more heavily shaded than the first half of Radio Walk. Ivy blankets the sloping backyards of the homes on either side of the stairs.

- You'll emerge on Franklin Ave., just north of Radio St. Turn right to cross Radio St. and continue on Franklin. You can catch occasional glimpses of Griffith Observatory between the houses on your right.

- Turn right just past 3818 Franklin to descend the Prospect Walk stairway, pausing at the top of steps to admire the eastward view along Hollywood Blvd., which stretches out below. Cross Hollyvista Ave. again and continue down the next set of steps.

- When you reach DeLoz Ave., turn right instead of descending the last flight of Prospect Walk. DeLoz is a quiet, sunny street with lots of cute Spanish-style houses and French and English cottages, as well as many traditional homes. The houses built into the steeply sloping hill on the right appear to be much larger than those on the left side of the street, but appearances can be deceiving with these hillside homes.

- Cross Prospect Ave. and continue on DeLoz Ave., passing the Radio Walk steps you ascended earlier. This is a bit of a tricky intersection, as it marks the connection of DeLoz, Prospect, and Melbourne, so just be sure to continue straight ahead on your path, rather than wandering off on one of these offshoots.

- DeLoz Ave. ends when it merges with Hollyvista Ave. Continue straight on what is now Hollyvista. At 2024 you'll notice a delightful home with blue awnings, a wood-shingled roof and a white picket fence—the picture of blissful domesticity. A large, austere, modern home sits in stark contrast at 2100 Hollyvista.

● Turn left at the next intersection to head west on Franklin Ave., and you will shortly return to your starting point just east of the Shakespeare Bridge.

route summary

1. Begin just east of the Shakespeare Bridge on Franklin Ave. Descend the stairway on the south side of the street next to the street sign for St. George St.

2. You'll emerge into the cul-de-sac at the north end of Sanborn Ave. Continue south on Sanborn.

3. Follow the road as it curves to the left, becoming Melbourne.

4. Continue straight across DeLoz Ave. and ascend the Radio Walk steps just to the right of 1856 DeLoz. Cross Hollyvista Ave. and continue up the next flight of steps.

5. You'll emerge on Franklin Ave., just north of Radio St. Turn right to cross Radio St. and continue on Franklin.

6. Turn right just past 3818 Franklin to descend the Prospect Walk stairway. Cross Hollyvista Ave. again and continue down the next set of steps.

7. When you reach DeLoz Ave., turn right instead of descending the last flight of Prospect Walk.

8. Cross Prospect Ave. and continue straight on DeLoz Ave.

9. DeLoz Ave. ends when it merges with Hollyvista Ave. Continue straight on what is now Hollyvista.

10. Turn left at the next intersection to head west on Franklin Ave. to return to your starting point just east of the Shakespeare Bridge.

Shakespeare Bridge

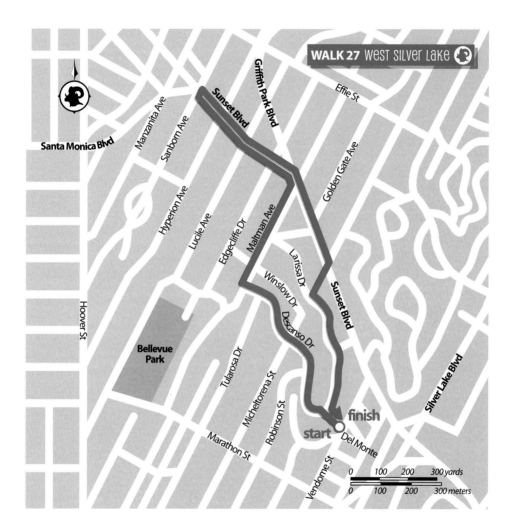

Effie St

Griffith Park Blvd

Sunset Blvd

Golden Gate Ave

Santa Monica Blvd

Manzanita Ave

Sanborn Ave

Hyperion Ave

Lucile Ave

Edgecliffe Dr

Maltman Ave

Larissa Dr

Winslow Dr

Descanso Dr

Sunset Blvd

Hoover St

Bellevue
Park

Tularosa Dr

Micheltorena St

Robinson St

Silver Lake Blvd

start

finish

Del Monte

Marathon St

Vendome St

| 0 | 100 | 200 | 300 yards |
| 0 | 100 | 200 | 300 meters |

27 WeST SILVer Lake: SUNSET JUNCTION, WHAT'S YOUR FUNCTION?

BOUNDARIES: **Sunset Blvd., Silver Lake Blvd., Marathon St., Hoover St.**
THOMAS GUIDE COORDINATES: **Map 594; C6**
DISTANCE: **Approx. 1¾ miles**
DIFFICULTY: **Moderate**
PARKING: **Free street parking is available on Vendome St.**

A short stretch of Sunset Blvd. in Silver Lake perfectly illustrates the unique dichotomy of this neighborhood. The intersection of Santa Monica and Sunset boulevards, known as Sunset Junction, illustrates the unique blending of cultures so prevalent in Silver Lake—that of predominantly white rockers, hipsters, and scruffy artists who have flocked to the area in recent years, and the Mexican-American families who have lived here for generations. Once a year in the summer, the Sunset Junction Neighborhood Alliance puts on a street fair to celebrate this diversity. This is a huge event that draws big crowds with performances by local bands and an endless variety of vendors hawking clothing, jewelry, incense and, of course, lots of great stuff to eat.

● Begin at the intersection of Vendome St. and Del Monte Dr., just south of Sunset Blvd. On the west side of Vendome, across from the intersection of Del Monte, are the famous Music Box Steps, immortalized in Laurel and Hardy's 1932 short film *The Music Box*, in which the duo attempted to move a piano up the 133 steps, and hilarity ensued.

● Ascend the staircase to Descanso Dr., climb another short flight of steps up to the second level of the split street, and then turn left.

● Follow Descanso Dr. as it curves around to the right. The island that divides the street into two narrow one-directional traffic lanes is pleasantly landscaped with trees and flowers. On the northwest corner of Descanso Dr. and Micheltorena St. is a cheerful home painted with sunflowers; the front gate is decorated with a mosaic angel. Continue on Descanso across Micheltorena, noticing how the homes become more attractively maintained as you head farther up the hill.

- When you reach the end of Descanso Dr., turn right on Maltman Ave. Follow the road over the crest of the hill, and then all the way down to Sunset Blvd.

- Turn left on Sunset Blvd. On the opposite side of the street are El Conquistador, a vibrant Mexican restaurant that serves up a mean margarita; Tantra, a sultry Indian eatery; and Cirxa, where you can feast on decadent Cajun and Creole fare.

Once you cross Lucile Ave., the abundance of funky specialty shops is a sure sign of this neighborhood's uniquely hip style of gentrification. Trendy home furnishings stores line the northeast side of Sunset, while the southwest side features an eclectic array of shops and cafes. Upscale gift shops and baby boutiques sit next door to vintage clothing stores and the Surplus Value Center, where you can stock up on Dickies gear and fatigues. Cute names like Den of Antiquity, Pull My Daisy, and Eat Well signal the creativity of Silver Lake's small business owners.

As you approach Sanborn Ave. you'll notice the Sunset Junction sign over the sidewalk. The cluster of shops on the corner, several of which are hidden from the street, include the Cheese Store of Silver Lake, a hair salon, and a flower shop.

- Turn around at Sanborn Ave. to retrace your steps back to Maltman Ave. Cross Maltman and continue along Sunset Blvd., passing the charming Madame Matisse café on the corner, and Millie's, a no-frills diner frequented by the neighborhood's edgier artists and rockers, located at 3524. The strip mall next door is home to Alegria on Sunset, whose unassuming exterior belies the vibrant atmosphere within— this is an excellent spot for *aguas frescas* and authentic Mexican specialties drenched in *mole* sauce.

- When you reach Micheltorena St., look for the short sidewalk that leads to a long stairway on your right; an interesting wooden rotunda sits in the enclosed yard to the left of the sidewalk. Ascend the Micheltorena steps as far as Larissa Dr. and turn left (don't climb the second flight of steps).

- Continue along Larissa, keeping to the right when the road splits, at which point it becomes Descanso Dr.

- Follow Descanso Dr. uphill, keeping an eye out for the short flight of steps that cuts across the meridian on your left.

- When you come to these steps, descend and then cross the other side of the street back to the Music Box Steps, which you climbed earlier. Head back downstairs to return to your starting point on Vendome St.

Sunset Junction sign

POINTS OF INTEREST

Surplus Value Center 3828 W. Sunset Blvd., Los Angeles, CA 90026, 323-662-8132

Eat Well 3916 W. Sunset Blvd., Los Angeles, CA 90029, 323-664-1624

Millie's 3524 W. Sunset Blvd., Los Angeles, CA 90026, 323-664-0404

Madame Matisse 3536 W. Sunset Blvd., Los Angeles, CA 90026, 323-662-4862

Alegria on Sunset 3510 W. Sunset Blvd., Los Angeles, CA 90026, 323-913-1422

Casbah Café 3900 W. Sunset Blvd., Los Angeles, CA 90029, 323-664-7000

Cirxa 3719 W. Sunset Blvd., Los Angeles, CA 90026, 323-663-1048

Tantra 3705 W. Sunset Blvd., Los Angeles, CA 90026, 323-663-8268

Café Stella 3932 W. Sunset Blvd., Los Angeles, CA 90029, 323-666-0265

El Conquistador 3701 W. Sunset Blvd., Los Angeles, CA 90026, 323-666-0265

Cheese Store of Silver Lake 3926 W. Sunset Blvd., Los Angeles, CA 90029, 323-644-7511

Den of Antiquity 3902 W. Sunset Blvd., Los Angeles, CA 90029, 323-666-3881

Pull My Daisy 3908 W. Sunset Blvd., Los Angeles, CA 90029, 323-663-0608

route summary

1. Begin at the intersection of Vendome St. and Del Monte Dr., just south of Sunset Blvd.

2. Ascend the staircase on your right to Descanso Dr., climb another short flight of steps up to the second level of the split street, and then turn left.

3. Follow Descanso Dr. as it curves around to the right.

4. When you reach the end of Descanso Dr., turn right on Maltman Ave.

5. Turn left on Sunset Blvd.

6. Turn around at Sanborn Ave. to retrace your steps back to Maltman Ave. Cross Maltman and continue on Sunset Blvd.

7. Turn right at Micheltorena St. following the sidewalk that leads to the long stairway. Ascend the Micheltorena steps as far as Larissa Dr. and turn left (don't climb the second flight of steps).

8. Continue on Larissa, keeping to the right when the road splits, at which point it becomes Descanso Dr.

9. Follow Descanso Dr. uphill, keeping an eye out for the short flight of steps that cuts across the meridian on your left.

10. Descend the stairs and cross the street to reach the Music Box Steps, heading back downstairs to return to your starting point on Vendome St.

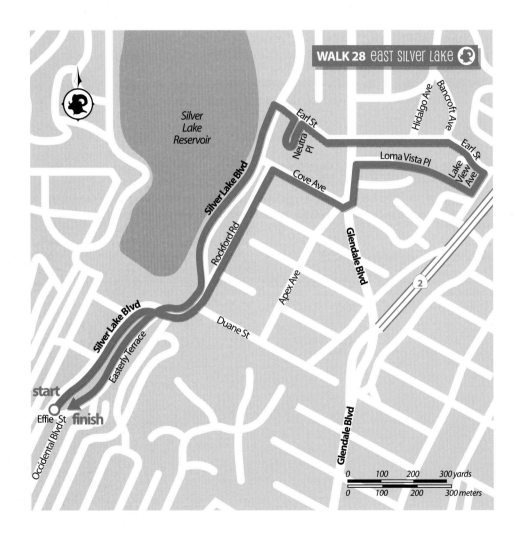

Silver
Lake
Reservoir

Earl St

Hidalgo Ave

Bancroft Ave

Earl St

Neutra Pl

Loma Vista Pl

Lake View Ave

Silver Lake Blvd

Cove Ave

Rockford Rd

Glendale Blvd

2

Apex Ave

Silver Lake Blvd

Duane St

Easterly Terrace

Glendale Blvd

start

Effie St finish

Occidental Blvd

0   100   200   300 yards
0   100   200   300 meters

28 east Silver Lake: Modern Masterpieces above Sparkling Waters

BOUNDARIES: **Silver Lake Blvd., Glendale Blvd., 2 Freeway, Earl St.**
THOMAS GUIDE COORDINATES: **Map 594; D6**
DISTANCE: **Approx. 2 miles**
DIFFICULTY: **Strenuous**
PARKING: **Free street parking is available on Silver Lake Blvd.**

Silver Lake is a popular destination for Los Angeles' gay, artist, and musician communities, as well as for culturally diverse young families who have found that the neighborhood's picturesque hills and lively community spirit make it a desirable alternative to more cost-prohibitive areas such as the west side or the Hollywood Hills. This route will start in one of the neighborhood's destinations for daytime shopping and nighttime music, before climbing into the hills overlooking the Silver Lake Reservoir, where you'll discover rustic, overgrown walkways and homes that seem so far removed from LA's urban sprawl you'll hardly believe you're only a few minutes from downtown.

- Begin on Silver Lake Blvd. near the intersection with Effie St. For the most part, Silver Lake Blvd. is lined with houses and apartment buildings, but this short stretch features a collection of cute stores and cafes. Yolk, a chic gift shop where you can choose from a selection of uniquely hip merchandise such as children's toys, home decorations, architectural books, and yummy-scented candles, sits at 1626 Silver Lake Blvd. Next to Yolk is a home interiors store called Rubbish. This fashionable stretch of Silver Lake Blvd. also features the Heartbeat House dance workout studio at 1638.

- Head north on Silver Lake Blvd. At 1700 you'll come to Netty's, a funky home-style café with a sign declaring it was "serving Silver Lake before it was hip." Next door to Netty's is the Back Door Bakery and Café, an informal eatery with an outdoor patio popular with locals and their dogs. Spaceland, Silver Lake's main venue for live music from about-to-break bands, resides at 1717 Silver Lake Blvd. After crossing

Van Pelt Pl., you'll see where all of the dogs at Back Door came from—the Silver Lake Recreation Center and off-leash dog park sits at the base of the reservoir for which the neighborhood is named on the east side of the street. At 1886 Silver Lake Blvd. is a charming Tudor Revival house with a little tower that looks like it belongs in a fairy tale.

● After crossing Duane St., you'll come to a fork in the road where Rockford Rd. splits off from Silver Lake Blvd. to the right. Follow Rockford uphill. At 1948 Rockford is a striking modern home with a shallow peaked roof and jutting eaves over the garage that give the structure a top-heavy feel. Next door is a mysterious gated compound with a long stairway that presumably leads up to Apex Ave., which runs parallel to Rockford. You can catch occasional glimpses down to the sparkling blue reservoir between the houses on your left.

● Turn right on Cove Ave. Up ahead, you'll see a wide stairway—ascend the shallow steps, stopping to turn and admire the spectacular vista of the reservoir, the hills of Silver Lake and, in the distance, the Hollywood sign, and the dome of Griffith Park observatory. The homes on either side of the stairway are concealed by lush vegetation—palm trees, ivy, and succulents.

● At the top of the stairs, continue to head straight on Cove for one more block to Apex Ave. and turn left, following it down the hill toward Glendale Blvd. You'll notice that, despite the picturesque surroundings, some of the homes in this neighborhood are unkempt, with peeling paint and junk-strewn yards.

● At the diagonal intersection of Apex Ave. and Glendale Blvd., *carefully* cross Glendale (there is no crosswalk) and then turn left to head north.

● Turn right on Loma Vista Pl. At 2384 you'll notice a whimsical house with wavy walls and colorful mosaics that bring to mind the architecture of Antonio Gaudi.

● Ascend the steps at the end of the cul-de-sac. This combination stairway and walkway may very well be the longest in Los Angeles. Heavily overgrown in places and lined on either side with bungalows and farmhouses, the Loma Vista Pl. path has a distinctly rural feel. Eventually, the shady staircase widens and starts to head downhill. At this point, you can hear the dull roar of the 2 Freeway just ahead, startling you back into awareness of your urban surroundings.

- When you reach the end of Loma Vista Pl. stairs, turn left on Lake View Ave., which runs right next to the freeway. Across the freeway you can see the hills of Elysian Park, LA's second largest urban wilderness, after Griffith Park.

- Turn left on Earl St. Bear right to remain on Earl St., avoiding Earl Ct.

- When you reach the intersection of Earl St. and Bancroft Ave., look for a stairway near the street sign. Ascend the Earl St. steps, an extensive, zig-zagging stairway that is quite overgrown in some places, giving it a wild feel.

- At the top of the stairs, continue straight on Earl St., which heads downhill at a sharp angle after it crosses Hidalgo Ave. As you descend the hill toward Glendale Blvd., the reservoir comes into view once more. You'll notice that many of the homes are elevated above the street and concealed behind dense thickets of trees and ivy; the residents obviously value their privacy.

- Once again, *carefully* cross Glendale Blvd. and continue to head straight on Earl St. This stretch of Earl features several architecturally interesting houses. At 2425 is a lovely Spanish home with vibrant blue trim and a mailbox covered in brightly colored tile. At 2434 Earl St., you'll notice a stepped structure covered in weathered wood shingles. This is the Treetops triplex, which was designed in 1980 by Dion Neutra, son of acclaimed modernist architect Richard Neutra. Next door to the Treetops at

Richard Neutra house

the corner of Earl St. and Neutra Pl., shrouded by bamboo and trees, is the headquarters for the Institute for Survival Through Design, headed up by Dion Neutra himself.

- Turn left on Neutra Pl. This short cul-de-sac is a showcase for the architecture of Dion's father, famed first-generation modernist architect Richard Neutra. You can see examples of his work at 2218, 2200 and 2210 Neutra Pl. The O'Hara House at 2210 is particularly striking; perched high above the street to afford views of the reservoir through its giant picture windows, the structure is a study of geometric shapes in glass and wood.

- Return to Earl St. and turn left toward Silver Lake Blvd.

- Turn left on Silver Lake Blvd. You're now level with the reservoir just across the street. This stretch of the boulevard is rather pleasant, shaded with towering pines and eucalyptus trees. As you head south on Silver Lake, you'll pass by another string of Richard Neutra-designed homes on your left, from 2226 to 2238 Silver Lake Blvd.

- Continue to walk alongside the reservoir on Silver Lake Blvd. for just under half a mile. After crossing Rockford St., you'll retrace your steps from earlier for a cou-

DESIGNER NAME: RICHARD NEUTRA

Born in Vienna in 1892, Richard Neutra unaccountably came to be one of the leaders of the Southern California modern architecture movement. After training with Otto Wagner in Austria, Neutra was drawn to the United States by American architectural legend Frank Lloyd Wright, and eventually settled in California, where he worked closely with another Viennese-born Modernist icon, Rudolph Schindler. Neutra's signature designs usually consist of a light metal frame with a stucco or wood finish and extensive use of glass, creating an effect that manages to be both light and industrial. His buildings also take advantage of the region's amenable climate by carefully integrating residential landscapes into the structural design.

Neutra found Silver Lake to be LA's most open-minded neighborhood in terms of innovative architecture, so he built his home and studio in the hills overlooking the reservoir, and also designed several more houses in this neighborhood.

ple of short blocks before turning left on Easterly Terr. and leaving the noisy boulevard behind. Easterly Terr. is an elevated residential street that runs roughly parallel to Silver Lake Blvd. Large homes sit high above on the steep hill to your left, some teetering on stilts.

- When you reach the fork in the road at Occidental Blvd., go right to head downhill on Occidental.

- Turn right on Effie St. There's no street sign, but it is the first street you'll come to on Occidental Blvd.

- Follow Effie for one short block to Silver Lake Blvd., where you'll find yourself back at your starting point.

POINTS OF INTEREST

Yolk 1626 Silver Lake Blvd., Los Angeles, CA 90026, 323-660-4315

Rubbish 1627 Silver Lake Blvd., Los Angeles, CA 90026, 323-661-5575

Netty's 1700 Silver Lake Blvd, Los Angeles, CA 90026, 323-662-8655

Back Door Bakery 1710 Silver Lake Blvd, Los Angeles, CA 90026, 323-662-7927

Heartbeat House Dance Studio 1638 Silver Lake Blvd., Los Angeles, CA 90026, 323-660-6192

Spaceland 1717 Silverlake Blvd, Los Angeles, CA 90026, 323-662-7728

Silver Lake Recreation and Dog Park 1850 Silver Lake Blvd., Los Angeles, CA 90026, 323-644-3946

route summary

1. Begin at the intersection of Silver Lake Blvd. and Effie St.
2. Head north on Silver Lake Blvd.
3. Bear right on Rockford Rd.
4. Turn right on Cove Ave. and ascend the stairway.
5. Turn left on Apex Ave.
6. Turn left on Glendale Blvd.
7. Turn right on Loma Vista Pl.
8. Ascend the stairway/walkway and follow it back downhill.
9. Turn left on Lake View Ave.
10. Turn left on Earl St. and bear right to avoid Earl Ct.
11. Ascend the stairs at intersection with Bancroft Ave.
12. At the top of the stairs, continue straight on Earl St.
13. Cross Glendale Blvd. and continue on Earl St.
14. Turn left on Neutra Pl.
15. Return to Earl St. and turn left.
16. Turn left on Silver Lake Blvd.
17. Turn left on Easterly Terr.
18. Bear right on Occidental Blvd.
19. Turn right on Effie St.
20. Return to the starting point at the intersection of Effie St. and Silver Lake Blvd.

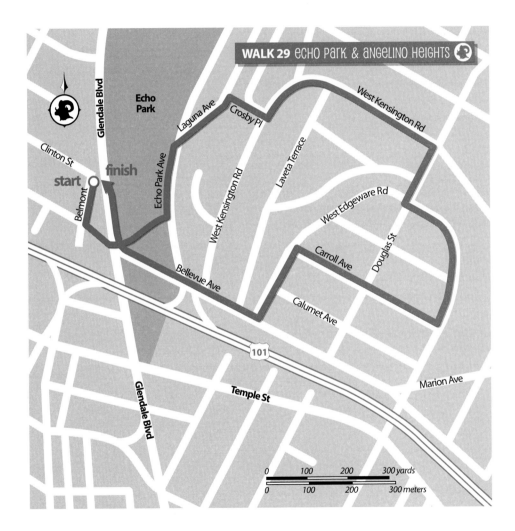

Echo Park

Clinton St

Glendale Blvd

Laguna Ave

Crosby Pl

West Kensington Rd

start

finish

Belmont

Echo Park Ave

West Kensington Rd

Laveta Terrace

West Edgeware Rd

Douglas St

Carroll Ave

Bellevue Ave

Calumet Ave

101

Glendale Blvd

Temple St

Marion Ave

| 0 | 100 | 200 | 300 yards |
| 0 | 100 | 200 | 300 meters |

29 ECHO PARK AND ANGELINO HEIGHTS: AN UNEXPECTED SLICE OF VICTORIANA

BOUNDARIES: **Alvarado St., Sunset Blvd., Bellevue Ave.**
THOMAS GUIDE COORDINATES: **Map 634; D1**
DISTANCE: **Approx. 2 miles**
DIFFICULTY: **Moderate**
PARKING: **Free street parking is available on Clinton St. (Pay attention to posted signs.)**

Echo Park is one of several east side neighborhoods populated by that uniquely LA combination of Latino families and twenty- to thirty-something hipsters. Located immediately northwest of downtown, this hilly region features some gorgeous homes, many with excellent views, and is convenient to many of the modish shopping/dining destinations that have popped up in the area, particularly along Sunset and Silver Lake Boulevards. Echo Park itself is also a draw—its picturesque lake is a convenient community gathering place and distinctive focal point of the region. Perhaps the most fascinating feature of this neighborhood, the gorgeous Victorian homes of Angelino Heights are located up on a hill just east of Echo Park Lake.

- Begin at the intersection of Clinton St. and Belmont Ave., where Clinton St. ends east of Alvarado St. Turn right to head south on Belmont Ave. You'll pass by a stairway at the end of Clinton, which leads down toward the Echo Park Lake.

- At the intersection of Bellevue Ave., turn left to follow the sidewalk that takes you to the steps leading down to Glendale Blvd. The walkway is marred somewhat by graffiti and litter, but nicely trimmed with bougainvillea and palm trees. Cross Glendale Blvd. at the bottom of the steps.

- Once across the street, follow the pathway on your left down into Echo Park and then bear right to continue on the path along the south end of the lake. Echo Park is a vibrant and scenic community center with a heavy Latino cultural influence, such as the *paleta* (popsicle) salesman circling the lake with his cart. Mothers push strollers along the path, as kids take the paddle boats out for a ride and older gentlemen cast fishing poles out into the placid green water. At the far end of the lake, several jets of water spout high into the air. Continue to follow the path up the east side of the lake, parallel to Echo Park Ave.

- When you reach the paddle boat rental area about halfway up the east side of the lake, follow the stairs on your right up out of the park and cross Echo Park Blvd. at the crosswalk.

- Continue on Laguna Ave., passing by a church on your left. This is a modest residential street, populated mostly with older apartment buildings.

- Ascend the Crosby Pl. stairway on your right (opposite 867 Laguna Ave.). The concrete steps are heavily graffiti-ed and bordered by overgrowth, but this vantage point affords a great view of the lake behind you. At the top of the steps, continue straight on Crosby Pl. A striking gray Colonial Revival duplex sits on the southwest corner of Crosby Pl. and West Kensington Rd. This is the first of many architecturally fascinating homes that you will encounter as you continue on your walk through Angelino Heights.

BACK STORY: L.A.'S VICTORIAN SUBURB

Before it was declared Los Angeles' very first Historic Preservation Overlay Zone in 1983, Angelino Heights had survived through boom and bust. Developers William W. Stilson and Everett E. Hall created this residential subdivision as one of the city's very first suburbs in 1886, a unique housing tract composed of ornate Queen Anne and Eastlake Victorian homes that was conveniently located on the outskirts of LA's then-bustling downtown area. Unfortunately, a banking recession in 1888 put a stop to the development, leaving about 50 of these amazing homes to admire today, most of which are concentrated on Carroll and Kellam Avenues. Kensington Road, which borders this timeless Victorian oasis, came to be populated with distinguished Craftsman houses during a second wave of development in the early 1900s. As a result, Angelino Heights now offers a rare selection of finely constructed, beautiful homes, and a combination of architectural styles that won't be found elsewhere in Los Angeles. The 1300 block of Carroll Avenue is listed on the National Register of Historic Places for its heavy concentration of Victorians, most of which have been lovingly restored and maintained by the current owners.

- Turn left on West Kensington Rd. Another charming Colonial Revival home sits at 1005 West Kensington. In stark contrast, a deep orange Spanish-style apartment building with a cactus garden in the front is right next door. Continue on West Kensington Rd. as it curves to the right, crossing Laveta Terrace. The houses on this street become larger and more elaborate as you head farther uphill; many of the Craftsmans date back to the early 1900s. You'll come to your first Victorian at 892 West Kensington Rd., looking incongruous among the many Craftsman and Colonial Revival homes.

- Turn right on Douglas St. and continue for about two blocks to West Edgeware Rd. A somber Victorian heavily shrouded by trees on the southwest corner of Douglas and West Edgeware has the look of a haunted house.

- Turn left on West Edgeware Rd. This street features a few historical Craftsman and Colonial Revival homes scattered among the mostly rundown apartment buildings that were built later in the century. As the road curves around to the south, a view of the nearby downtown skyscrapers opens up ahead.

- Turn right on Carroll Ave., where you'll be transported into another era. Developed as a suburban housing tract for Los Angeles' downtown professionals in the 1880s, the Queen Anne and Eastlake Victorian homes along the 1300 block of Carroll have been immaculately restored and maintained thanks to a devoted preservation effort, and are now listed on the National Register of Historic Places. The juxtaposition of these intricately ornamented homes with the sleek downtown high-rises that lie immediately beyond is a sight to see

Victorian home in Angelino Heights

indeed. This street makes an excellent Halloween destination, as nearly all of the residents get into the spirit by decking out their old-fashioned homes with giant spiderwebs and hanging dummies.

- At the end of Carroll Ave., turn left on West Edgeware Rd., where the quality of the residences deteriorates rapidly. Head down the hill toward the noisy 101 Freeway.

- Turn right on Bellevue Ave., which runs parallel to the freeway. As you cross Echo Park Ave., you'll see a swimming pool, part of the Echo Park Recreation Center, immediately adjacent to the freeway onramp. It seems like a bizarrely inappropriate location for a kids' pool. You'll pass by Echo Park Lake on your right and the rec center playground and picnic area, which is usually lively with some celebration or another, on your left.

- Cross Glendale Blvd. at the signal and then turn right on the other side to head toward the Clinton St. stairway you passed at the start of your walk. This is the second of three stairways along this block, the first being the Bellevue Ave. stairs you descended earlier.

- Ascend the Clinton St. steps, a double stairway that leads back up to the junction of Clinton St. and Belmont Ave., where you began your journey.

route summary

1. Begin at the intersection of Clinton St. and Belmont Ave., where Clinton St. ends east of Alvarado St. Turn right to head south on Belmont Ave.

2. At the intersection of Bellevue Ave., turn left to follow the sidewalk that takes to the steps leading down to Glendale Blvd. Cross Glendale Blvd. at the bottom of the steps.

3. Once across the street, follow the pathway on your left down into Echo Park and then bear right to continue on the path along the south end of the lake. Continue to follow the path up the east side of the lake, parallel to Echo Park Ave.

4. Exit the park at the stairs near the paddle boat rental area and cross Echo Park Blvd.

5. Continue on Laguna Ave.

6. Ascend the Crosby Pl. stairway on your right (opposite 867 Laguna Ave.). At the top of the steps, continue straight on Crosby Pl.

7. Turn left on West Kensington Rd.

8. Turn right on Douglas St.

9. Turn left on West Edgeware Rd.

10. Turn right on Carroll Ave.

11. Turn left on West Edgeware Rd.

12. Turn right on Bellevue Ave.

13. Cross Glendale Blvd. at the signal and turn right.

14. Ascend the Clinton St. stairway to return to your starting point.

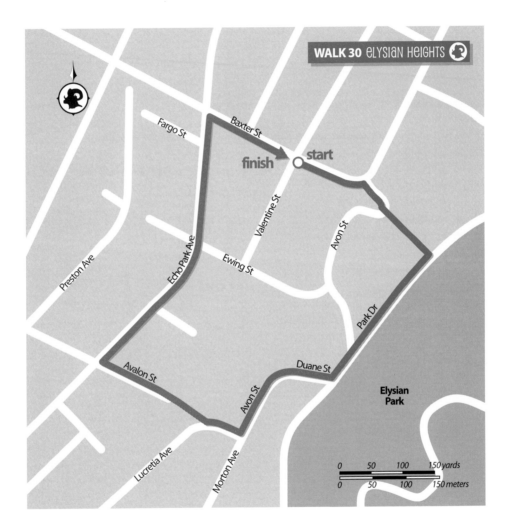

Fargo St

Baxter St

finish

start

Echo Park Ave

Valentine St

Avon St

Preston Ave

Ewing St

Park Dr

Avalon St

Avon St

Duane St

Elysian Park

Lucretia Ave

Morton Ave

| 0 | 50 | 100 | 150 yards |

| 0 | 50 | 100 | 150 meters |

30 ELYSIAN HEIGHTS: LOOKING DOWN ON LA'S OLDEST PUBLIC PARK

BOUNDARIES: **Alvarado St., Baxter St., Park Dr.,**
THOMAS GUIDE COORDINATES: **Map 564; F6**
DISTANCE: **Approx. ¾ mile**
DIFFICULTY: **Moderate**
PARKING: **Free street parking is available on Baxter St.**

Founded in 1781, Elysian Park is Los Angeles' second largest urban oasis (right behind Griffith Park). Its 600 acres are planted with native chaparral and eucalyptus and ficus trees, and provide hiking trails, picnic areas, and playing fields to the nature-craving residents of central and eastern Los Angeles. The park is also home to Dodger Stadium. The hilly neighborhood of Elysian Heights abuts the western border of the park, thus providing a delightful escape for residents who wish to forget for a little while that they live in one of the nation's most heavily populated cities.

● Begin at the intersection of Valentine St. and Baxter St. (east of Echo Park Ave.) and head east toward the hill. An elementary school is on your right. This is a peaceful residential neighborhood; the cute cottage-like homes on the left side of the street are lushly landscaped with assorted indigenous plant life: fruit trees, cactus, and more colorful floral varieties.

● Turn right on Avon St. At this point, the neighborhood starts to have an increasingly rustic feel, with fewer homes and more open space. This may be changing, however, as there are signs of new construction everywhere. Ascend the steps on your left, a very long zig-zagging stairway that appears to be carefully maintained—there are even new street lights installed alongside the steps. Up above on the hill are a few relatively new modern homes. At one point, a dirt path travels off across the grassy slope to your left, but you'll continue up the steps, stopping every once awhile to admire the stunning view behind you, which stretches from Century City to Griffith Park.

- Turn right at the top of the stairs onto Park Dr. Elysian Park is directly across the street, a lush green basin with dirt paths winding down to the bottom. This 600-acre park features an arboretum, countless dirt hiking paths, and picnic areas. Through the eucalyptus trees, you can catch an excellent view of downtown to the southeast. Joggers and dog-walkers travel the dirt path just a few yards below, and if you're so inclined, you can hop down the short slope and join them in exploring this big rustic oasis.

- Continue along Park Dr. to Duane St. and turn right. Duane has the feel of a narrow country lane as it curves downhill to the left and turns into Avon St.

- Turn right on Lucretia, and just after the road curves to the left, look for a narrow sidewalk on your right—follow it to the next stairway, nearly as long as the one you ascended earlier, which zig zags down to Avalon St. As you descend, admire more fabulous views all the way to the coast (on a clear day) to the west, and of the San Gabriel Mountains to the northeast.

- Continue straight on Avalon St. for one block to Echo Park Ave.

- Turn right on Echo Park Ave. The next few blocks are considerably less idyllic than the elevated portion of this walk; some of the houses are run down and the commercial options don't extend much beyond a liquor store and a hair salon.

- When you reach the elementary school near your starting point, turn right on Baxter St., and follow it back to the intersection with Valentine, where you began.

route summary

1. Begin at the intersection of Valentine St. and Baxter St., (east of Echo Park Ave.) and head east.
2. Turn right on Avon St. and ascend the long zig-zagging staircase on your left.
3. Turn right at the top of the stairs onto Park Dr.
4. Turn right on Duane St. and follow it as it curves to the left and turns into Avon St.
5. Turn right on Lucretia, and just after the road curves to the left, look for a narrow sidewalk on your right—follow it to the next stairway and descend.
6. Continue straight on Avalon St. for one block to Echo Park Ave.
7. Turn right on Echo Park Ave.
8. Turn right on Baxter St., and follow it back to the intersection with Valentine St.

View of downtown LA through Elysian Park

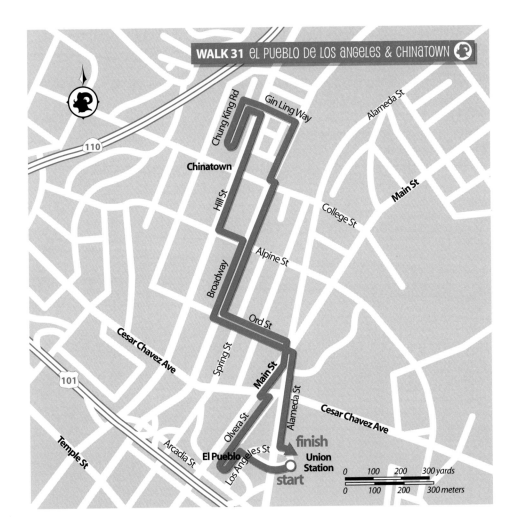

WALK 31 EL PUEBLO DE LOS ANGELES & CHINATOWN

110

Chung King Rd

Gin Ling Way

Alameda St

Chinatown

Hill St

College St

Main St

Broadway

Alpine St

Ord St

Cesar Chavez Ave

101

Spring St

Main St

Olvera St

Alameda St

Cesar Chavez Ave

Temple St

Arcadia St

El Pueblo

Los Angeles St

finish

Union
Station

start

0   100   200   300 yards
0   100   200   300 meters

31 EL PUEBLO DE LOS ANGELES AND CHINATOWN: WHERE HISTORY, CULTURE AND TOURISM COLLIDE

BOUNDARIES: **101 Freeway, Alameda St., 110 Freeway**
THOMAS GUIDE COORDINATES: **Map 634: G3**
DISTANCE: **Approx. 2 miles**
DIFFICULTY: **Easy**
PARKING: **You will find paid parking lots on Alameda St. and Los Angeles St. There is also limited metered parking available on Alameda across from Union Station, as well as on surrounding side streets, but we recommend you take the Metro public rail system to this walk. After all, it does begin at the hub of LA's (admittedly limited) subway system.**

This walk is about as diverse as it gets, exploring both El Pueblo de Los Angeles, home to the area's first Mexican settlers, and Chinatown, which is both a thriving hub for the city's Chinese-American community and a standard tourist attraction. Both neighborhoods now serve as enduring tributes to the history of the non-Caucasian settlers and immigrants who have contributed to the development of the greater Los Angeles multicultural society. Your journey begins at one of the city's most recognizable Art Deco landmarks and its central hub for public transit, Union Station.

● Begin at Union Station at 800 N. Alameda St. This wonderfully romantic building was established in 1939 and combines the influence of Art Deco and Spanish Colonial Revival architecture to splendid effect. If you traveled here by car, enter the station through the colossal arched entryway and spend a few minutes taking in the gorgeous painted ceilings, intricate inlaid marble floors and walls, ornate black iron chandeliers, and historic Art Deco furnishings of America's "last great rail station." On the north side of the station is an enclosed patio with a colorful tiled wall fountain. Union Station's resident upscale eatery, Traxx restaurant and bar, offers *al fresco* dining on this patio.

● After you've finished exploring the station, exit through the south doorway and walk across the brick-paved plaza to the Metropolitan Water District building to admire the lovely circular fountain out front, which is tiled in a brilliant fish scale design. Return to the plaza and head west out toward Alameda St.

- Follow Los Angeles St. across Alameda to enter El Pueblo de Los Angeles, the approximate site of the original town founded by settlers in 1781, back when California still belonged to Mexico. You'll pass by the grassy area known as Father Serra Park, which features a statue of the beloved Franciscan priest.

- Continue straight along the pedestrian walkway known as Paseo de la Plaza. As you approach the gathering center of the plaza—an enormous gazebo that acts as a stage for mariachi bands and street performers—you'll pass the Biscailuz Building on your right. This former home to the Mexican Consulate General now houses the Mexican Cultural Institute. A vibrant mural by Leo Politi entitled, *Blessing of the Animals* graces one wall of the building.

- Head south across the plaza to check out some of El Pueblo's historic buildings. At the corner of Main St. and Arcadia St. are the Masonic Hall (est. 1858); Los Angeles' first theatrical house, the Merced Theatre (est. 1870); and the Pico House, an extravagant, Italianate luxury hotel commissioned by the last governor of Mexican California, Pío Pico in 1870. Los Angeles' first fire station, Firehouse No.1 (est. 1884), sits at the southeast corner of the plaza; the restored building is now a museum for late 19th century firefighting memorabilia.

- Walk north back across the plaza and look for the entrance to Olvera Street, which is identified by a large brown cross. The rich aroma of leather emanates from the purse and belt vendor stalls that crowd the entrance. This one-block pedestrian alley is a popular tourist attraction designed to recreate the type of thriving Mexican marketplace you might find in Tijuana or Ensenada. At 10 Olvera Street, you'll come to the Avila Adobe, the oldest existing house in Los Angeles, built by Don Francisco Avila in 1818. As you continue to make your way through the alley, you'll pass an eclectic mix of stalls and shops selling souvenirs, western clothing, jewelry, Mexican artwork, candies, *pan dulce*, and other treats. If you prefer to forego the snack food stalls and sit down to a full, authentic Mexican meal, Casa la Golondrina at 17 Olvera Street is a popular spot.

- You'll emerge from Olvera Street onto Cesar E. Chavez Ave. Turn left here.

- In less than a block you'll come to Main St.—turn right on Main St. and follow it to where it merges with Alameda St.

- Turn left on Alameda St. and then immediately turn left again onto Ord St. Philippe the Original occupies the northwest corner of this intersection. Even if you don't plan to eat at the legendary deli and French Dip slinger, you ought to step inside to check out the joint's singular ambience. The interior appears to have changed little since it was established in 1908; sawdust covers the floors and long communal picnic tables lined with benches occupy most of the floor space. The building is huge, offering private booth seating in the rear of the first floor and several private rooms upstairs. In addition to the legendary sandwich, you can purchase all manner of deli items behind the busy counter, as well as Philippe's famous nine-cent cup of coffee. Public restrooms are also available here.

- Exit back on to Ord. St. and turn right to continue west for three short blocks to Broadway.

- Turn right on Broadway, staying on the east side of the street—you're now proceeding along Chinatown's main drag. As you head north on Broadway, you'll pass jewelry and clothing stores, a pungent fish market, and several tiny shops selling Chinese dried goods and spices.

- Cross Alpine St. and you'll come to the 800 block of Broadway, which is home to several malls—Dynasty Center, Chinatown Plaza, and Saigon Plaza. The plaza most worth poking your head into is Saigon, an outdoor collection of vendor stalls selling

Interior of Union Station

clothing, shoes, slippers, and a delectable array of deep-fried treats.

- When you reach College St., cross over to the west side of Broadway and continue north. You'll pass a beautiful tiled mural next door to the Big China Restaurant at 911 Broadway.

- Pass the first Chinese gateway you come to, which leads into an alley, and continue to the East Gate, the magnificent entryway to Chinatown's Central Plaza. The colorful wooden portal is an example of Neo-Chinese architecture, which is carried through in the gorgeous tile work and gaily painted balconies inside the plaza.

- Enter through the East Gate, following Gin Ling Way into Central Plaza. The Wonder Food Bakery is just inside the entrance on your left, and a lovely fountain trickles on your right. Gin Ling Way is hung with red and white paper lanterns and lined with tourist shops selling a variety of Chinese tchotchkes. Gin Ling Way is also home to Mountain Bar, whose dimly lit, deep red interior attracts artists and hipsters. On your left-hand side just before Mei Ling Way, you'll pass a massive wishing well sculpture that dates back to 1939, where you can toss your coins toward little signs representing "Health," "Money," "Love," and other good

Back Story: el Pueblo and Chinatown

Interestingly enough, both El Pueblo de Los Angeles and Chinatown have been moved from their original sites. The actual location where Mexican settlers established their village in 1781 was closer to the Los Angeles River, just east of where Union Station stands today, but flooding forced them to move to higher ground in 1818—the current site of El Pueblo. For its part, the original neighborhood known as Chinatown was rudely displaced to make way for construction of Union Station in the 1930s. And so the Chinese immigrants eventually developed the thriving community a few blocks to the northwest that is now more appropriately referred to as "*New Chinatown.*"

fortunes. As you cross Mei Ling Way, look to your left to see the five-tier pagoda atop Hop Louie restaurant and bar. This distinctive Chinatown landmark was constructed in 1941.

● Cross Hill St. and continue into Chinatown's West Plaza by way of Chung King Court. Chung King Court dead-ends at Chung King Rd., another pedestrian walkway that has attracted a spate of avant-garde artists in recent years, making the West Plaza a major destination for hot new gallery openings on weekend evenings.

● Exit West Plaza back onto Hill St. by way of Chung King Court and turn right to head south. If you've managed to hold out this long, Foo Chow restaurant on the southwest corner of Chung King Court and Hill St. is an excellent place to stop in for a generous helping of noodles, seafood, or moo shu for not a lot of money. On the east side of Hill St., just south of Gin Ling Way, you'll notice an empty lot in which large white letters have been erected to spell "Chinatownland"—a cute homage to the original "Hollywoodland" sign above Beachwood Canyon.

● Cross College St. and continue south on Hill St., admiring the view of the downtown skyline straight ahead. At 825 Hill St. you'll come to the Chinese United Methodist Church; appropriately enough, this house of worship incorporates elements of both Chinese- and Western-style architecture.

● Turn left on Alpine St. and continue for one block back to Broadway.

● Turn right on Broadway, remaining this time on the west side of the street. Cathay Bank, the first Chinese-American-owned bank in Southern California, sits on the south-

Hop Louie restaurant and bar

west corner of Alpine and Broadway. Continue south on Broadway, passing the Far East Plaza on your right. This shopping mall is home to numerous restaurants serving a variety of Far East regional cuisines, as well as the Wing Hop Fung Ginseng and China Products Center, which sells a rich variety of herbs, teas, and Chinese arts and crafts.

● Turn left on Ord St., retracing your steps for a few blocks back to Alameda St.

● Turn right on Alameda. On the east side of the street at 900 N. Alameda you'll see the imposing Mission/Spanish Revival façade of the United States Post Office Terminal Annex, which was designed by Gilbert S. Underwood in 1938.

● Cross Cesar E. Chavez to return to your starting point at Union Station.

POINTS OF INTEREST

Traxx Restaurant and Bar 800 N. Alameda St. (inside Union Station), Los Angeles, CA 90012, 213-625-1999

Firehouse No. 1 134 Paseo de la Plaza, Los Angeles, CA 90012. Free tours are offered for Firehouse No. 1. Call 213-628-1274 for more information.

Avila Adobe 10 Olvera Street, Los Angeles, CA 90012. Free tours are offered for the Avila Adobe. Call 213-628-1274 for more information.

Casa la Golondrina 17 Olvera St., Los Angeles, CA 90012, 213-628-4349

Philippe the Original 1001 N. Alameda St., Los Angeles, CA 90012, 213-628-3781

Mountain Bar 475 Gin Ling Way, Los Angeles, CA 90012, 213-625-7500

Hop Louie Restaurant and Bar 950 Mei Ling Way (inside Central Plaza), Los Angeles, CA 90012, 213-628-4244

Foo Chow Restaurant 949 N. Hill St., Los Angeles, CA 90012, 213-485-1294

Wing Hop Fung Ginseng and China Products Center 727 N. Broadway, Los Angeles, CA 90012, 213-626-7200

route summary

1. Begin at Union Station at 800 N. Alameda St.
2. Exit the station through the south doorway and head west through the plaza toward Alameda St.
3. Follow Los Angeles St. across Alameda to enter El Pueblo de Los Angeles.
4. Continue straight along the pedestrian walkway known as Paseo de la Plaza.
5. Head south across the plaza to check out some of El Pueblo's historic buildings.
6. Walk north back across the plaza and continue through Olvera Street.
7. Emerge from Olvera Street onto Cesar E. Chavez Ave. and turn left.
8. Turn right on Main St. and follow it to where it merges with Alameda St.
9. Turn left on Alameda St. and then immediately turn left again onto Ord St. Stop in at Philippe the Original.
10. Exit back on to Ord. St. and turn right to continue west for three short blocks to Broadway.
11. Turn right on Broadway, staying on the east side of the street.
12. Cross Alpine St. and explore the shopping plazas on the 800 block of Broadway.
13. When you reach College St., cross over to the west side of Broadway and continue north.
14. Pass the first Chinese gateway you come to, and continue to the East Gate.
15. Enter Central Plaza through the East Gate, following Gin Ling Way.
16. Cross Hill St. and continue into Chinatown's West Plaza by way of Chung King Ct. Chung King Ct. dead-ends at Chung King Rd.
17. Exit West Plaza back onto Hill St. by way of Chung King Ct. and turn right to head south.
18. Cross College St. and continue south on Hill St.
19. Turn left on Alpine St. and continue for one block back to Broadway.
20. Turn right on Broadway, remaining this time on the west side of the street.
21. Turn left on Ord St., retracing your steps for a few blocks back to Alameda St.
22. Turn right on Alameda.
23. Cross Cesar E. Chavez to return to your starting point at Union Station.

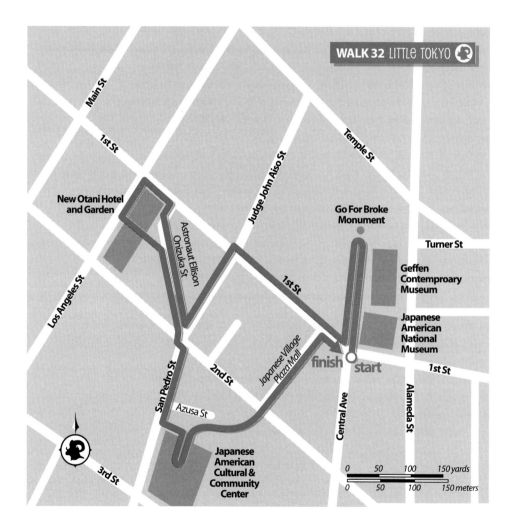

WALK 32 LITTLE TOKYO

Main St

1st St

Temple St

Judge John Aiso St

New Otani Hotel and Garden

Go For Broke Monument

Turner St

Astronaut Ellison Onizuka St

1st St

Geffen Contemproary Museum

Los Angeles St

Japanese American National Museum

San Pedro St

2nd St

Japanese Village Plaza Mall

finish start

1st St

Azusa St

Central Ave

Alameda St

3rd St

Japanese American Cultural & Community Center

0   50   100   150 yards
0   50   100   150 meters

32 LITTLE TOKYO: A PROUD TRIBUTE TO JAPANESE IMMIGRANT HISTORY

BOUNDARIES: **Temple St., Los Angeles St., 3rd St., Alameda St.**
THOMAS GUIDE COORDINATES: **Map 634; G4**
DISTANCE: **Approx. ¾ mile**
DIFFICULTY: **Easy**
PARKING: **Metered street parking is available on 1st St.**

Located in downtown Los Angeles just south of the 101 Freeway and next door to the artists loft district is Little Tokyo, a neighborhood that simultaneously projects multicultural urban cool while retaining its ties to Japanese-American history. There's plenty to draw locals and tourists alike to this region, such as authentic Japanese eateries too numerous to count, spas offering affordable shiatsu treatments, shops selling colorful knick knacks, the Japanese-American Museum, and even the Geffen Contemporary extension of the Museum of Contemporary Art.

● Begin at the intersection of Central Ave. and 1st. St., where Central Ave. ends and transforms into an open pedestrian plaza. On the east side of the clearing is the new site of the Japanese American National Museum, a graceful sandstone, metal, and glass building. This modern building was designed by Gyo Obata, who also designed the Air and Space Museum in Washington D.C. The former site of the museum sits on the west side of the plaza. This lovely old brick building (est. 1925) was originally the site of the Nishi Hongwanzi Buddhist Temple and is now home to the National Center for the Preservation of Democracy.

● Head north through the plaza toward the Geffen Contemporary branch of the Museum of Contemporary Art (MOCA), the site for installation pieces that are too large to fit in the museum's downtown California Plaza location. After you pass the warehouse-like home of MOCA's easternmost satellite, you'll come to the Go For Broke monument, which commemorates over 16,000 Japanese-American veterans of World War II who voluntarily went to Europe and the Pacific Rim to fight for the same country that installed their families in concentration camps back in the States. Surviving veterans volunteer as guides at the monument, and if you have the time to talk to one of these incredibly brave and patriotic men, you'll no doubt be amazed at the stories he has to tell.

- Return to the intersection of Central and 1st and turn right to head west for one block on 1st St., passing a crowded collection of Japanese sweet shops, sushi restaurants, and shiatsu spas. Glance downward along the north side to see Little Tokyo's history engraved in the pavement—this is Little Tokyo's Historic District.

- Turn left on San Pedro St. (Judge John Aiso St. in the opposite direction). As you continue south, you'll come to the site of Seiji Kunishima's Stonerise sculpture, which sits in a quiet garden on the north side of the Union Bank building.

- At the northwest corner of San Pedro and 2nd you'll come to the entrance to Weller Ct., also known as Astronaut Ellison S. Onizuka St., for the first Japanese-American astronaut. This pedestrian walking street is marked by Shinkichi Tajiri's Friendship Knot sculpture. As you walk through Weller Ct., you'll pass Marukai Market, a large grocery store where you can purchase all manner of authentic Japanese goodies. About halfway through the court you'll come to a replica of the Challenger Space Shuttle, aboard which Onizuka launched his final space mission.

- At the end of Weller Ct., turn left on Los Angeles St. and proceed to the main entrance of the New Otani Hotel. Enter the lobby and take the elevator on your right up to the garden level. You'll emerge into a lovely rooftop Japanese garden—the two-level oasis features waterfalls and walking paths, and provides an excellent view of the downtown skyline to the southwest.

- Return to the elevator booth, but instead of re-boarding, follow the sign for Weller Ct., descending the stairs on the east side of the garden. You'll walk down through a multilevel food court offering udon, curry, and other Japanese fare before returning to ground level in Weller Ct. Turn right to head back to the intersection of San Pedro St. and 2nd St. and cross 2nd.

- Cross to the east side of San Pedro St. and turn right to head south. In front of the bank on the southeast corner is a bronze statue of prominent Japanese farmer Sontoku (Kinjiro) Ninomiya, sometimes known as the "peasant sage of Japan."

- After crossing the Azusa St. alley, you'll come to the Japanese American Culture and Community Center. Enter the spacious brick-paved plaza, designed by Isamu Noguchi. The imposing concrete façade of the Center lies directly to the south.

- Enter the Community Center through the massive glass doors and take the elevator down to the basement level, where you can explore the beautiful James Irvine Japanese Garden, a carefully tended paradise that lies in stark contrast to the rather ugly building that towers above.

- Return to ground level and walk back across the plaza to the Azusa St. alley. Follow the short alley through to 2nd St.

- Cross 2nd. St. and continue through the Japanese Village Plaza Mall, bearing right at the split to continue on the path toward 1st St. This is the heart of Little Tokyo's shopping district, offering sushi and noodle cafes, shabu shabu dining, knick knack shops, shiatsu massage, sweets, and plenty of other opportunities to indulge yourself.

- After grabbing a snack, meal, or massage in the plaza, exit onto 1st St., where you'll find yourself back at your starting point at the intersection of Central Ave.

Go For Broke monument

POINTS OF INTEREST

Japanese American National Museum 369 E. 1st St., Los Angeles, CA 90012, 213-625-0414

MOCA at the Geffen Contemporary 152 N. Central Ave., Los Angeles, CA 90013, 213-626-6222

Japanese American Cultural and Community Center 244 S. San Pedro St., Suite #505, Los Angeles, CA 90012, 213-628-2725

The New Otani Hotel and Garden 120 S. Los Angeles St., Los Angeles, CA 90012, 213-629-1200

route summary

1. Begin at the intersection of Central Ave. and 1st St.
2. Head north through the plaza to the Go For Broke monument.
3. Return to the intersection of Central Ave. and 1st St. and turn right to head west for one block on 1st St.
4. Turn left on San Pedro St.
5. Enter Weller Ct. (aka Astronaut Ellison S. Onizuka St.) at the northwest corner of San Pedro and 2nd St.
6. At the end of Weller Ct., turn left on Los Angeles St. Enter the lobby of the New Otani Hotel and take the elevator on your right up to the garden level.
7. From the rooftop garden, follow the sign for Weller Ct., descending the stairs on the east side of the garden. Turn right at the bottom to head back to the intersection of San Pedro St. and 2nd St. and cross 2nd.
8. Cross to the east side of San Pedro St. and turn right to head south.
9. After crossing the Azusa St. alley, enter the plaza of the Japanese American Culture and Community Center.
10. Enter the Community Center and take the elevator down to the James Irvine Japanese Garden at basement level.
11. Return to ground level and walk back across the plaza to the Azusa St. alley. Follow the short alley through to 2nd St.
12. Cross 2nd. St. and continue through the Japanese Village Plaza Mall, bearing right at the split to continue on the path toward 1st St.
13. Exit the mall onto 1st St., returning to your starting point at the intersection of Central Ave.

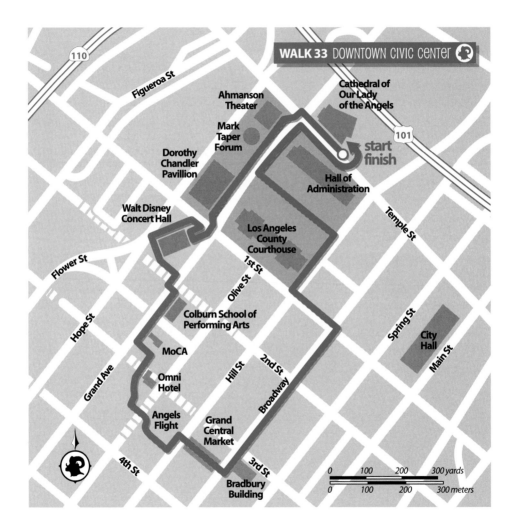

110

Figueroa St

Ahmanson Theater

Cathedral of Our Lady of the Angels

101

Mark Taper Forum

Dorothy Chandler Pavillion

start finish

Hall of Administration

Walt Disney Concert Hall

Los Angeles County Courthouse

Temple St

Flower St

1st St

Olive St

Colburn School of Performing Arts

Hope St

MoCA

Spring St

City Hall

Grand Ave

Omni Hotel

Hill St

2nd St

Main St

Angels Flight

Broadway

Grand Central Market

4th St

3rd St

Bradbury Building

0   100   200   300 yards
0   100   200   300 meters

33 DOWNTOWN CIVIC CenTer: reviTaLizaTion in THe WorKs

BOUNDARIES: **101 Freeway, Hope St., Broadway St., 4th St.**
THOMAS GUIDE COORDINATES: **Map 634; F3**
DISTANCE: **Approx. 1½ miles**
DIFFICULTY: **Moderate**
PARKING: **Like every building downtown, the Cathedral of Our Lady of Angels, where this route begins, requires that you pay for parking. Your best bet is to do this walk on a weekend or on a weekday after 4:00 P.M., when you can park for a fairly reasonable flat fee. Provided that you attend Sunday Mass, you can park for three hours for free. Alternatively, you can take the Metro Red Line to the Civic Center stop, and then walk half a block south to your starting point at the Cathedral. Finally, you can always try your luck with metered parking on the surrounding streets.**

The Civic Center, as the area of downtown just south of the 101 Freeway and just east of the 110 is called, has been subject to some eccentric developments over the past few years as part of a revitalization effort, and the overhaul is far from over. Over the next several years, numerous ugly parking structures will be leveled to make way for more commercial, residential, retail, and hotel space. Presently, the effect of all this expansion is occasionally successful, as in the case of the majestic Walt Disney Concert Hall, and at other times discordant; witness the decidedly ungraceful design of the Cathedral of Our Lady of Angels. Today's walk will explore these new additions to the downtown cityscape, as well as institutions that form the city's historic core, such as City Hall and Grand Central Market.

● **Begin at the Cathedral of Our Lady of Angels at 555 W. Temple St. Whether you park in the structure or walk from the Metro station, you will enter the cathedral grounds by way of a lower courtyard that is graced with a waterfall fountain. Ascend the stairs into the main courtyard, which gives access to the cathedral itself and also features a little café and even a gift shop. Before proceeding toward the church, wander over to the northeast corner of the upper courtyard, where you'll discover an interesting sculpture garden featuring an assortment of wild and domestic creatures. Upon approach, the cathedral looms formidably. Architect Rafael Moneo constructed the** massive edifice out of adobe-colored concrete, creating an oddly striated effect with his layered formation of the outer walls.

Enter the Cathedral of Our Lady of Angels by way of the great bronze doors on the left side of the façade. The starkly modern interior feels refreshingly cool on a hot day and carries through the exterior theme of neutral tones in stone, wood, and marble. Watery sunlight filters through the gray-tinted Spanish alabaster windows. Take a few moments to explore, sticking to the perimeter of the building if there is a service underway, and you'll find a collection of sculptures and framed oil paintings that are oddly dwarfed by the dimensions of the interior space. Perhaps the most striking trappings are the hand-painted tapestries that line the walls of the inner sanctuary, portraying a diverse sampling of the Catholic community.

● After exploring the Cathedral, exit back into the plaza, return to street level and turn right to head west along Temple St.

● After crossing Grand Ave., cross to the south side of Temple so that you are on the southwest corner of the intersection. Ascend the stairs up to Music Center complex.

● Turn left at the top of the stairs to walk through the Los Angeles Times Garden Courtyard, which is not so much a garden as a paved walkway between towering concrete columns. On your right, you'll pass the Ahmanson Theatre and then the Mark Taper Forum, a striking cylindrical theatre decorated all-around with an abstract bas-relief. Note that there are public restrooms available on your left.

After passing the reflecting pools that front the Mark Taper, you'll emerge into the main courtyard of the Music Center. The classy outdoor Pinot Grill operates in the evenings here, and you can also grab a quick, inexpensive bite at the Spotlight Café if you're so inclined. The centerpiece of the plaza is an elevated dancing fountain built around an expressive and semi-religious sculpture entitled "Peace on Earth." This large monument was dedicated by artist Jacques Lipchitz in 1969 as "a Symbol of Peace to the Peoples of the World," according to the inscription on the base of the fountain. Take a few minutes to enjoy your vantage point here in the mist of the Music Center complex. To the west you'll see the glass and steel Department of Water and Power building, flanked by its own magnificent high-spouting fountains.

The distinctive City Hall tower (est. 1929), which incorporates classical and Art Deco design elements to elegant effect, rises beyond the sunken parkway directly to the southeast.

Before descending the stairway down to Grand Ave. on the east side of the fountain, take a second to admire the metal sculpture of an open doorway by Robert Graham. The piece is called "Dance Door" and features a bas-relief of nude dancers reminiscent of Degas' ballerinas.

- At the bottom of the stairs, turn right. You'll pass the County Courthouse on your left just before reaching 1st St., at which point the burnished, mellifluous wings of Frank Gehry's Walt Disney Concert Hall come into view. This world-renowned architectural masterpiece is the new permanent home of the Los Angeles Philharmonic.

- Cross 1st St. and enter the visitors lobby through the glass doors on the east side of the building (facing Grand Ave.). The lobby is a study in curved surfaces— white-painted walls and ceilings with blonde wood finishing. This is a tourist spot, after all, so you'll find another gift shop and café here. Self-guided audio tours of the architectural highlights of the concert hall itself are available for a small fee.

- Exit Disney Hall back onto Grand Ave. and then turn left to backtrack slightly to the corner of 1st St. Turn left on 1st St., remaining on the same side of the street as the concert hall.

- Continue west on 1st for almost one block. Just before reaching Hope St., turn left to follow the stairway up to the community park hidden behind the concert hall. This garden is lovely

Civic Center fountain with City Hall in background

195

and green, with plentiful shade trees and chairs to rest on. Continue to walk through the park and you'll come to the centerpiece, a gently burbling fountain in the shape of a giant rose. This unique sculpture is covered in a mosaic of broken blue-and-white china pieces, and was designed by Gehry as a tribute to Lillian Disney on behalf of her children and grandchildren.

- Proceed toward the far end of the park and then turn left to cut through the charming outdoor Children's Amphitheatre. Descend the stairway back down to Grand Ave. and turn right.

- Cross 2nd St. and then cross Grand Ave. so that you are on the same side of the street as the Colburn School of Performing Arts. Continue to head south on Grand and you'll come upon the brick-colored walls of the Museum of Contemporary Art (MOCA). The museum's roofline is eccentrically punctuated with pyramid-shaped skylights.

- Turn left to enter MOCA's outdoor plaza, which is identified by a looming sculpture that is essentially a top-heavy junk pile of wrecked airplane parts.

- Turn right to follow the narrow courtyard built around a long strip of reflecting pool and shaded by magnolia trees, passing the Omni Hotel on your left. As the plaza opens up, you'll find yourself overlooking the spectacular Watercourt fountain, which doubles as a stage for free outdoor concerts during the summer.

- Descend either the escalator or the stairway to your right, which will deposit you in a covered hallway of numerous quick lunch spots for the suit-and-tie crowd. You can grab a bite here, but you'd be better off choosing something more interesting from the variety at the Grand Central Market, which you will be coming to shortly. Turn right to emerge into the light on the same level of the Watercourt fountain.

- Walk around the front of the Watercourt, and then look for the stairway on your right that leads to the park below. Descend the first set of steps, and then continue down the next long stairway, which runs parallel to the no-longer-operational Angels Flight funicular. The sloping grassy park on your right is populated with some of the city's homeless.

- At the bottom of the stairs, cross Hill St. to reach the entrance of Grand Central Market (est. 1917), where you can choose from a rich variety of culinary delights, including pizza, Thai, Chinese, burgers, sandwiches, ice cream, fresh-squeezed juices, Salvadorian, or any number of Mexican dining options. You can easily grab a sustaining meal for under five bucks here. Walk all the way through the market until you emerge onto Broadway.

- Turn left on Broadway. At the southeast corner of Broadway and 3rd St. is the Bradbury building, which was designed by George H. Wyman in the 1890s. You must check out the inside of this architectural landmark, which is open to the public. The interior is lit by natural light filtering through the translucent domed roof high above the atrium. The elaborate stairways are composed of cast iron in an eclectic Victorian design. You may recognize the distinctive surroundings from the climactic fight scene in *Blade Runner*.

- Return to the street and continue north along Broadway. This part of town is rather shabby compared to the business district surrounding the Music Center, but offers its share of interesting sites. For example, you'll notice the delightfully tacky Guadalupe Wedding Chapel, featuring a Romanesque façade ornamented with faux Corinthian columns—very Vegas—on the west side of the street just after you cross 3rd St. As you approach 2nd St., check out the elaborate bas-relief artwork depicting a stylized history of the colonization of California that decorates the Los Angeles Times parking structure on your right. The imposing concrete façade of the Times building itself sits at the northeast corner of Broadway and 2nd.

Walt Disney Concert Hall

Continue for one more block to 1st St., where you'll get a closer view of the distinctive City Hall tower.

● Turn left on 1st St., passing the Los Angeles County Law Library on your right as you make your way uphill.

● After crossing Hill St., turn right to head north on Hill; passing the entrance to the County Courthouse before turning left into the pleasant public park that runs between the courthouse and the Hall of Administration. Continue to head west through the park; at the far end is a magnificent circular fountain that projects a refreshing mist over the surrounding benches—a lovely place to take one last break before the end of the walk.

● On the other side of the fountain, ascend the stairs back up to Grand Ave. and turn right.

● Continue for half a block to Temple St. and turn right, where you'll find yourself back at your starting point at the Cathedral.

POINTS OF INTEREST

Cathedral of Our Lady of Angels 555 West Temple St., Los Angeles, CA 90012, 213-680-5200. For information about free group tours, call 213-680-5215

Music Center (Dorothy Chandler Pavilion, Ahmanson Theatre, Mark Taper Forum) 135 N. Grand Ave., Los Angeles, CA 90012, 213-972-7211. For additional tour information about the Music Center venues, call 213-972-4399

Walt Disney Concert Hall 111 S. Grand Ave., Los Angeles, CA 90012, 213-972-7211 For additional tour information about Disney Hall, call 213-972-4399

Museum of Contemporary Art 250 S. Grand Ave., Los Angeles, CA 90012, 213-626-6222

Omni Hotel 251 S. Olive St., Los Angeles, CA 90012, 213-671-3300

Grand Central Market 317 S. Broadway St., Los Angeles, CA 90012, 213-624-2378

route summary

1. Begin at the Cathedral of Our Lady of Angeles on Temple St. between Grand Ave. and Hill St.
2. Exit the cathedral courtyard and turn right on Temple St.
3. Cross Grand Ave., cross to the south side of Temple, and ascend the stairs to the Music Center complex.
4. Turn left and cross through the Music Center plaza.
5. Descend the stairs on the east side of plaza back down to Grand Ave.
6. Turn right on Grand.
7. Cross 1st St. and enter the Walt Disney Hall lobby through the doors on Grand Ave.
8. Exit back onto Grand and turn left to return to the corner of 1st St., and then turn left on 1st.
9. Ascend the stairway on your left just before Hope St. and walk through the elevated park.
10. At far end of park, turn left to cut through the Children's Amphitheatre and then descend the stairs back down to Grand Ave.
11. Cross 2nd St., then cross Grand Ave. and continue to head south on Grand.
12. Turn left to enter the MOCA outdoor plaza.
13. Turn right to walk through a narrow courtyard, emerging into the main plaza above the Watercourt fountain.
14. Descend the escalator on your right and turn right at the bottom.
15. Walk around the front of the Watercourt fountain and descend the stairs on the east side of the plaza.
16. At the bottom of the stairs, cross Hill St. and then walk through Grand Central Market.
17. Turn left on Broadway St. and then enter the Bradbury building on the southeast corner of Broadway and 3rd St.
18. Return to the street and continue north along Broadway.
19. Turn left on 1st St.
20. Turn right on Hill St. and then turn left to cut through park.
21. Ascend the stairs back up to Grand Ave. and turn right.
22. Turn right on Temple St. to return to your starting point at the cathedral.

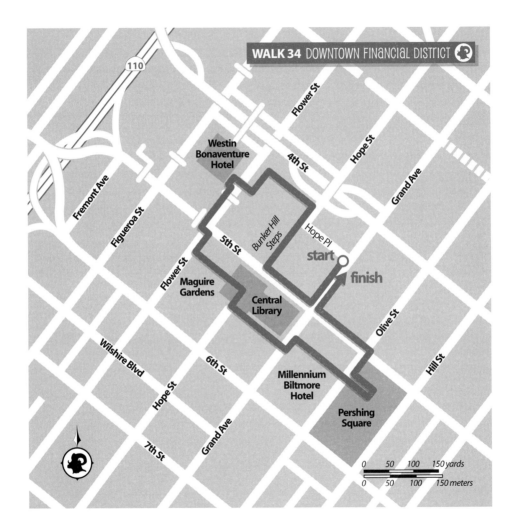

110

Flower St

Westin
Bonaventure
Hotel

4th St

Hope St

Grand Ave

Fremont Ave

Figueroa St

5th St

Bunker Hill
Steps

Hope Pl

start

finish

Flower St

Maguire
Gardens

Central
Library

Olive St

Wilshire Blvd

6th St

Millennium
Biltmore
Hotel

Hill St

Hope St

Grand Ave

Pershing
Square

7th St

| 0 | 50 | 100 | 150 yards |
| 0 | 50 | 100 | 150 meters |

34 DOWNTOWN FINANCIAL DISTRICT: MORE THAN MEETS THE EYE

BOUNDARIES: **Hill St., 4th St., Figueroa St., 6th St.**
THOMAS GUIDE COORDINATES: **Map 634; E4**
DISTANCE: **Approx. 1 mile**
DIFFICULTY: **Moderate**
PARKING: **Metered parking is available on Grand Ave. north of Hope Pl.**

At first glance, downtown Los Angeles' financial district doesn't have much personality, comprised as it is of anonymous mirrored glass skyscrapers that could belong to just about any modern metropolis. But take some time to explore what's hidden among all those tall buildings and you'll discover several of downtown's treasures, such as the innovative architecture of the Central Library, the extravagant interiors of the Millennium Biltmore Hotel, and the thoughtfully designed Bunker Hill steps, as well as numerous public art projects.

● Begin on Grand Ave. between Hope Pl. and 5th St. and head south toward 5th St.

● Turn right on 5th St. You'll notice the stately brick tower of the Millennium Biltmore Hotel rising on the southeast corner of Grand and 5th St. As you round the northwest corner, notice the classical Art Deco high-rise known as One Bunker Hill. This 14-story building is composed of solid limestone and buff-colored terra cotta and used to be home to Southern California Edison.

● Ascend the gracefully curving Bunker Hill staircase on your right. An elevated fountain built to resemble a stony brook runs down the center of the wide steps, which are also known as LA's own Spanish Steps. Opposite the steps on the other side of 5th St. is the north entrance to the Central Library; an inscription carved into the stone façade reads, "Books alone are liberal and free: They give to all who ask. They emancipate all who serve them faithfully." As you make your way up the shallow steps, notice the cylindrical Library Tower reaching skyward on your right. The tallest building in downtown LA, this distinctive landmark was recently branded with the US

Bank logo on its lofty lighthouse, an unfortunate but inevitable sign of the times. The Citicorp building, or "*LA Law* building," is on your left.

- At the top of the steps, you'll come to a small circular plaza built around a fountain sculpture of a nude woman in bronze. McCormick & Schmick's, a sophisticated seafood restaurant and bar fashioned in dark wood, brass, and leather, is on your right. This is a popular haunt of the district's attorneys and bankers, who are lured by the bar's cheap and tasty happy hour food specials. Continue straight ahead onto Hope St., noticing the gleaming wings of Walt Disney Concert Hall several blocks to the north.

- When you reach the YMCA building on your left, just before 4th St., turn left to cut through the outdoor plaza. You'll see various metal sculptures depicting male and female figures in athletic pursuits gracing the patio.

- As you continue through the plaza, the mirrored glass cylindrical towers of the Westin Bonaventure Hotel loom up ahead. Follow the first pedestrian walkway you come to into the building and then descend the spiral stairway all the way down to the lobby. (Or, if you prefer, take a ride down in one of the building's famous glass elevators so that you can admire the view.) Built in 1978, the inside of the Bonaventure now appears dated, with lots of concrete and very little natural light. Once you've reached the lobby, exit the hotel through the glass doors on your left to Flower St.

- Turn right on Flower St. and then cross to the southeast corner of Flower St. and 5th St. so that you're on the same corner as the Central Library.

- Follow the long stepped walkway leading to the library's entrance, admiring the unique façade of the 1920s-era public building, which successfully incorporates elements of modern urban architecture with the ancient influence of Egyptian, Roman, Byzantine, and Islamic civilizations. The library's solitary tower is capped with a colorful tiled pyramid depicting a sunburst and torch to represent the light of knowledge. A tiled reflecting pool runs down the center or the path leading up to the library entrance, and a lovely wall of spouting fountains lies in an alcove off to the right of the main entryway plaza. Café Pinot, an upscale restaurant serving

California/French cuisine, is off to your left. The grassy public space and decorative fountains surrounding the library are known as the Maguire Gardens.

● Enter the library through the striking west-facing portal. Continue through the dark hallway into the main lobby, which is graced with a vibrantly painted ceiling. LA's Central Library is worth taking some time to explore; of particular architectural interest is the newly added Tom Bradley Wing at the east end of the building, which consists of a dramatic, light-filled eight-story atrium. You should also head upstairs to admire the Lodwrick M. Cook Rotunda with its intricate stenciled ceiling and enormous chandelier.

● After exploring the interior of the library, return to the main lobby on the first floor and leave the building through the south-facing exit (toward Hope St.).

● Once outside, descend the first two sets of stairs and then turn left to follow the sidewalk (do not descend the last set of stairs down to street level). You'll pass by the Hilton Checkers Hotel on your right, a nicely restored 1920s building with ornate molded details.

● When you reach Grand Ave., carefully cross the street and then turn left. When you reach the valet parking area of the Millennium Biltmore Hotel, turn right to proceed to the hotel's rear entrance. This Beaux Arts landmark opened for business in 1923 and remains one of LA's finest classical hotels. You'll find yourself in the hotel's splendid lobby, ornamented with a richly carved and painted ceiling, thick rugs, and distinguished furnishings.

Central Library

- Continue straight through the lobby and then turn right into the building's grand hallway, which is lined with intricately carved stone pillars. Turn left at the elevators and descend the stairs down into the front lobby—it doesn't seem possible, but this massive, high-ceilinged room is even more magnificent than the first lobby you entered, featuring an impressive arched ceiling with an intricate inlaid wood design and a lovely central fountain. Walk through the lobby to exit onto Olive St.

- Cross Olive St. to Pershing Square. This public park is still considered a major landmark in downtown Los Angeles, but has fallen hard from its former glory as a lush oasis in the center of the city. Today this mostly concrete-paved space looks outdated with its colorful geometric walls and sculptures, but does afford a convenient raised clearing from which to survey the surrounding architecture. To the west is the distinguished brick façade of the Biltmore Hotel you just exited; immediately north of the Biltmore is the dramatic marble-and-steel high-rise belonging to the Gas Company, made unique by a curved, boat-like glass atrium at the very top. North of Pershing Square you'll see the Art Deco-style Title Guarantee and Trust building, which dates back to 1930. And if you look toward the southwest you can catch a glimpse of the outdoor clock

BACK STORY: WHAT EVER HAPPENED TO BUNKER HILL?

The region currently referred to as the Financial District sits atop Bunker Hill, a former residential neighborhood that was leveled to make way for the skyscrapers that mark downtown Los Angeles today. Once a bustling residential community for Los Angeles professionals and their families, Bunker Hill degenerated over time and eventually become populated with unsavory rooming houses. In the 1960s, LA's Community Redevelopment Agency demolished what was left of the neighborhood's Victorian residences to make way for a "new downtown," complete with shiny skyscrapers to signal the city's prosperity and status as an international commercial and banking center.

(colorfully neon-lit at night) that overlooks the patio outside the Oviatt building pent-house, another Art Deco landmark. At the south end of the park a towering fountain that resembles a giant rain gutter spills a murky stream of water into a shallow stone-lined pool.

- Exit Pershing Square back onto Olive St. and turn right.

- Turn left on 5th St. and continue for one block, passing between the towering edi-fices of the Biltmore Hotel and the Gas Company Tower.

- Turn right on Grand Ave. to return to your starting point.

View of skyscrapers from Pershing Square

POINTS OF Interest

Central Library 630 W. 5th Street, Los Angeles, CA 90071, 213-228-7000

McCormick & Schmick's 633 W. Fifth St., Los Angeles, CA 90071, 213-629-1929

Westin Bonaventure Hotel 404 S. Figueroa St., Los Angeles, CA 90071, 213-612-4743

Café Pinot 700 W. 5th St., Los Angeles, CA 90071, 213-239-6500

Millennium Biltmore Hotel 506 S. Grand Ave., Los Angeles, CA 90071, 213-624-1011

route summary

1. Begin on Grand Ave. between Hope Pl. and 5th St. and head south toward 5th St.
2. Turn right on 5th St.
3. Ascend the Bunker Hill steps on your right.
4. At the top of the steps, continue straight ahead onto Hope St.
5. When you reach the YMCA building on your left, just before 4th St., turn left to cut through the outdoor plaza.
6. Follow the first pedestrian walkway into the Bonaventure Hotel and then descend the spiral stairway to the lobby. Exit the hotel through the glass doors on your left to Flower St.
7. Turn right on Flower St. and then cross to the southeast corner of Flower St. and 5th St.
8. Follow the walkway to the entrance of the Central Library.
9. Pass through the library's entrance and continue through the dark hallway into the main lobby. Explore the interior of the library, including the upstairs rotunda and the eastern Bradley wing.
10. Return to the main lobby on the first floor and leave the building through the south-facing exit (toward Hope St.).
11. Descend the first two sets of stairs and then turn left to follow the sidewalk (do not descend the last set of stairs down to street level).
12. Cross Grand Ave. and turn left. When you reach the valet parking area of the Millennium Biltmore Hotel, turn right to proceed to the hotel's rear entrance.
13. Continue straight through the lobby and then turn right into the building's grand hallway. Turn left at the elevators and descend the stairs down into the front lobby. Walk through the lobby to exit onto Olive St.
14. Cross Olive St. to enter Pershing Square.
15. Exit Pershing Square back onto Olive St. and turn right.
16. Turn left on 5th St. and continue for one block.
17. Turn right on Grand Ave. to return to your starting point.

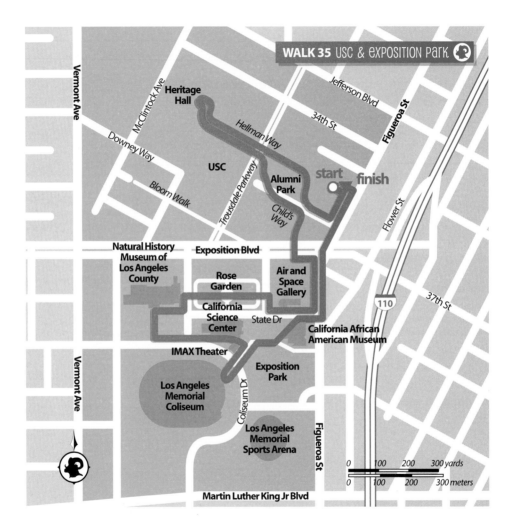

Vermont Ave

Jefferson Blvd

McClintock Ave

Heritage Hall

34th St

Downey Way

Hellman Way

Figueroa St

USC

Bloom Walk

Trousdale Parkway

Alumni Park

start

finish

Child's Way

Flower St

Natural History Museum of Los Angeles County

Exposition Blvd

Air and Space Gallery

Rose Garden

California Science Center

State Dr

110

37th St

IMAX Theater

California African American Museum

Coliseum Dr

Exposition Park

Los Angeles Memorial Coliseum

Los Angeles Memorial Sports Arena

Figueroa St

0   100   200   300 yards
0   100   200   300 meters

Martin Luther King Jr Blvd

Vermont Ave

35 USC aND ExPOSITION Park: HIGHEr LEarNING

BOUNDARIES: Figueroa St., Jefferson Blvd., Vermont Ave., Martin Luther King Jr. Blvd.
THOMAS GUIDE COORDINATES: Map 634; B1
DISTANCE: Approx. 1½ miles
DIFFICULTY: Easy
PARKING: Paid parking is available in USC's Parking structure X, just inside Gate 3 off Figueroa St. Parking in this structure is free if you schedule a tour of the campus ahead of time. Call 213-740-6605 to make a tour reservation. Metered parking is available on Exposition Blvd.

The University of Southern California is a world-renowned private learning institution with a state-of-the-art campus, where students are extremely well cared for, and at the same time held to very high expectations. The attractive college grounds are located south of downtown Los Angeles. Just across the street is Exposition Park, a university-owned property that is home to numerous museums and outdoor educational displays, the classically inspired Los Angeles Memorial Coliseum, and a magnificent rose garden.

The following walking route is written in such a way that you can embark independently, but we suggest you take advantage of the free, one-hour guided tours USC offers throughout the week, not only to learn more about this remarkable campus, but also to take advantage of free parking in the university parking structure conveniently located just off of Figueroa St. Call 213-740-6605 to make a tour reservation.

● From the parking structure, walk east out through the gate onto Figueroa and turn right to proceed to the next campus entrance. (If you parked on Exposition Blvd., head east toward Figueroa and then turn left to reach the campus entrance.) Just inside the gate is the Admissions office, which shares a building with Trojan Residence Hall at 615 Child's Way. This is where you'll check in if you're taking the guided tour.

● Continue west on Child's Way. At 635, you'll come to the Alumni House. This simple but elegant white clapboard building was dedicated in 1880 as the original University of Southern California. According to the plaque in front of the structure, this is the oldest university building in all of Southern California.

- Turn right and then cut diagonally across the Alumni House plaza, heading northwest toward McCarthy Quad. You'll emerge into the expansive open lawn area, where students gather to lounge around in the sun, or frantically complete assignments on their laptops (the entire campus is equipped with wireless Internet access). The quad is bordered to the north by Leavey Library, and by Doheny Library to the south—you can see the top of the Shrine Auditorium just beyond Leavey on the other side of Jefferson Blvd.

- Turn left, heading west with Doheny Library on your left and the quad on your right. Continue straight along Hellman Way—you'll pass Alumni Park on your left before coming to the very collegiate-looking (even by USC architectural standards) Bovard Administration building. As you walk past the north side of the building, you can even peek into University President Sample's opulent office, which occupies the northwest corner of the first floor. Next you'll pass the renowned Annenberg School for Communication on your right and the Physical Education building on your left.

- Turn right just past the Annenberg building, and then turn left to enter Heritage Hall. In the lobby, you can admire every sports trophy USC has ever won, including countless Heismans awarded to the Trojan football team. Quite impressive, if you're into that sort of thing.

- Exit Heritage Hall and retrace your steps back along Hellman Way past Bovard before turning right to cut diagonally across Alumni Park (heading southeast). Stop to admire the graceful Prentiss Memorial Fountain in the center of the park, entitled "The Four Corner Stones of American Democracy." You'll have to circle the fountain to discover each of these cornerstone values; the words are engraved into the fountain and illustrated by pretty little statues.

- Once through the park, turn left to head east on Child's Way, passing the Alfred Newman Recital Hall on your right, which is, oddly enough, decorated with an elaborate bas-relief of prehistoric mammals, and Hubbard Hall.

- Turn right just past the entrance to Lewis Hall, following the brick-paved passageway south toward Exposition Blvd.

- Exit through the gate onto Exposition Blvd. and cross the street at the crosswalk before turning left toward Figueroa St.

- Turn right on Figueroa and continue to State Dr., where you'll turn right to enter Exposition Park. An old United Airlines jet is suspended on your right, one of the Aerospace Museum's several outdoor air/spacecraft displays.

- As you continue west on State Dr., you'll pass the Aerospace Museum building, which was designed by Frank Gehry in 1984.

- Turn right just past the Aerospace Museum, passing the red brick façade of the old Armory building, which is now home to the California Science Center's Annenberg wing.

- You'll see Exposition Park's spectacular rose garden on your left. Pause to admire the carefully ordered plots of colorful rosebushes stretching out before you, with the ornate domed building of the original Los Angeles County Historical and Art Museum (now the east wing of the Natural History Museum) forming a picture-perfect backdrop. Walk through the garden toward the museum, breathing in deeply the sweetly scented air.

- Emerge from the garden and turn left, and then turn right at the next footpath, which you'll follow to the imposing entrance of the Natural History Museum. You can explore the

Exposition Park Rose Garden

grand interior architecture and educational displays of the museum for a moderate fee, or just continue on your walk to the California Science Center, which offers free admission.

- Turn left to follow the path leading south away from the museum entrance toward the Los Angeles Memorial Coliseum.

- Turn left at the next path and follow the walkway up into the remarkable plaza of the California Science Center. This area is covered by a huge cylindrical metal structure from which strings of gold balls hang down. We're unsure of the scientific premise of this contraption, but it's fun to look at and provides a shady place to sit. Admission to the Science Center's permanent exhibit galleries is free, so take some time to explore this truly educational *and* entertaining museum. The IMAX Theatre is next door—if you have an extra hour or two and around eight bucks to spend, watching a film on one of the enormous screens is a sensory treat. After exploring the California Science Center, exit back out into the plaza and turn left (heading in the opposite direction of the Natural History Museum).

- Just before you reach the parking structure adjacent to the IMAX Theatre, turn right to follow the sidewalk, cross Coliseum Dr., and then turn left on the other side of the street to head toward the main entrance of the Coliseum. This 92,516-seat stadium saw its first football game (USC versus Pomona College) in 1923 and has since hosted two Olympiads, two Super Bowls, and a World Series. Stop to check out the headless, anatomically correct statues of a male and female Olympian in front of the stadium entrance.

- Cross Coliseum Dr. once again to head back toward the parking structure and then descend the staircase that leads down into the sunken garden to the left of the structure.

- Follow the pleasant path past educational displays about hummingbirds and butter-flies. An interactive exhibit on the top level of the parking structure shows kids how to use a lever to lift up an actual pickup truck—pretty cool. Continue to follow the path around the structure as it turns to the right, passing under an A-12 Blackbird spycraft built in the 1960s.

- Ascend the stairs on your left and continue straight ahead, passing in front of the entrance to the California African American Museum. If the museum's open, take advantage of the no-cost admission to learn more about the cultural and artistic contributions that African-Americans have made, particularly in California and the West.

- When you find yourself back at the jet exhibit at the intersection of State Dr. and Figueroa St., exit Exposition Park back out onto Figueroa and turn left.

- As you approach the intersection, turn right to cross the short sidewalk, and then left to follow another crosswalk across Exposition Blvd./37th St.

- Continue to head north on Figueroa with USC on your left. Ahead you'll see the giant neon sign for Felix Chevrolet/Cadillac, a pop cultural landmark graced with the likeness of the lovable cartoon cat himself.

- You'll pass the first gate into USC, and then turn left into the second entrance, which leads back to parking structure X.

POINTS OF INTEREST

Exposition Park Rose Garden 701 State Dr., Los Angeles, CA 90037, 213-763-0114.
Note: Closed during January and February for pruning.

Natural History Museum 900 Exposition Blvd., Los Angeles, CA 90007, 213-763-3466

California Science Center 700 State Dr., Los Angeles, CA 90037, 323-724-3623, 213-744-7400 (for IMAX Theatre information)

California African American Museum 600 State Dr., Los Angeles, CA 90037, 213-744-7432

Los Angeles Memorial Coliseum 3911 S. Figueroa St., Los Angeles, CA 90037, 213-747-7111

route summary

1. From university parking structure X, walk east out through the gate onto Figueroa and turn right to proceed to the next campus entrance. Just inside at 615 Child's Way is the Admissions office, where you'll check in if you're taking the guided tour.

2. Continue west on Child's Way. At 635, you'll come to the Alumni House.

3. Turn right and then cut diagonally across the Alumni House plaza, heading northwest toward McCarthy Quad.

4. Turn left, heading west on Hellman Way past Doheny Library, Alumni Park, the Bovard Administration building, the Annenberg School for Communication and the Physical Education building.

5. Turn right just past the Annenberg building, and then turn left to enter Heritage Hall.

6. Exit Heritage Hall and retrace your steps back along Hellman Way past Bovard before turning right to cut diagonally across Alumni Park (heading southeast).

7. Once through the park, turn left to head east on Child's Way past the Alfred Newman Recital Hall and Hubbard Hall.

8. Turn right just past the entrance to Lewis Hall, heading south toward Exposition Blvd.

9. Exit through the gate onto Exposition Blvd. and cross the street at the crosswalk before turning left toward Figueroa St.

10. Turn right on Figueroa and continue to State Dr., where you'll turn right to enter Exposition Park.

11. Continue west on State Dr., passing the Aerospace Museum on your right.

12. Turn right just pass the Aerospace Museum, passing the red brick façade of the old Armory building.

13. Enter the Rose Garden on your left and walk the length of the garden.

14. Emerge from the garden and turn left, and then turn right at the next footpath, heading toward the main entrance of the Natural History Museum.

15. Turn left to follow the path leading south away from the museum entrance toward the Los Angeles Memorial Coliseum.

16. Turn left at the next path and follow the walkway up into the plaza of the California Science Center. Continue straight through the plaza.

17. Just before you reach the parking structure adjacent to the IMAX Theatre, turn right to follow the sidewalk, cross Coliseum Dr., and then turn left on the other side of the street to head toward the main entrance of the Coliseum.

18. Cross the Coliseum Dr. once again toward the parking structure and then descend the staircase that leads down into the sunken garden to the left of the structure.

19. Follow the garden path adjacent to the parking structure, continuing along the sidewalk as it turns to the right.

20. Ascend the stairs on your left and continue straight ahead, passing by the entrance to the California African American Museum.

21. When you reach the intersection of State Dr. and Figueroa St., exit Exposition Park back out onto Figueroa and turn left.

22. As you approach the intersection, turn right to cross the short sidewalk, and then left to follow another crosswalk across Exposition Blvd./37th St.

23. Continue to head north on Figueroa.

24. Pass the first gate into USC, and then turn left into the second entrance, which leads back to parking structure X.

Los Angeles Memorial Coliseum

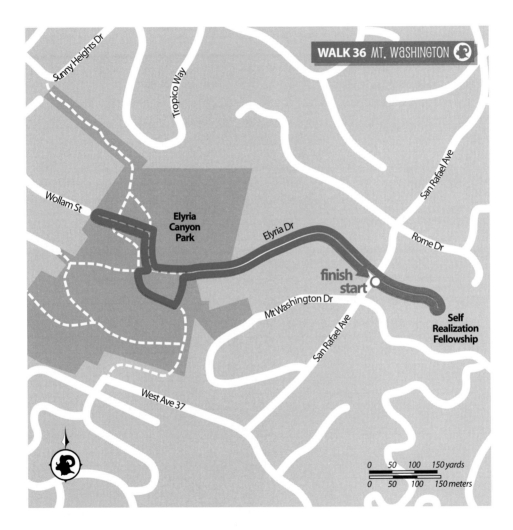

Sunny Heights Dr

Tropico Way

San Rafael Ave

Wollam St

Elyria Canyon Park

Elyria Dr

Rome Dr

finish
start

Mt Washington Dr

San Rafael Ave

Self Realization Fellowship

West Ave 37

| 0 | 50 | 100 | 150 yards |
| 0 | 50 | 100 | 150 meters |

36 MT. WASHINGTON: Far From The CITY IN Spirit

DIRECTIONS: **This route starts at the peak of Mt. Washington, and can therefore be tough to find. Follow these driving directions in order to successfully navigate the twists and turns of the narrow canyon roads:**
- **Begin at the intersection of Figueroa Ave. and Marmion Way.**
- **Head north on Marmion Way.**
- **Turn left on Ave. 45.**
- **Turn right on Cañon Crest Dr.**
- **Turn left on Ave. 46.**
- **Turn left on Rome Dr.**
- **Turn left on San Rafael Ave.**
- **Arrive at the intersection with Elyria Dr.**

THOMAS GUIDE COORDINATES: **Map 594; J4**
DISTANCE: **¼ mile to 1½ miles, depending on route chosen**
DIFFICULTY: **Easy to Strenuous**
PARKING: **Free parking is available just inside the gates of the Self-Realization Fellowship grounds.**

Mt. Washington is one of several idyllic communities hidden in the hills between downtown Los Angeles and Pasadena. This rustic neighborhood is populated with a collection of artistic, laid-back, nature-loving individuals, so it's no surprise that it is also home to the world headquarters of the Self-Realization Fellowship. Founded in 1920 by Paramahansa Yogananda, this worldwide religious organization seeks to bring together people of all creeds in the pursuit of world peace and harmony—a noble goal, to be sure.

This walk can be whatever you make of it—either a short stroll through the grounds of the Fellowship, where you can pause to meditate on the beauty of your serene surroundings atop the hill and enjoy panoramic views of the city below, or a genuine hike that takes you from these carefully manicured grounds down through the rustic beauty of nearby Elyria Canyon Park and back up again.

● **Begin just inside the gates of the Self-Realization Fellowship International Headquarters at the intersection of San Rafael Ave. and Elyria Dr. A small visitor** center is just inside the gate to your left—here you can speak to a volunteer or browse through literature to learn more about this popular pan-religious movement.

- Head into the fellowship grounds, passing a large lawn area on your right before you come to a tennis court. Descend the steps and cut lengthwise across the court. To your right is a sundial set around with benches—from here, you can sit and enjoy a view of the downtown high-rises a few miles south of Mt. Washington.

- Continue along the gravel path, which leads through a lush garden of ferns, ficus trees, and palms. Private alcoves set back into the vegetation on either side of the path offer a place to contemplate or meditate, serenaded by the sound of a trickling fountain. Eventually you'll come to a table and chairs carved out of stone that sit beneath a stand of pine trees—another lovely spot to stop for a rest, engage in deep thought, or stop thinking altogether.

- Follow the path past the stone table and chairs as it turns to the left, ascending a short flight of steps and then passing by a planter filled with water and lily pads. Continue up the next set of steps, passing through a rose garden before you emerge back into the paved parking area.

- As you head back toward the entrance to the Fellowship, you'll pass the main building on your right. The distinctive three-story, flat-roofed structure was established as the Mt. Washington Inn, a popular resort for Hollywood stars and society types in the late 1800s and early years of the 20th century. The Mt. Washington Development Company even built a short railway leading up and down the hill to get patrons to and from the inn. The railway has long since shut down, but the former passenger depot still stands down the hill at the corner of Ave. 43 and Marmion Way.

After passing the former hotel, you'll also notice a small gazebo on your right—inside is a wishing well decorated with peaceful greetings and wishes from Paramahansa Yogananda himself.

At this point, you can return to your car and end the walk, or you could opt for a real workout by continuing on the following route down into Elyria Canyon Park, which is located down the street from the Self Realization Fellowship:

Addendum:

- Exit the Fellowship Grounds and continue straight on Elyria Dr., crossing San Rafael Ave. A stunning shingled Craftsman sits on the corner on your right.

- Follow the road as it turns to the left. You can see the chaparral-covered hills of Elyria Canyon sloping down on your right. Continue all the way to the end of the street, where you'll come to a trailhead.

- Follow the trail as it starts to descend through the grassy meadowland into the canyon. Elyria Canyon Park is part of the Santa Monica Mountains Conservancy park-land. The park spans over 35 square acres, and is notable as home to one of the last remaining stands of California black walnut in the greater Los Angeles area. If you've brought your dog along for the hike, be sure to keep him on-leash in the park. You should also watch out for poison oak, although you should be safe as long as you stick to the clearly marked trails.

- When you come to the first split in the trail, take the right-hand path that affords a view of Glendale in the distance.

- At the next split, continue to follow your path as it curves to the right. The trail widens slightly here and shows rem-nants of asphalt paving. Continue downhill along the shady trail.

- At the next split in the trail, follow the path that curves downhill to your left a short distance down to the floor of the canyon and the Elyria Canyon Park entrance at Wollam St.

Elyria Canyon Park

- Head back up the trail, bearing right at the split to continue along the same path you took down.

- When you return to the point where the path widens, take the narrow dirt trail that branches off to the right (instead of continuing back up the same trail you first followed into the park). Follow the trail as it curves to the left, affording a view of the other side of the canyon and the large homes perched high on the ridge above.

- At the next split, take the narrow trail to the left that heads uphill and follow it as it curves around through the bushes, past a bench and trash can before it reconnects with your original path.

- Turn right and take the trail back up to your starting point at the end of Elyria Dr.

- Follow Elyria Dr. back to the entrance to the Self Realization Fellowship headquarters where you began.

POINT OF INTEREST

Self-Realization Fellowship Headquarters 3880 San Rafael Dr., Los Angeles, CA 90065, 323-225-2471

route summary

1. Begin at the entrance to the Self-Realization Fellowship International Headquarters at the intersection of San Rafael Ave. and Elyria Dr.

2. Head into the Fellowship grounds, and then descend the stairs into the tennis court on your right. Cut lengthwise across the court.

3. Follow the gravel path through the garden.

4. Continue to follow the path as it turns to the left, and then continue up the steps, eventually ending at the parking lot.

5. Return to your starting point just inside the entrance.

Addendum:

6. Exit the gates of the Self Realization Fellowship and continue straight on Elyria Dr.

7. Follow the road as it turns to the left and continue all the way to where the street ends.

8. Follow the dirt hiking trail into Elyria Canyon Park.

9. When you come to the first split in the trail, take the right-hand path.

10. At the next split, continue to follow your path as it curves to the right and continue downhill.

11. At the next split in the trail, follow the path that curves downhill to your left and follow it to the park entrance at Wollam St.

12. Head back up the trail, bearing right at the split to continue along the same path you took down.

13. When you return to the point where the path widens, take the narrow dirt trail that branches off to the right and follow the trail as it curves to the left.

14. At the next split, take the narrow trail to the left that heads uphill back to the point where it reconnects with your original path.

15. Turn right and take the trail back up to your starting point at the end of Elyria Dr.

16. Follow Elyria Dr. back to the entrance to the Self Realization Fellowship headquarters where you began.

APPENDIX 1: WaLKS BY THeMe

PeoPLe WaTCHING

Northwest Santa Monica (Walk 2)
Venice Beach (Walk 4)
Sunset Strip (Walk 14)
West Hollywood (Walk 15)
Miracle Mile (Walk 16)
Whitley Heights and Hollywood Boulevard
    (Walk 19)
Larchmont Village and Windsor Square
    (Walk 23)
West Silver Lake (Walk 27)

arTS aND CULTUre

Southeast Santa Monica (Walk 3)
UCLA Campus (Walk 7)
Leimert Park Village (Walk 10)
NoHo Arts District (Walk 11)
Miracle Mile (Walk 16)
Chinatown and El Pueblo (Walk 31)
Little Tokyo (Walk 32)
Downtown Civic Center (Walk 33)
Downtown Financial Center (Walk 34)
USC and Exposition Park (Walk 35)

DINING, SHOPPING, aND eNTerTaINMeNT

Northwest Santa Monica (Walk 2)
Venice Beach (Walk 4)
North Culver City (Walk 8)
Downtown Culver City (Walk 9)
Leimert Park Village (Walk 10)
NoHo Arts District (Walk 11)
Studio City (Walk 12)
Sunset Strip (Walk 14)
West Hollywood (Walk 15)
Miracle Mile (Walk 16)
Larchmont Village and Windsor Square
    (Walk 23)
Koreatown/Wilshire Center (Walk 24)
West Silver Lake (Walk 27)
Chinatown and El Pueblo (Walk 31)
Little Tokyo (Walk 32)

arCHITeCTUraL TourS

Mar Vista (Walk 5)
North Culver City (Walk 8)
Carthay Circle and South Carthay (Walk 17)
Melrose Hill (Walk 22)
Los Feliz (Walk 25)
East Silver Lake (Walk 28)
Echo Park and Angelino Heights (Walk 29)

peaceful escapes

Castellammare (Walk 1)
Ballona Wetlands (Walk 6)
Laurel Canyon (Walk 13)
High Tower and Hollywood Bowl (Walk 18)
Lower Beachwood Canyon (Walk 20)
Upper Beachwood Canyon (Walk 21)
Franklin Hills (Walk 26)
Elysian Heights (Walk 30)
Mt. Washington (Walk 36)

serious workouts

Castellammare (Walk 1)
Downtown Culver City (Walk 8)
Upper Beachwood Canyon (Walk 21)
Los Feliz (Walk 25)
East Silver Lake (Walk 28)

APPENDIX 2: POINTS OF INTEREST

FOOD AND DRINK

101 Coffee Shop 6145 Franklin Ave, Los Angeles, CA 90028, 323-467-1175
Abbot's Habit 1401 Abbot Kinney Blvd., Venice, CA 90291, 310-399-1171
Alegria on Sunset 3510 W. Sunset Blvd., Los Angeles, CA 90026, 323-913-1422
Aroma Coffee and Tea Co. 4360 Tujunga Ave., Studio City, CA 91604, 818-508-6505
Back Door Bakery 1710 Silver Lake Blvd., Los Angeles, CA 90026, 323-662-7927
Back on Broadway 2024 Broadway Blvd., Santa Monica, CA 90404, 310-453-8919
BCD Tofu House 3575 Wilshire Blvd., Los Angeles, CA 90010, 213-382-6677
Beachwood Market 2701 Belden Dr., Los Angeles, CA 90068, 323-464-7154
Beacon 3280 Helms Ave., Culver City, CA 90034, 310-838-7500
Cabo Cantina 8301 W. Sunset Blvd, West Hollywood, CA 90069, 323-822-7820
Café Bizou 2450 Colorado Ave., Santa Monica, CA 90404, 310-582-8203
Cafe Chapeau 236 N. Larchmont Blvd., Los Angeles, CA 90004, 323-462-4985
Café du Village 139½ N. Larchmont Blvd., Los Angeles, CA 90004, 323-466-3996
Café Pinot 700 W 5th St., Los Angeles, CA 90071, 213-239-6500
Café Stella 3932 W. Sunset Blvd., Los Angeles, CA 90029, 323-666-0265
Caioti Pizza Café 4346 Tujunga Ave., Studio City, CA 91604, 818-761-3588
California Roll & Sushi 125 N. Larchmont Blvd., Los Angeles, CA 90004, 323-841-5458
Canyon Country Store 2100 Laurel Canyon Blvd., Los Angeles, CA 90046, 323-654-8583
Casa la Golondrina 17 Olvera St., Los Angeles, CA 90012, 213-628-4349
Carney's Restaurant 8351 W. Sunset Blvd, West Hollywood, CA 90069, 323-654-8300
Casbah Café 3900 W. Sunset Blvd., Los Angeles, CA 90029, 323-664-7000
Chan Dara Restaurant 310 N. Larchmont Blvd., Los Angeles, CA 90004, 323-467-1052
Cheese Store of Silver Lake 3926 W. Sunset Blvd., Los Angeles, CA 90029, 323-644-7511
Cirxa 3719 W. Sunset Blvd., Los Angeles, CA 90026, 323-663-1048
Citrine Restaurant 8360 Melrose Ave., West Hollywood, CA 90069, 323-655-1690
Culver City Farmers Market Main St. between Culver Blvd. and Venice Blvd. Tuesdays 3:00 to 7:00 P.M.

The Derby 4500 Los Feliz Blvd., Los Angeles, CA 90027, 323-663-8979

Diedrich Coffee 732 Montana Ave., Santa Monica, CA 90403, 310-656-7838

Dresden Restaurant and Bar 1760 N. Vermont Ave., Hollywood, CA 90027, 323-665-4294

Eat Well 3916 W. Sunset Blvd., Los Angeles, CA 90029, 323-664-1624

Eclectic Café 5156 Lankershim Blvd., North Hollywood, CA 91601, 818-760-2233

El Conquistador 3932 W. Sunset Blvd., Los Angeles, CA 90029, 323-666-0265

Electric Lotus 4656 Franklin Ave., Los Angeles, CA 90027, 323-953-0040

Elephant Walk Restaurant 4336 Degnan Blvd., Los Angeles, CA 90008, 323-299-1765

Elixir Tonics and Teas 8612 Melrose Ave., West Hollywood, CA 90069, 310-657-9300

Erewhon Natural Foods Market 7660 Beverly Blvd., Los Angeles, CA 90036, 323-937-0777

Espresso Roma Cafe 124 N. Larchmont Blvd., Los Angeles, CA 90004, 323-465-3461

Farmers Market 6333 West 3rd St., Los Angeles, CA 90036, 323-933-9211

Foo Chow Restaurant 949 N. Hill St., Los Angeles, CA 90012. 213-485-1294

Fred 62 1850 N. Vermont Ave., Los Angeles, CA 90027, 323-667-0062

Gladstone's 4 Fish 17300 Pacific Coast Hwy, Pacific Palisades, CA 90272, 310-454-3474

Grand Casino French Bakery 3826 Main St., Culver City, CA 90232, 310-202-6969

Grand Central Market 317 S. Broadway St., Los Angeles, CA 90012, 213-624-2378

Home Restaurant 1760 Hillhurst Ave., Los Angeles, CA 90027, 323-669-0211

Hop Louie Restaurant and Bar 950 Mei Ling Way (inside Central Plaza), Los Angeles, CA 90012, 213-628-4244

J.J.'s Cafe 3599 Hayden Ave., Culver City, CA 90232, 310-837-3248

Joe's Restaurant 1023 Abbot Kinney Blvd., Venice, CA 90291, 310-399-5811

Kitchen on 43rd Place 3347½ W 43rd Pl., Los Angeles, CA 90008, 323-299-7799

La Bottega Marino 203 N. Larchmont Blvd., Los Angeles, CA 90004, 323-962-1325

La Dijonaise 8703 Washington Blvd., Culver City, CA 90232, 310-287-2770

La Luna Ristorante 113 N. Larchmont Blvd., Los Angeles, CA 90004, 323-962-2130

Leonidas Belgian Chocolates 201 N. Larchmont Blvd., Los Angeles, CA 90004, 323-860-7966

Le Petit Greek 127 N. Larchmont Blvd., Los Angeles, CA 90004, 323-464-5160

Lilly's 1031 Abbot Kinney Blvd., Venice, CA 90291, 310-314-0004

Louise's Trattoria 232 N. Larchmont Blvd., Los Angeles, CA 90004, 323-962-9510

Lucy Florence Coffee House and Le Florence Gallery 3351 W. 43rd St., Los Angeles, CA 90008, 323-293-1356

M&M Soul Food Restaurant 4317 Degnan Blvd., Los Angeles, CA 90008, 323-298-9898

Madame Matisse 3536 W. Sunset Blvd., Los Angeles, CA 90026, 323-662-4862

Mani's Bakery 519 S. Fairfax Ave., Los Angeles, CA 90036, 323-938-8800

Marmalade Café and Catering 710 Montana Ave., Santa Monica, CA 90403, 310-395-9196

McCormick & Schmick's 633 W Fifth St., Los Angeles, CA 90071, 213-629-1929

Mexico City 2121 Hillhurst Ave., Los Angeles, CA 90027, 323-661-7227

Millie's 3524 W. Sunset Blvd., Los Angeles, CA 90026, 323-664-0404

Miyagi's 8225 W. Sunset Blvd, West Hollywood, CA 90046, 323-650-3524

Mountain Bar 475 Gin Ling Way, Los Angeles, CA 90012, 213-625-7500

Musso & Frank Grill 6667 Hollywood Blvd., Los Angeles, CA 90028, 323-467-7788

Netty's 1700 Silver Lake Blvd., Los Angeles, CA 90026, 323-662-8655

New School of Cooking 8690 Washington Blvd., Culver City, CA 90232, 310-842-9702

Pace 2100 Laurel Canyon Blvd., Los Angeles, CA 90046, 323-654-8583

Palermo Italian Restaurant 1858 N. Vermont Ave., Los Angeles, CA 90027, 323-663-1178

Philippe the Original 1001 N. Alameda St., Los Angeles, CA 90012, 213-628-3781

Phillip's BBQ 4307 Leimert Blvd., Los Angeles, CA 90008, 323-292-7613

Pig n' Whistle 6714 Hollywood Blvd., Los Angeles, CA 90028, 323-463-0000

Pioneer Boulangerie 804 Montana Ave., Santa Monica, CA 90403, 310-451-4998

Pit Fire Pizza Co. 5108 Lankershim Blvd., North Hollywood, CA 91601, 818-980-2949

Porch Restaurant 8430 W. Sunset Blvd, West Hollywood, CA 90069, 323-848-5100

Prado Restaurant 244 N. Larchmont Blvd., Los Angeles, CA 90004, 323-467-3871

Psychobabble 1866 N. Vermont Ave., Los Angeles, CA 90027, 323-664-7500

Saddle Ranch Chop House 8371 W. Sunset Blvd, West Hollywood, CA 90069, 323-656-2007

Spumoni Italian Restaurant 713 Montana Ave., Santa Monica, CA 90403, 310-393-2944

Stroh's Gourmet 1239 Abbot Kinney Blvd., Venice, CA 90291, 310-450-5119

Sweet Lady Jane 8360 Melrose Ave., West Hollywood, CA 90069, 323-653-7145

Tangiers Lounge 2138 Hillhurst Ave., Los Angeles, CA 90027, 323-666-8666

Tantra 3705 W. Sunset Blvd., Los Angeles, CA 90026, 323-663-8268

Tortilla Grill 1357 Abbot Kinney Blvd., Venice, CA 90291, 310-581-9953

Tokyo Delve's Sushi Bar 5239 Lankershim Blvd., North Hollywood, CA 91601, 818-766-3868

Traxx Restaurant and Bar 800 N Alameda St. (inside Union Station), Los Angeles, CA 90012, 213-625-1999

Urth Caffe 8565 Melrose Ave., West Hollywood, CA 90069, 310-659-0628

Venice Beach Farmers Market Corner of Dell Ave. and South Venice Blvd., Venice, CA 90291. Fridays 7 A.M. to 11 A.M.

Village Coffee Shop 2695 N. Beachwood Dr., Los Angeles, CA 90068, 323-467-5398

Village Pizzeria 131 N. Larchmont Blvd., Los Angeles, CA 90004, 323-465-5566

Wahoo's Fish Taco 6258 Wilshire Blvd., Los Angeles, CA 90048, 323-933-2480

Yamashiro 1999 N. Sycamore Ave., Los Angeles, CA 90068, 323-466-5125

Z Pizza 123 N. Larchmont Blvd., Los Angeles, CA 90004, 323-466-6969

HOTELS

Argyle Hotel 8358 W. Sunset Blvd, West Hollywood, CA 90069, 323-654-7100

Chateau Marmont 8221 W. Sunset Blvd, West Hollywood, CA 90046, 323-656-1010

Culver Hotel 9400 Culver Blvd., Culver City, CA 90232, 888-328-5837

Millennium Biltmore Hotel 506 S. Grand Ave., Los Angeles, CA 90071, 213-624-1011

The New Otani Hotel and Garden 120 S. Los Angeles St., Los Angeles, CA 90012, 213-629-1200

Omni Hotel 251 S. Olive St., Los Angeles, CA 90012, 213-671-3300

Standard Hotel 8300 W. Sunset Blvd, West Hollywood, CA 90069, 323-650-9090

Westin Bonaventure Hotel 404 S. Figueroa St., Los Angeles, CA 90071, 213-624-1000

ENTERTAINMENT AND NIGHTLIFE

5th Street Dick's Coffee Company 3347 W. 43rd Pl., Los Angeles, CA 90008, 323-296-3970

Avery Schreiber Theatre 11050 Magnolia Blvd., North Hollywood, CA 91601, 818-761-0704

Babe Rickey's Inn 4339 Leimert Blvd., Los Angeles, CA 90008, 323-295-9112

Comedy Store 8433 W. Sunset Blvd, West Hollywood, CA 90069, 323-656-6225

Deaf West Theatre 5112 Lankershim Blvd., North Hollywood, CA 91601, 818-762-2998

The Derby 4500 Los Feliz Blvd., Los Angeles, CA 90027, 323-663-8979

Egyptian Theatre 6712 Hollywood Blvd., Hollywood, CA 90028, 323-466-3456

El Capitan Theatre 6838 Hollywood Blvd., Los Angeles, CA 90068, 323-467-7674

Grauman's Chinese Theatre 6925 Hollywood Blvd., Hollywood, CA 90028, 323-464-6266

House of Blues 8430 W. Sunset Blvd, West Hollywood, CA 90069, 323-848-5100

Jazz Bakery 3233 Helms Ave., Culver City, CA 90034, 310-271-9039

Kitchen on 43rd Place 3347½ W 43rd Pl., Los Angeles, CA 90008, 323-299-7799

Lucy Florence Coffee House and Le Florence Gallery 3351 W. 43rd St., Los Angeles, CA 90008, 323-293-1356

The Magic Castle 7001 Franklin Ave., Los Angeles, CA 90068, 323-851-0800

Music Center (Dorothy Chandler Pavilion, Ahmanson Theatre, Mark Taper Forum) 135 N. Grand Ave., Los Angeles, CA 90012, 213-972-7211. For additional tour information, call 213-972-4399

NoHo Arts Center 11136 Magnolia Blvd., North Hollywood, CA 91601, 866-811-4111

Pantages Theatre 6233 Hollywood Blvd., Los Angeles, CA 90028, 323-468-1770

Regency West Theatre 3339 W. 43rd St., Los Angeles, CA 90008, 323-292-5143

Spaceland 1717 Silverlake Blvd, Los Angeles, CA 90026, 213-833-2843

Two Roads Theatre 4348 Tuhunga Ave., Studio City, CA 91604, 818-762-7488

Walt Disney Concert Hall 111 S. Grand Ave., Los Angeles, CA 90012, 213-972-7211. For additional tour information, call 213-972-4399.

Wiltern Theatre 3790 Wilshire Blvd, Los Angeles, CA 90010, 213-380-5005

World Stage Performance Gallery 4344 Degnan Blvd., Los Angeles, CA 90008, 323-293-2451

MUSEUMS AND GALLERIES

American Heritage Masonic Museum 4357 Wilshire Blvd., Los Angeles, CA 90010, 323-930-9806

Bergamot Station 2525 Michigan Ave., Santa Monica, CA 90404, 310-829-5854

California African American Museum 600 State Dr., Los Angeles, CA 90037, 213-744-7432

California Science Center 700 State Dr., Los Angeles, CA 90037, 323-724-3623, 213-744-7400 (for IMAX Theatre information)

Erotic Museum 6741 Hollywood Blvd, Hollywood, CA 90028, 323-463-7684

Frederick's of Hollywood Lingerie Museum 6608 Hollywood Blvd., Hollywood, CA 90028, 323-466-8506

Geffen Contemporary 152 N. Central Ave., Los Angeles, CA 90013, 213-621-2766

Hollywood Bowl Museum 2301 N. Highland Ave, Los Angeles CA 90068, 323-850-2058

Hollywood Heritage Museum 2100 N. Highland Ave., Los Angeles, CA 90068, 323-874-4005

Japanese American National Museum 369 E. 1st St., Los Angeles, CA 90012, 213-625-0414

LA Art Exchange 2451 Broadway Blvd., Santa Monica, CA 90404, 310-828-6866

Lankershim Arts Center 5108 Lankershim Blvd., North Hollywood, CA 91601, 818-760-1278

Los Angeles County Museum of Art 5905 Wilshire Blvd., Los Angeles, CA 90036, 323-857-6000

The Lowe Gallery 2034 Broadway Blvd., Santa Monica, CA 90404, 310-449-0184

Lucy Florence Coffee House and Le Florence Gallery 3351 W. 43rd St., Los Angeles, CA 90008, 323-293-1356

Museum in Black 331 Degnan Blvd., Los Angeles, CA 90008, 323-292-9528

Museum of Contemporary Art 250 S. Grand Ave., Los Angeles, CA 90012, 213-626-6222

Natural History Museum 900 Exposition Blvd., Los Angeles, CA 90007, 213-763-3466

NoHo Ceramics Gallery 5100 Lankershim Blvd., North Hollywood, CA 91601, 818-505-2100

NoHo Modern 11225 Magnolia Blvd., North Hollywood, CA 91601, 818-505-1297

Pacific Design Center 8687 Melrose Ave., West Hollywood, CA 90068, 310-657-0800

Page Museum 5801 Wilshire Blvd., Los Angeles, CA 90036, 323-934-7243

Schindler House and MAK Center for Design 835 North Kings Road, West Hollywood, CA 90068, 323-651-1510

Sunny Meyer Fine Art 11223 Magnolia Blvd., North Hollywood, CA 91601, 818-985-6630

eDUCaTIOnaL anD CULTUraL CenTers

Central Library 630 W. 5th Street, Los Angeles, CA 90071, 213-228-7000

Japanese American Cultural and Community Center 244 S. San Pedro St., Suite #505, Los Angeles, CA 90012, 213-628-2725

HISTOrICaL LanDMarKS anD MOnUMenTS

American Heritage Masonic Museum 4357 Wilshire Blvd., Los Angeles, CA 90010, 323-930-9806

Avila Adobe 10 Olvera Street, Los Angeles, CA 90012. Free tours available. Call 213-628-1274 for more information.

Barnsdall Art Park/Hollyhock House 4800 Hollywood Blvd., Los Angeles, CA 90027, 323-644-6269 (Call to schedule a tour)

Central Library 630 W. 5th Street, Los Angeles, CA 90071, 213-228-7000

Ebell Club of Los Angeles 743 S. Lucerne Blvd., Los Angeles, CA 90005, 323-931-1277

Egyptian Theatre 6712 Hollywood Blvd., Hollywood, CA 90028, 323-466-3456

Ennis-Brown House 2607 Glendower Ave., Los Angeles, CA 90027, 323-668-0234 (Call to schedule a tour)

Firehouse No. 1 134 Paseo de la Plaza, Los Angeles, CA 90012. Free tours available. Call 213-628-1274 for more information.

Grauman's Chinese Theatre 6925 Hollywood Blvd., Hollywood, CA 90028, 323-464-6266

Hollywood Heritage Museum 2100 N. Highland Ave., Los Angeles, CA 90068, 323-874-4005

Musso & Frank Grill 6667 Hollywood Blvd., Los Angeles, CA 90028, 323-467-7788

Pantages Theatre 6233 Hollywood Blvd., Los Angeles, CA 90028, 323-468-1770

Wiltern Theatre 3790 Wilshire Blvd, Los Angeles, CA 90010, 213-380-5005

Wilshire Boulevard Temple 3663 Wilshire Blvd., Los Angeles, CA 90010, 213-388-2401

Spiritual Institutions

American Heritage Masonic Museum 4357 Wilshire Blvd., Los Angeles, CA 90010, 323-930-9806

Cathedral of Our Lady of Angels 555 West Temple St., Los Angeles, CA 90012, 213-680-5200.
   For information about free group tours, call 213-680-5215

Self-Realization Fellowship Headquarters 3880 San Rafael Dr., Los Angeles, CA 90065, 323-225-2471

Vedanta Society of Southern California 1946 Vedanta Place, Hollywood, CA 90068, 323-465-7114

Wilshire Boulevard Temple 3663 Wilshire Blvd., Los Angeles, CA 90010, 213-388-2401

Shopping

Bodhi Tree Bookstore 8585 Melrose Ave., West Hollywood, CA 90069, 310-659-1733

Chevalier's Books 126 N. Larchmont Blvd., Los Angeles, CA 90004, 323-465-1334

Den of Antiquity 3902 W. Sunset Blvd., Los Angeles, CA 90027-4748, 323-666-3881

The Grove 189 The Grove Dr., Los Angeles, CA 90036, 888-315-8883

Heritage Bookshop 8540 Melrose Ave., West Hollywood, CA 90069, 310-659-3674

Hollywood & Highland 6801 Hollywood Blvd., Los Angeles, 90028, 323-960-2331

Hollywood Toys & Costumes 6600 Hollywood Blvd., Hollywood, CA 90028, 323-464-4444

Landis General Store 142 N. Larchmont Blvd., Los Angeles, CA 90004, 323-465-7998

Larchmont Beauty Center 208 N. Larchmont Blvd., Los Angeles, CA 90004, 323-461-0162

Magart Mexican Furnishings 11221 Magnolia Blvd., North Hollywood, CA 91601, 818-755-3904

Pull My Daisy 3908 W. Sunset Blvd., Los Angeles, CA 90029, 323-663-0608

Rubbish 1627 Silver Lake Blvd., Los Angeles, CA 90026, 323-661-5575

Scentsabilities Gift Boutique 4336 Tujunga Ave., Studio City, CA 91604, 818-761-7727

Skylight Books 1818 N. Vermont Ave., Los Angeles, CA 90027, 323-660-1175

Surplus Value Center 3828 W. Sunset Blvd., Los Angeles, CA 90026, 323-662-8132

Wing Hop Fung Ginseng and China Products Center 727 N. Broadway, Los Angeles, CA 90012, 213-626-7200

Yolk 1626 Silver Lake Blvd., Los Angeles, CA 90026, 323-660-4315

Zambezi Bazaar 4334 Degnan Blvd., Los Angeles, CA 90008, 323-299-6383

Beauty and Health

Aroma Spa and Sports 3680 Wilshire Blvd., Los Angeles, CA 90010, 213-387-0212
Center for Yoga 230½ Larchmont Blvd., Los Angeles, CA 90004, 323-464-1276
The Dance Collective 4327 Degnan Blvd., Los Angeles, CA 90008, 323-291-1538
Foundation Yoga 1720 Main St., Venice, CA 90291, 310-305-1888
Heartbeat House Dance Studio 1638 Silver Lake Blvd., Los Angeles, CA 90026, 323-660-6192
Larchmont Beauty Center 208 N. Larchmont Blvd., Los Angeles, CA 90004, 323-461-0162
Massage Garage 3812 Main St., Culver City, CA 90232, 310-202-0082
The Massage Place and Petit Spa 625 Montana Ave, Santa Monica, CA 90403, 310-393-7007
Spoiled: A Day Spa 4338 Tujunga Ave., Studio City, CA 91604, 818-508-9772

Parks and Gardens

Exposition Park Rose Garden 701 State Dr., Los Angeles, CA 90037, 213-763-0114.
Note: Closed January and February for pruning.
La Cienega Park Community Center 8400 Gregory Way, Beverly Hills, CA 90211, 310-550-4625
Mildred E. Mathias Botanical Gardens University of California, Los Angeles, Los Angeles, CA 90095,
310-825-1260. Please call ahead to make sure the gardens are open at the time of your visit.
Pan Pacific Park 7600 Beverly Blvd., Los Angeles, CA 90036, 323-939-8874
Silver Lake Recreation and Dog Park 1850 Silver Lake Blvd., Los Angeles, CA 90026, 323-644-3946
Westminster Off-Leash Dog Park 1234 Pacific Ave., Venice, CA 90291, 310-301-1550
William S. Hart Park 8341 DeLongpre Ave., West Hollywood, CA 90069, 323-848-6308

Miscellaneous

Academy of Television Arts and Sciences 5220 Lankershim Blvd., North Hollywood, CA 91601,
818-754-2800
Sony Pictures Studios 10202 West Washington Blvd., Culver City, CA 90232, 323-520-TOUR

APPENDIX 3: CaLories BurneD Per WaLk

Calorie estimates are based on the duration of the walk and the approximate rate at which individuals of given weights burn calories at each speed.

Walk		110–130 lbs	130–150 lbs	150–170 lbs	170–200 lbs	200–230 lbs
	CALORIES BURNED AT 2.5 mph					
1.	Castellammare	90–106	106–122	122–139	139–163	163–188
2.	Northwest Santa Monica	120–142	142–163	163–185	185–218	218–250
3.	Southeast Santa Monica	75–88	88–102	102–116	116–136	136–156
4.	Venice Beach	120–142	142–163	163–185	185–218	218–250
5.	Mar Vista	45–53	53–61	61–69	69–82	82–94
6.	Playa Vista	30–35	35–41	41–46	46–54	54–63
7.	UCLA Campus	105–124	124–143	143–162	162–191	191–219
8.	North Culver City	90–106	106–122	122–139	139–163	163–188
9.	Downtown Culver City	210–248	248–286	286–324	324–381	381–438
10.	Leimert Park Village	27–32	32–37	37–42	42–49	49–56
11.	Noho Arts District	45–53	53–61	61–69	69–82	82–94
12.	Studio City's Woodbridge Park	90–106	106–122	122–139	139–163	163–188
13.	Laurel Canyon	15–18	18–20	20–23	23–27	27–31
14.	Sunset Strip	60–71	71–82	82–93	93–109	109–125
15.	West Hollywood	120–142	142–163	163–185	185–218	218–250
16.	Miracle Mile	150–177	177–204	204–231	231–272	272–313
17.	Carthy Circle & South Carthy	120–142	142–163	163–185	185–218	218–250
18.	High Tower & Hollywood Bowl	60–71	71–82	82–93	93–109	109–125
19.	Whitley Heights & Hollywood Blvd	120–142	142–163	163–185	185–218	218–250

CALORIES BURNED AT 3.5 MPH

110–130 lbs	130–150 lbs	150–170 lbs	170–200 lbs	200–230 lbs
81–96	96–111	111–126	126–148	148–170
108–128	128–148	148–167	167–197	197–227
68–80	80–92	92–105	105–123	123–142
108–128	128–148	148–167	167–197	197–227
41–48	48–55	55–63	63–74	74–85
27–32	32–37	37–42	42–49	49–57
95–112	112–129	129–147	147–172	172–198
81–96	96–111	111–126	126–148	148–170
190–224	224–259	259–293	293–345	345–396
24–29	29–33	33–38	38–44	44–51
41–48	48–55	55–63	63–74	74–85
81–96	96–111	111–126	126–148	148–170
14–16	16–18	18–21	21–25	25–28
54–64	64–74	74–84	84–98	98–113
108–128	128–148	148–167	167–197	197–227
135–160	160–185	185–209	209–246	246–283
108–128	128–148	148–167	167–197	197–227
54–64	64–74	74–84	84–98	98–113
108–128	128–148	148–167	167–197	197–227

CALORIES BURNED AT 2.5 mph

Walk	110–130 lbs	130–150 lbs	150–170 lbs	170–200 lbs	200–230 lbs
20. Lower Beachwood Canyon	120–142	142–163	163–185	185–218	218–250
21. Upper Beachwood Canyon	120–142	142–163	163–185	185–218	218–250
22. Melrose Hill	30–35	35–41	41–46	46–54	54–63
23. Larchmont Village & Windsor Square	120–142	142–163	163–185	185–218	218–250
24. Koreatown/Wilshire Center	90–106	106–122	122–139	139–163	163–188
25. Los Feliz	90–106	106–122	122–139	139–163	163–188
Los Feliz with Addendum	210–248	248–286	286–324	324–381	381–438
26. Franklin Hills	30–35	35–41	41–46	46–54	54–63
27. West Silver Lake	105–124	124–143	143–162	162–191	191–219
28. East Silver Lake	120–142	142–163	163–185	185–218	218–250
29. Echo Park & Angelino Heights	120–142	142–163	163–185	185–218	218–250
30. Elysian Heights	45–53	53–61	61–69	69–82	82–94
31. El Pueblo de Los Angeles & Chinatown	120–142	142–163	163–185	185–218	218–250
32. Little Tokyo	45–53	53–61	61–69	69–82	82–94
33. Downtown Los Angeles	90–106	106–122	122–139	139–163	163–188
34. Downtown Financial District	60–71	71–82	82–93	93–109	109–125
35. USC & Exposition Park	90–106	106–122	122–139	139–163	163–188
36. Mt. Washington	15–18	18–20	20–23	23–27	27–31
Mt. Washington with Addendum	90–106	106–122	122–139	139–163	163–188

CALORIES BURNED AT 3.5 MPH

110–130 lbs	130–150 lbs	150–170 lbs	170–200 lbs	200–230 lbs
108–128	128–148	148–167	167–197	197–227
108–128	128–148	148–167	167–197	197–227
27–32	32–37	37–42	42–49	49–57
108–128	128–148	148–167	167–197	197–227
81–96	96–111	111–126	126–148	148–170
81–96	96–111	111–126	126–148	148–170
190–224	224–259	259–293	293–345	345–396
27–32	32–37	37–42	42–49	49–57
95–112	112–129	129–147	147–172	172–198
108–128	128–148	148–167	167–197	197–227
108–128	128–148	148–167	167–197	197–227
41–48	48–55	55–63	63–74	74–85
108–128	128–148	148–167	167–197	197–227
41–48	48–55	55–63	63–74	74–85
81–96	96–111	111–126	126–148	148–170
54–64	64–74	74–84	84–98	98–113
81–96	96–111	111–126	126–148	148–170
14–16	16–18	18–21	21–25	25–28
81–96	96–111	111–126	126–148	148–170

INDEX

(*Italicized* page numbers indicate photos.)

101 Freeway, 107
7 Fountains apartments, 77

A

Abbot Kinney Boulevard, 22–23
Abrams, Dover, 60
Academy Awards, 110
Academy of Television Arts and Sciences, 60, 61, *61*, 62
Actors Studio, 77
Adelaide steps, 9–10
Aerospace Museum, 211
Ahmanson Theatre, 194, 198
Ain, Gregory, 27–29
Air and Space Museum, Washington D.C., 187
Allison, David, 36
Alumni House, 209–210
Ambassador Hotel, 139, 141
American Cinematheque, 109
American Heritage Masonic Museum, 132
American Renegade Theatre. *See* NoHo Arts Center
Angelino Heights, 168–173
Angels Flight, 196
Apple Store, 90
Argyle Hotel, 76, 77, 78
Aroma Spa and Sports Center, 138, *139*, 140–141
Artisans' Patio, 109
artists loft district, 187
Avery Schreiber Theatre, *59*, 62
Avila Adobe, 180, 184
Avila, Don Francisco, 180

B

Babylon Court, *109*, 110
Ballona Creek, 49
Ballona Wetlands, 30–33, *33*
Barnsdall Art Park, 143, 145–148
Barrymore, John, 2
Bautista de Anza, Juan, 96

Beachwood Canyon stairways, 121–125
Beachwood Canyon, 115–119, 120–125
Bellevue Avenue stairway, 172
Belushi, John, 75–76
Berendo stairway, 143–144
Bergamot Station, 15, 18
Biltmore Hotel. *See* Millennium Biltmore Hotel
Biscailuz Building, 180
Blade Runner, 144, 197
Blessing of the Animals, 180
Bonaventure Hotel. See Westin Bonaventure Hotel
Bradbury building, 197
Brady Bunch, The 65–66
Brown Derby plaza, 139
Bunker Hill Steps 201–202
Bunker Hill, 201, 204

C

Calder, Alexander, 35
California African American Museum, 213
California black walnut, 219
California Romanza architecture, 147
California Science Center, 211–212, 213
Canyon Country Store, 71–72, 73
Carroll Avenue, 170–172
Carthay Circle Elementary School, 97
Carthay Circle Park, 96
Carthay Circle, 94–99
Casa Real, 77
Caselotti, Adriana, 132
Castellammare, 2–7
Cathay Bank, 183
Cathedral of Our Lady of Angels, 193–194, 198
Center for Yoga, 134
Central Library, 201–203, *203*, 206
Central Plaza, 182
Challenger Space Shuttle, 188
Chaplin, Charlie, 107
Chateau Marmont, 75, 79, 78
Children's Amphitheatre, 196
Chinatown Plaza, 181
Chinatown, 179, 181–184
Chinese United Methodist Church, 183
Chung King Road, 183
City Hall tower, 193, 195, 198

City of Los Angeles Cultural Heritage Commission, 123
Civic Center. *See* Downtown Civic Center
Clinton Street stairway, 172
Cocoanut Grove nightclub, 139
Colburn School of Performing Arts, 196
Colorado Center, 16
Community Redevelopment Agency, 60, 204
Consulate General of the Republic of Indonesia, 138
County Courthouse, 195, 198
Crosby Place stairway, 170
Culver City Farmers Market, 48, 51
Culver City Hall, 48
Culver City Park, 49–50
Culver City Transportation Center, 48
Culver City, 40–45, 45–51
Culver Hotel, 47, 50
Culver Studios, 47, *49*, 50

D

Dance Door, 195
Deaf West Theatre, 60, 62
Debbie Allen Dance Academy, 40
DeMille Studios, 47
Department of Water and Power building, 194
Derby, The, 143, 148
Desilu Studios, 47
Disney Hall. *See* Walt Disney Concert Hall
Disney, Lillian, 196
Disney, Walt, 59
Dodger Stadium, 175
dog parks, 21, 23, 25, 76, 84, 162, 166
Doors, The, 71
Downtown Civic Center, 192–199
Downtown Culver City, 46–51
Downtown Financial District, 200–207
Dresden restaurant and bar, 143, 146, 148
Dynasty Center, 181

E

Earl Street stairway, 163
East Silver Lake, 160–167
Eastlake Victorian homes. *See* Victorian homes.

Ebell Club of Los Angeles. *See* Wilshire Ebell Theatre and Club House
Echo Park Lake, 169–170, 172
Echo Park Recreation Center, 172
Echo Park, 168–173
Eckbo, Garrett, 27, 28
Egyptian Theatre, 109, 112
El Capitan Theatre, 110, 113
El Pueblo de Los Angeles, 179–182
Elyria Canyon Park, 217–220, *219*
Elysian Heights, 174–177
Elysian Park, 175–176, *177*
Ennis-Brown House, 143–144, 146–147, 148
Equitable building, 139
Erotic Museum, 110, 112
Exposition Park Rose Garden, 209, 211, *211*, 213
Exposition Park, 208–215

F
Fallingwater, 146
Fame, 41
Far East Plaza, 184
Farmers Market, The 89, 92
Father Serra Park, 180
Felix Chevrolet/Cadillac sign, 213
Fields, Tim, 61
Financial District. *See* Downtown Financial District
Firehouse No. 1, 180, 184
Fleur de Lis apartments, 108
Fontenoy Apartments, 108
Ford, Harrison, 144
Foundation Yoga, 24, *25*
Fowler Museum of Cultural History, 36
Franklin D. Murphy Sculpture Garden, 35
Franklin Hills, 150–153
Fred 62 diner, 146, 148
Frederick's of Hollywood Lingerie Museum, 109, 112

G
Gallery of Functional Art, 15
Garland, Judy, 107
Gas Company Tower, 204–205, *205*
Gaylord Apartments, 139
Geffen Contemporary, 187, 190
Gehry, Frank, 195–196, 211

Gin Ling Way, 182
Go For Broke monument, 187–188, 189
Gone With the Wind, 47
Graham, Robert, 35, 195
Grand Central Market, 193, 196–197, 198
Grauman's Chinese Theatre, 110, 113
Griffith Observatory, 143
Griffith Park, 143
Griffith, D.W., 110
Grove, The, 89–90, 92
Guadalupe Wedding Chapel, 197
Guggenheim Museum, 146

H
Haines Hall, 36
Hall of Administration, 198
Hancock Park, 88, 131
Hart Park. *See* William S. Hart Park
Helms Bakeries, 41–43, *43*
Helms Bakery Museum, 43
Hendrix, Jimi, 109
High Tower, 101–103, *103*
Highland-Camrose Park, 101, 104
Hilton Checkers Hotel, 203
Historic Preservation Overlay Zones, 90–92, 95–99, 107–108, 127, 131–132
Hollyhock House, 143, 145–148, *147*
Hollywood & Highland, 107, *109*, 110–111, 113
Hollywood Ardmore apartments, 108
Hollywood Boulevard, 109–110
Hollywood Bowl Museum, 103–104
Hollywood Bowl, 101, 103–104, 107
Hollywood Heights, 100–105
Hollywood Heritage Museum, 107, 112
Hollywood Roosevelt Hotel, 110
Hollywood sign, 121, 122
Hollywood Toys & Costumes, 109, 112
Hollywood Walk of Fame, 109
Hollywoodland gates, 121, 123
Hollywoodland Realty Company, 121
Hollywoodland stairways. *See* Beachwood Canyon stairways
Hollywoodland, 121–125
Hotel Hunt. *See* Culver Hotel
House of Blues, 76, 78
Howard Hughes, 76
HPOZ. *See* Historic Preservation Overlay Zones

I
Ince, Thomas H., 47
Institute for Survival Through Design, 164
Intolerance, 110

J
James Irvine Japanese Garden, 189
Janss Steps, 36
Japanese American Culture and Community Center, 189–190
Japanese American National Museum, 187, 190
Japanese gardens, 188–189
Japanese Village Plaza Mall, 189
Japanese-American WWII veterans, 187–188
John Storer House, 146
Junior Arts Center, 146

K
Kelham, George, 36
Kennedy, Robert F., 139
Kerkhoff Hall, 37
Kings Road Park, 84
Kinjiro, peasant sage of Japan. *See* Ninomiya, Sontoku
Kinney, Abbot, 21, 24
Kinsey Hall, 36
Kodak Theatre, 110
Koenig, Pierre, 5
Koreatown, 136–141
Krotona Colony, 116
Kunishima, Seiji, 188

L
LA Art Exchange, 16, 18
La Bottega Marino, 134
La Brea Tar Pits, 87–88, *89*
La Cienega Park, 95, 98
La Leyenda building, 108
LACMA. *See* Los Angeles County Museum of Art
LaDou, Ed, 65
Lake Hollywood reservoir, 122
Lankershim Art Gallery, 60
Lankershim Arts Center, 60, 62
Larchmont Village, 131, 134
Laurel and Hardy, 155
Laurel Canyon, 70–73

Le Florence Gallery, 53, 56
Leimert Park Village, 52–57
Leimert Plaza Park, 54
Lemon Grove Park and Recreation Center, 127
Library Tower, 201–202, *205*
Liman, Doug, 143
Lipchitz, Jacques, 35, 194
Little Armenia, 146
Little Tokyo Historic District, 188
Little Tokyo, 186–191
Lodwrick M. Cook Rotunda, 203
Loma Vista stairway, 162–163
Los Angeles County Historical and Art Museum, 211
Los Angeles County Museum of Art, 87–88, 92
Los Angeles Historic Cultural Monument, 137
Los Angeles Memorial Coliseum, 209, 212, 213, *215*
Los Angeles Municipal Arts Gallery, 146
Los Angeles Philharmonic, 195
Los Angeles public libraries, 140
Los Angeles River, 66, 182
Los Feliz 3 movie theatre, 146
Los Feliz Village, 143, 145–146
Los Feliz, 142–149
Loteria, 89
Love Street, 71
Lowe Gallery, The, 16, 18
Lower Beachwood Canyon, 115–119

M

M&M Soul Food Restaurant, 54, *55*, 56
MacArthur Park, 139
Magic Castle, The, 111
Maguire Gardens, 203, *203*
MAK Center for Art and Architecture, 81–82, 85
Mann's Chinese Theatre. *See* Grauman's Chinese Theatre
Mar Vista, 26–29
Mark Taper Forum, 194, 198
Mark Taper Foundation, 60
Masonic Hall, 180
Matisse, Henri, 35
Meisner Center for the Arts, 60
Melrose Hill, 126–129
Merced Theatre, 180

Metro stations, 137, 179, 193
Metropolitan Water District building, 179–180
Mexican Consulate General, 180
Mexican Cultural Institute, 180
MGM Plaza. *See* Colorado Center
Micheltorena stairway, 156
Mildred E. Mathias Botanical Gardens, 38, 39
Millard House, 146
Millennium Biltmore Hotel, 101, 203–204, *205*, 206
Miracle Mile district, 86–93, 94–99
MOCA at the Geffen Contemporary. *See* Geffen Contemporary
MOCA. *See* Museum of Contemporary Art
Modernique Homes, 27
Molly Malone's Irish Pub, 89
Moneo, Rafael, 193
Montana Avenue, 9–11
Morrison, Jim, 71, 75
Mt. Washington Development Company, 218
Mt. Washington Inn, 218
Mt. Washington, 217–221
Museum in Black, 54, 56
Museum of Contemporary Art, 83–84, 196
Music Box Steps, 155, 157
Music Box, The, 155
Music Center, 194–195, 198

N

National Center for the Preservation of Democracy, 187
National Registrar of Historic Places, 170–171
Natural History Museum, 211–212, 213
Neutra, Dion, 163–164
Neutra, Richard, 28, 163–164
New Chinatown. *See* Chinatown.
New Otani Hotel, 188, 190
Ninomiya, Sontoku, 189
Nishi Hongwanzi Buddhist Temple, 187
Noguchi, Isamu, 189
NoHo Actors Studio, 61
NoHo Arts Center, 57, 62
NoHo Arts District, 58–63
NoHo Ceramics Gallery, 60, 62

NoHo Modern, 61, 62
North Culver City, 40–45
North Hollywood Gym, 60
North Hollywood, 58–63
Northwest Santa Monica, 8–13

O

Obata, Gyo, 187
Ocean Front Walk. *See* Venice Beach Boardwalk
O'Hara House, 164
Olive Hill, 146–147
Olvera Street, 180–181, *181*
Omni Hotel, 196, 198
One Bunker Hill, 201
Onizuka, Ellison S., 188
Oviatt building, 205

P

Pacific Coast Highway, 3, 6
Pacific Design Center, 81, 83–85
Pacific Palisades, 2–7
paddle boats, 170
Page Museum, 87–88, 92
Palisades Park, 11
Pan Pacific Park, 90, 92
Pantages Theatre, 111
Park La Brea, 89, 91
Paseo de la Plaza, 180
Pavilion for Japanese Art, 88
Peace on Earth, 194
Pershing Square, 204–205
Piccadilly Apartments, 140
Pico House, 180
Pico, Pío, 180
Playa Vista, 30–33
Playboy Studio West, 16
Plaza at the Arboretum, 17
Pleistocene Epoch, 88
Politi, Leo, 180
Powell Library, 36
Prentiss Memorial Fountain, 210
Prospect Trail steps, 72
Prospect Walk stairway, 152

Q

Queen Anne Victorian homes. *See* Victorian homes.

R

Radio Walk stairway, 152
Rancho Higuera, 41, 43
Regency West Theatre, *55*, 56
Renaissance Hotel, 110
RKO Studios, 47
Road Theatre Company, 60
Robert F. Kennedy Memorial Parkway, 140
Rodin, Auguste, 35
Ross, A.W., 96
Royce Hall, 36, 37
Rudolph Valentino, 107
Rustic Canyon, 9
Ryman Program for Young Artists, 61

S

Saigon Plaza, 181
Samuel Freeman House, 146
Samy's Camera, 89
Santa Monica, 8–13, 14–19
Santa Monica Mountains Conservancy, 219
Santa Monica Museum of Art, 15
Schindler House, 28, 81–82, 84–85, *83*
Schindler, Rudolph, 28, 82, 144, 164
Scottish Rite Masonic Temple, 132
Self-Realization Fellowship, 217–218, 220
Shakespeare Bridge, 151, 153, *153*
Shoshana Wayne Gallery, 15
Shrine Auditorium, 210
Siegel, Bugsey, 76
Silver Lake dog park. *See* Silver Lake Recreation Center and Dog Park
Silver Lake Recreation Center and Dog Park, 162, 166
Silver Lake Reservoir, 161–164
Silver Lake, 154–159, 160–169
Sirhan, Sirhan, 139
Skylight Theatre, 146
Snow White, 132
Sony Entertainment, 47
Sony Pictures Plaza, 48
Sony Pictures Studios, 47–48, 51
South Carthay, 93–99
South Venice, 21
Southeast Santa Monica, 14–19
Southern California Edison building, 201
Spaceland, 161, 166

Spanish Steps. *See* Bunker Hill Steps
St Basil's Catholic Church, 138, 141
Standard Hotel, 76, 78
Stanwyck, Barbara, 115
Stonerise sculpture, 188
Studio City, 64–69
Sunny Meyer Fine Art, 61, 62
Sunset Junction Neighborhood Alliance, 155
Sunset Junction, 155–156, *157*
Sunset Strip, 75–79
Sunset Tower, 76
Swingers, 143, 148

T

Tavern Trail steps, 72
textile block architecture, 111, 144, 146
Theosophical movement, 116
Title Guarantee and Trust Building, 204
Todd, Thelma, 4
Tom Bradley Wing, 203
Track 16 Gallery, 15
Treetops triplex, 163
Tujunga Village, 65–67
Two Roads Theatre, *65*, 68

U

UCLA, 34–39
UCLA botanical gardens. *See* Mildred E. Mathias Botanical Gardens
Underwood, Gilbert S., 184
Union Station, 179, 182, 184
United States Post Office Terminal Annex, 184
Universal/Sony Music complex, 17
University of California, 35
University of Southern California, 209
Upper Beachwood Canyon, 120–125
USC, 208–215
USC Trojans, 210

V

Valley Village, 64–69
Vedanta Society of Southern California, 117, 118
Venice Beach Boardwalk, 24
Venice Beach Farmers Market, 22, 25
Venice Beach, 20–25
Venice Canals, 20–22, *22*, 24

Venice of America Amusement Park, 23, 24
Victorian homes, 169–172, *171*, 204

W

Wagner, Otto, 164
Walk of Fame. *See* Hollywood Walk of Fame
Walt Disney Concert Hall, 193, 195–196, *197*, 198
Water Garden, The, 15–17, *17*
Watercourt fountain, 196
Wayne, John, 76
West Hollywood Park, 84
West Hollywood, 28, 75–79, 80–85
West Plaza, 183
West Silver Lake, 154–159
Westin Bonaventure Hotel, *202*, 206
Westminster Avenue School, The, 23
Westminster dog park, 21, 23, 25
Westwood, 34–39
Whitley Heights, 106–113
Whitley Market, 111
Whitley Terrace steps, 107, 112
William S. Hart Park, 76, 78
Wilshire Boulevard Temple, 138, 141
Wilshire Center Farmers Market, 139, 141
Wilshire Center, 136–141
Wilshire Christian Church, 138, 141, *141*
Wilshire Colonnade, 140
Wilshire Country Club, 131
Wilshire Ebell Theatre and Club House, 132, 134
Wilshire United Methodist Church, 133
Wilshire, Henry Gaylord, 139
Wiltern Theatre, 137, 141
Windsor House, 132
Windsor Square Association, 132
Windsor Square, 131–135
Windward Circle, 23
Wing Hop Fung Ginseng and China Products Center, 184
Wizard of Oz, The 47
Woodbridge Park, 64–69
Woodruff, S.H., 121
World Stage Performance Gallery, 54, 56
Wright, Frank Lloyd, 111, 143–147, 164
Wyman, George H., 197

about the author

Southern California native Erin Mahoney loves to walk, yet she's lived most of her life in areas that wouldn't typically be considered pedestrian-friendly. Undaunted, she makes it a point to hoof it whenever possible. She finds walking to be meditative, invigorating, and almost always rewarding, as there are so many fascinating features and landmarks in Los Angeles that are easy to miss when whizzing by in a car.

Erin is also the founder and editor of ChillOutLA.com, a guide to health, beauty, and relaxation deals in Los Angeles. She currently lives in the Hollywood Hills with her husband Tony and her Golden Retriever/Chow mix Tuffy, both of whom patiently accompanied her on many of the walks featured in this book.